America's Armories

America's Armories

Architecture, Society, and Public Order

Robert M. Fogelson

Harvard University Press
Cambridge, Massachusetts, and London, England   1989

This book is printed on acid-free paper, and its binding
materials have been chosen for strength and durability.

Library of Congress Cataloging in Publication Data

Fogelson, Robert M.
   America's armories : architecture, society, and
public order /
Robert M. Fogelson.
      p.   cm.
   Includes bibliographical references and index.
   1. Armories—United States. 2. United States—
National Guard. 3. Military architecture—United
States. 4. United States—Social conditions—
1865–1918. I. Title.
UA42.F64 1989
355.7—dc19   89-30999
ISBN 0-674-03110-5 (alk. paper)   CIP

Designed by Gwen Frankfeldt

To Maria
and
to the memory of my father

Contents

Illustrations

Preface

Eighty years ago an Englishman named A. W. A. Pollock made a trip to the United States on what today would seem a rather odd mission. He had read a couple of articles about the American national guard and the national guard armories, which, in his words, were "springing up all over the Union." Wondering whether the American armory would be appropriate for the British Territorial Force, he decided to take a close look at it. There was much to see. During the late nineteenth and early twentieth centuries, hundreds of armories, nearly all of which looked like medieval castles and fortresses, had been built in urban America, most of them in the Northeast and Midwest. Pollock saw only a handful of them, but he came away much impressed—and with good reason. He visited New York City's imposing Seventh Regiment Armory, the most famous armory in the country. Built in the late 1870s, it was more like a "military palace than a regimental armory," wrote a Boston journalist. He also visited Buffalo's huge Sixty-fifth Regiment Armory. A sprawling castle that had just been finished, it was then the largest (and perhaps the finest) armory in the world. To erect even the least pretentious of the American armories in Britain was "absolutely out of the question," Pollock concluded, though it might be possible to build a smaller and less costly version.

Pollock saw the armories in their heyday. Since then many of them have been destroyed. Some, including Buffalo's Sixty-fifth

Regiment Armory, have burned down. Others have been torn down, either because the national guard did not need the buildings or because other groups wanted the sites. Of the armories still standing, many have been sold or given away and are now used by nonmilitary groups for nonmilitary purposes. And of the armories that still house the national guard, most have been turned into part-time coliseums, community centers. and emergency facilities. Even New York's Seventh Regiment Armory, which is now dwarfed by tall office buildings and apartment houses, also serves as a shelter for some of the city's many homeless people. But through the eyes of Pollock and other observers—and with the help of documents and illustrations of the period—it is possible to envision the armories in the late nineteenth and early twentieth centuries, a time when these formidable, often defensible, structures loomed over the landscape of urban America. A time when the armories were the place where the national guard, then the country's principal peacekeeping and strikebreaking force, stored its arms and ammunition; drilled, socialized, and held meetings; and assembled in the event of an uprising. A time when the armories served not only as the home of the guardsmen, but also as schoolhouse, clubhouse, fortress, and symbol—a symbol of the might of the state and its determination to maintain order at any cost.

I have long been aware of armories. I grew up in the Bronx, not far from the Kingsbridge Armory, the largest armory ever built. I remember playing tennis with my father in the Twenty-second Regiment Armory in Upper Manhattan. I also taught at Columbia for a few years and lived on the Upper East Side, a block from the Eighth Regiment Armory and a mile or so from the home of the Seventh Regiment. From time to time I walked by these imposing buildings and, like many New Yorkers, wondered when and why they had been erected. I did not try to find out until many years later, when I started to teach a course at MIT on the history of the built environment in urban America. Among the subjects around which the course was organized were parks, suburbs, tenements, skyscrapers, zoos, cemeteries—and armories. I included armories because I felt that here was a good opportunity to learn about the building and design of these formidable structures. What I learned was so interesting that I decided to write a book about them.

The result, it should be stressed, is not so much architectural history as social history, albeit social history of a building type—a relatively new and peculiarly American building type. At the heart of the book are three sets of questions. First, why were the armories built? And when and for whom? Also, what purposes did they serve? Second, why were so many of them located in the most fashionable neighborhoods, far from the groups most likely to riot and the institutions most likely to be their targets? Third, why were virtually all the armories erected before 1900 designed to look like medieval castles and fortresses? And why did the architects completely and permanently abandon the castellated style after 1910? *America's Armories* is not only about buildings. Since, as Louis Sullivan once wrote, buildings reveal "the mental state of those who make them and those for whom they are made," it is also about the architects who designed the armories and the guardsmen whom they housed. It is about the upper-middle and upper classes, about their hopes and fears, and especially about the fears of class warfare that inspired the building of the armories and influenced their design. Not least of all, it is about urban America and some of the ways in which it has changed since the great wave of armory building began slightly over a century ago.

Acknowledgments

A good many people and institutions helped me write *America's Armories*. I am indebted to the Graham Foundation for Advanced Study in the Fine Arts, which awarded me a grant that covered much of the expense. My thanks to the foundation and its director, Carter H. Manny, Jr. Additional support came from the MIT Provost's Fund in Humanities, Arts, and Social Sciences. My thanks to Provost John M. Deutch and Deans John de Monchaux and Nan Freidlander. I am also grateful to MIT for a sabbatical, during which I wrote part of the book.

For their help, I would like to thank the MIT libraries; Harvard University's Widener, Fine Arts, and Loeb libraries; Special Collections Division, Boston University's Mugar Library; Library of Congress; Pennsylvania Collection, Carnegie Library of Pittsburgh; Burton Historical Collection, Detroit Public Library; and Baltimore, Boston, Brooklyn, Cleveland, Cincinnati, Erie County, San Francisco, and Seattle public libraries. Special thanks to Terry Tobin, Tom Kiely, and Margaret DePopolo, head of Rotch Library, and her colleagues.

Also helpful were the New-York Historical Society; Maryland Historical Society; Pennsylvania Historical Society; California Historical Society; New York City Municipal Archives and Records Center; Massachusetts Adjutant-General's Office (and Brigadier-General Louis J. Ferrari); National Archives; Prints and Photographs Division of the Library of Congress (especially Mary Ison of the Committee for the Preservation of Architectural Records); and Marjorie Johnson and Wesley Haynes, each of whom gave me a hard-to-find illustration.

Michael Holleran, Andrew Altman, Michael Kerr, and Cris Nelson helped with the research. Tom Brown, Sally Deutsch, Bernie Frieden, David Friedman, David Handlin, Michael Holleran, Pauline Maier, Larry Susskind, and Gwen Wright read an earlier version of the manuscript and suggested ways to revise it. Robert Forget made the maps. John Cook photographed most of the illustrations, often improving on the originals. Carol Leslie and Nancy Kirk edited the manuscript. Aida Donald and Elizabeth Suttell saw it through publication. I would like to thank all of them—as well as John, Bea, and Sue Whiting, in whose farmhouse much of this book (and parts of two others) was written.

If we would know why certain things are as they are, in our architecture, we must look to the people; for our buildings as a whole are an image of our people as a whole, although specifically they are the individual images of those to whom, as a class, the public has delegated and entrusted its power to build. Therefore, by this light, the critical study of architecture becomes, not the study of an art—for that is but a minor phase of a great phenomenon—but in reality a study of the social conditions producing it.

Louis Sullivan, *Kindergarten Chats*

A New Building Type

Early in the afternoon of November 17, 1879, New York's Seventh Regiment marched out of the old Tompkins Market Armory, its home for almost twenty years. Nearly one thousand strong, resplendent in full uniform and accompanied by the regimental band, the officers and men paraded uptown to the Fifth Avenue Hotel. There they waited for President Rutherford B. Hayes, who appeared a few minutes later and, after bowing to the crowd, stepped into his carriage. Riding with him were Secretary of State William B. Evarts, Mayor of New York Edward Cooper, and George W. Curtis, a well-known author and celebrated orator. Escorted by the regiment and cheered on by a large crowd that lined the sidewalks, the presidential carriage moved north on Fifth Avenue. It turned east in the upper Sixties and then south on Park (then known as Fourth) Avenue, where the regiment formed a line in front of the spectators. As the troops presented arms and the band played "Hail to the Chief," the carriage came to a halt between Sixty-sixth and Sixty-seventh streets, directly in front of the new Seventh Regiment Armory. Colonel Emmons Clark, commander of the regiment, greeted the presidential party and escorted them into the building. There they joined the roughly five thousand New Yorkers, many of them prominent merchants, financiers, and property owners, who had come to celebrate the formal opening of the Seventh Regiment's new armory.[1]

After the regiment filed into the drill hall, Mayor Cooper asked its chaplain to offer a prayer, gave a brief speech of his own, and introduced Curtis. Curtis began by praising the Seventh Regiment for its gallant service in the Civil War, de rigueur in an address of this sort, and commending America's volunteer militia. Warming to his task, which was to articulate the audience's assumptions about the regiment and its new armory, he declared that they provided protection "not only against the foreign peril of war, but the domestic peril of civil disorder."

> In the last dire extremity, behind the policeman's club, glistens your bayonet [said Curtis of New York's volunteer militia], and its stern radiance guards this Commonwealth like a wall of fire. Because of this armory, and of all similar armories around us, the great city sleeps in peace. Every honest man goes quietly to his work, because he knows that, should lawful order be assaulted and overthrown, these reservoirs of the will of the State would overflow with resistless power.

The Seventh Regiment is a deterrent to riot—which, Curtis stressed, is "the unpardonable sin" in a nation "where the people govern" and "every wrong can be lawfully redressed." Its new armory, "worthy of the imperial State and the imperial City, is really a temple of peace. It is the memorial, also, of the gratitude of this community to a representative regiment of its Militia."[2]

The Seventh Regiment Armory did not look like a temple, much less a temple of peace. Designed by Charles W. Clinton, a young New York architect and former member of the regiment, it resembled a fortress—a fortress, one reporter wrote, that had been designed with due regard for both "architectural effect" and "easy defense." The administration building, a three-story structure that faced Park Avenue, was dominated by an ornamental tower flanked on each side by a square tower with a turreted roof. A massive cornice—much like "the machicolated cornices of the middle ages," wrote Colonel Clark—crowned the towers, while a bronze gate, bronze portcullis, and solid oak door, half a foot thick, defended the main entrance. Behind the administration building was the huge drill hall, which measured two hundred by three hundred feet. Its roof held up by iron trusses and thus its floor free of posts and pillars, the hall was one of the largest unobstructed spaces in the city. It was more than adequate for all regimental maneuvers. At the far end of the hall were three strong wooden doors, each protected by a heavy iron gate. Long, narrow windows, most of them guarded by iron bars or iron shutters, pierced the walls. "At every angle there are loop-holes for riflemen, enfilading all approaches," wrote the *National Guardsman,* "and twenty sharpshooters would keep all enemies at a respectful distance." If need be, one journalist said, "possibly two or three Gatling guns could be mounted in the tower and sweep the avenue."[3]

The Seventh Regiment's new quarters amazed most visitors, one of whom called it the "finest armory in the world." There was nothing to match it in the United States. Standing on the entire block bounded by Park and Lexington avenues and Sixty-sixth and Sixty-seventh streets, the armory covered about eighty-two thousand square feet (or nearly two acres), more than four times as much land as the Tompkins Market Armory. It dwarfed Chicago's First Regiment Armory and Philadelphia's First City Troop Armory, both of which had been built only a few years before. Far better than any other armory, the Seventh Regiment's new home embodied the special quality of the volunteer militia, which was a cross between a military force and a social club. As one observer put it: "The New York Seventh wanted for an armory neither a barracks nor a fort. It sought something between a military club-house and a barracks-arsenal—a structure that should look like the home of an active military organization, and speak in its plain, massive walls and noble aspect of the utility and dignity and firmness and strength of the National Guard." Not only was the armory formidable, it was elegant as well. The interior, with its carved ceilings, paneled walls, and hardwood floors, had the sort of luxury found only in the wealthiest homes and finest clubs. One journalist was so dazzled by the rooms and halls that he thought "the place rather deserves the name of a military palace than a regimental armory."[4]

The volunteer militia, of which the Seventh Regiment was perhaps the most illustrious unit, was as American as the republic itself. It grew out of the longstanding opposition to standing armies—which, in the words of the Continental Congress, were "inconsistent with the principles of republican governments, dangerous to the liberties of a free people, and generally converted into destructive engines for establishing despotism." Part of the English antimilitary tradition, this opposition emerged early in the colonial period, gathered momentum in the eighteenth century, and reached a peak in the revolutionary era, when the British attempted to reestablish their authority by stationing troops in Boston. In the wake of the Boston Massacre, which seemed to confirm their worst fears, the colonists strongly opposed the presence of a standing army. And they later incorporated their opposition into the Declaration of Independence. Opposition to a standing army was written into many of the new state constitutions too; and though the framers of the Constitution withstood intense pressures to prohibit a standing army, they created powerful safeguards to prevent its abuse. Although the United States went to war with England and with Mexico in the first half of the nineteenth century, opposition to a standing army remained so deep-seated that on the eve of the Civil War the nation had only sixteen thousand regular soldiers.[5]

In the absence of a large standing army, the new republic initially relied for its defense on what was known as the regular or enrolled militia. A form of compulsory military service, to which most able-bodied white males were liable, the militia was an English institution that took hold in the colonies. By independence it was commonly regarded as the alternative to a standing army—or, in the phrase of the Virginia Constitutional Convention, as "the proper, natural, and safe defence of a free state." During the early nineteenth century, however, the regular militia gradually fell apart. Finding military service burdensome, doctors, ministers, and other citizens asked for exemptions. Other Americans simply refused to serve, even at the risk of fine or imprisonment. Still others dropped out after being castigated by pacifists and mocked by young men who marched about the cities wearing outlandish costumes and carrying broomstick muskets and wooden swords. Although one president after another urged Congress to act to revitalize the militia, its decline was irreversible. As the years passed, most Americans came to believe—as Missouri Governor John C. Edwards put it—that "it is idle and useless, in time of peace, to force men to perform military duty who do so against their will." Following this reasoning, many states abolished compulsory military service in the 1840s; and by the 1850s the regular militia was defunct.[6]

The fall of the regular militia was more than offset by the rise of the volunteer militia. A form of voluntary association that appealed to young men with an interest in martial arts, a passion for pomp and circumstance, and a desire to socialize with individuals of their own class and ethnicity, the volunteer militia was another English institution that took root in the colonies. Before independence it was made up largely of a small number of elite companies, whose members were well-to-do Americans from long-established families; afterwards many other citizens, some of them working-class German and Irish Americans, organized companies of their own. By the middle of the nineteenth century, nearly every small town had at least one such company, and some big cities had a dozen or more. The companies picked their members, elected their officers, raised their funds, designed their uniforms, wrote their rules and regulations, and otherwise enjoyed a great degree of autonomy. But as the regular militia fell apart, the elected officials realized that the volunteer companies were the only reliable military units available and incorporated them into the state militias.[7] Although the volunteers still retained much of their autonomy, state officials could now order them to mobilize in the event that violent protests and other uprisings posed a threat to life, property, and public order.

Observers called attention to the striking diversity of the volunteer militia, pointing out that its members came from every social class and ethnic group. Strictly speaking, this was not so. Like most antebellum institutions, the volunteer militia was closed to blacks and women; and as its members were obliged to buy weapons and uniforms and pay dues and other charges, it was much too expensive for the poor. By the standards of the time, however, the volunteers were quite heterogeneous. Hartford had the Putnam Phalanx, two companies that consisted largely of what *Harper's Weekly* called the "solid men" of the city, affluent merchants, manufacturers, and professionals. But it also had one company that was made up mainly of clerks in the local wholesale houses. Bridgeport had two units that were composed of saddlers and mechanics, and New London had several outfits whose members were clerks and artisans. St. Louis had the Continental Rangers, a pro-British company that left the country to fight in the Crimean War. But it also had five Irish units, one Swiss unit, five German units, and even one unit, the Washington Blues, whose members were recruited mainly from Father Mathew's Temperance Society.[8] During the heyday of nativism, many cities even had companies that limited membership to the sons of native-born Americans. In this array of military units, voluntary associations of citizen-soldiers, Americans saw the alternative to a standing army.

The volunteer militia played an active part in the three major wars that took place after independence. A good many volunteers fought in the War of 1812; and a few companies, among them the Pittsburgh Blues and the New Orleans Volunteers, distinguished themselves. The war, however, was extremely unpopular in New England. As a result both Massachusetts and Connecticut turned down President James Madison's request for troops, though later they ordered detachments to guard the coast, which released a few regular soldiers for combat duty. Many more volunteers fought in the war with Mexico which erupted in 1846, by which time the regular militia was well on the wane. In response to a call from President James K. Polk, nineteen of the twenty-nine states sent the equivalent of seventy regiments. So many volunteers turned up, especially from the Southwest, where the war was very popular, that General Zachary Taylor had to leave six thousand of them behind when he went on the offensive. When the Civil War broke out in 1861, both the North and the South (which, of course, did not have an army of its own) issued calls for volunteers. At the start many states met or even exceeded their quotas, though in the end both sides resorted to conscription. For four bloody years the volunteers fought alongside the regulars and conscripts, compiling a record in which their companies and regiments took great pride long after the war was over.[9]

The volunteer militia served a number of other purposes, the most important of which was social. Much like Masonic lodges and other antebellum voluntary associations, the militia companies were social clubs. The members drilled and dined together, gave parties (and an occasional military ball), and otherwise socialized in ways that provided an alternative to the routine of daily life. The volunteers also visited other cities, usually at the invitation of local militia companies; these visits were gala events, highlighted by parades, reviews, huge dinners, and sometimes a sham battle. Some volunteers even spent a week at summer encampments, where they lived in tents, improved their martial skills, engaged in "manly" competition, and, not least of all, escaped domestic problems. Through these social activities the volunteer militia brought together men of similar background and viewpoints and set them apart from their fellow Americans. It gave them a sense of identity and a feeling of belonging, both of which were much sought after in so amorphous a society. By so doing, the historian Marcus Cunliffe has written, the volunteer militia attracted both native Americans, seeking to preserve the cohesion of their communities, and newcomers, trying to create cohesive communities of their own.[10]

The volunteer militia also served a ceremonial purpose, which was distinct from its social purpose. Throughout the antebellum years, Americans expected the militia to turn out for public events (and sometimes for private ones as well). They were seldom disappointed. The volunteers paraded in honor of the anniversary of American Independence, the birthday of George Washington, and, among other notable events, the founding of their military companies. They escorted prominent (and sometimes not-so-prominent) visitors—among them President Franklin Pierce, the Hungarian patriot Louis Kossuth, and José Antonio Paez, a former president of Venezuela in exile from his homeland. They marched in funeral processions for Andrew Jackson, Daniel Webster, and Henry Clay; and upon the death of a local official or militia officer, they accompanied the casket to the gravesite. Besides celebrating martial skills, the parades stimulated patriotic sentiments. They commemorated the nation's history, its victories, heroes, and beliefs, highlighting what bound Americans together rather than what set them apart. And as Inspector-General George S. Batcheller of the New York State National Guard pointed out, the parades did more than convey "the idea of national grandeur"; they also reminded the people of the might of the state and inspired in them "the peaceful sentiment of respect and obedience."[11]

The volunteer militia served a repressive purpose as well, especially in the second third of the century, a time of widespread rioting in urban America. As riots broke out in one city after another, the elected officials found that they could not count on the local police—which was ill equipped, unreliable, and, in many cities, nonexistent—or the federal army—which was very small and scattered all over the frontier. For lack of an alternative, they called on the volunteer militia. And though the militia was originally a defensive force, whose mission was to fight wars not to maintain order, the volunteers responded. Starting in the 1830s, they put down (or helped put down) bread riots, election-day riots, theater riots, gangland riots, and labor riots as well as anti-bank riots, anti-Catholic riots, anti-abolitionist riots, and, much the worst of all, anti-draft riots. Between 1834 and 1864 New York's Seventh Regiment (known as the Twenty- seventh until 1847) was summoned for riot duty at least eight times. Many citizens objected to using the volunteer militia to restore order. Adhering to the traditional view of popular uprisings as extralegal ways to maintain the status quo, some held that the elected officials should not intervene at all. Others insisted that they should rely on moral suasion or, if necessary, local police. But as the riots continued, many other Americans came to believe, as General Gustavus Adolphus Scroggs of Buffalo's Sixty-fifth Regiment said in 1855, that "an organized militia force is indispensable for the preservation of the peace and protection of property in this country."[12]

The volunteers took great pride in their weapons, uniforms, and encampments, but when it came to their armories, they had very little to boast about. During most of the antebellum period, very few of the militia companies had quarters of their own of any kind. For meetings, most companies rented rooms in taverns and hotels, on the upper floors of stables, and in Masonic halls and Odd Fellows halls. For company parties, regimental balls, and other festivities, the volunteers hired theaters and music halls. When the weather was mild, the militia drilled on the Common in Boston, the Washington Square Parade Ground in New York, and other large open spaces. When it turned cold, the infantry units rented the so-called long rooms in local taverns, many of which were not big enough for company drills, much less for regimental maneuvers. The cavalry units leased nearby riding academies. Not only were these quarters unimposing, but, as a result of periodic fires and changes in ownership, they were often temporary as well. Between 1800 and 1850 Philadelphia's First Troop, an elite cavalry unit, held its meetings and drills in dozens of different places, including Thomas Swann's riding school, the Shakespeare Hotel, and the Sign of the Lamb tavern.[13]

Through the first third of the nineteenth century, the volunteers found these arrangements satisfactory. But shortly thereafter several changes took place which led many of them to conclude that a rented room no longer sufficed for an armory. One was that the states supplied the volunteers with weapons, a practice that began soon after the volunteer companies were incorporated into the state militia. It was plain that taverns, hotels, and quasi-public halls were not suitable places to store arms and ammunition. Another change was that the militia leaders called for more frequent company drills and regimental maneuvers. If the citizen-soldiers were to drill in all seasons the militia companies would have to obtain drill halls much larger than even the largest of the long rooms. Yet another change was that the militia companies grew more important as social clubs. Besides objecting to being forced to lease space for social activities, often at a stiff price, the volunteers feared that their companies would not thrive unless they acquired their own quarters. A final change was that the volunteers took a more active role in the suppression of civil disorders. To many of them, it now became vital to secure permanent quarters to serve as rallying points, where the militia would assemble in an emergency, put on their uniforms, pick up their weapons, and await the order to move out.[14]

Convinced of the need for spacious and permanent quarters of their own, the volunteers called on the states for help. In response, a few states ordered the cities to furnish suitable armories for the militia, and one even offered the volunteers a small subsidy towards the construction of regimental armories. But rather than build armories for the militia, most local officials opted to rent quarters for them. The volunteers also appealed to the cities, a few of which were willing to accommodate them. New York is a case in point. Late in the 1830s the Second Company of the Twenty-seventh Regiment, stressing the need for "a suitable rendezvous" in time of disorder, petitioned the city council to provide an armory for the militia. The volunteers lined up solidly behind the petition. Two years later the council granted the Second Company and several other militia units the use of three large rooms on the second floor of the recently constructed public market on Centre Street. A few years later the Seventh Regiment started to look into the feasibility of erecting an armory of its own. Nothing came of these efforts until the mid-1850s, when the butchers began to urge the city to rebuild Tompkins Market. Seizing this opportunity, the Seventh proposed that the two upper floors be made into a regimental armory. Swayed by the Seventh's impressive record and political clout, the council went along. In 1860 the regiment moved into its new quarters.[15]

A few other armories were built in the late 1850s and early

1860s—by the cities, the volunteers, or a combination of the two. Brooklyn's volunteers prevailed on local officials to build the City (or Henry Street) Armory in 1858. A four-story structure, it housed the Thirteenth Regiment and several other militia units. Six years later local officials erected the Armory and Firemen's Hall, a two-story building, part of which consisted of company and drill rooms for the Forty-seventh Regiment and the rest of offices and meeting rooms for the fire department. Philadelphia's National Guards decided to build an armory of their own after a fire destroyed their temporary quarters in 1854. A three-story building, which was paid for by private subscriptions, it was completed in 1857. Seven years later Philadelphia's First Troop erected an armory. A two-story structure with a riding hall in the rear, it was financed by the sale of bonds, most of which were bought by members of the troop. Intent on bringing its scattered companies together under one roof, New York's Twenty-second Regiment put up an armory of its own in 1863—though only after the Board of Supervisors agreed to lease a site for it on West Fourteenth Street. A two-story building that provided space for company rooms and regimental headquarters, the armory cost roughly $20,000, which the regiment raised by issuing bonds.[16]

By the end of the Civil War, however, the volunteers had good cause to be discouraged. Most of the militia still lacked quarters of their own of any kind. With the exception of the Seventh and Twenty-second regiments—as well as several companies of the Sixth, Eighth, Eleventh, and Seventy-first, which shared the Centre Market drill rooms—New York's regiments rented space in quasi-public buildings. Most of these places were "miserable affairs," wrote one New Yorker in 1859, "wholly unfit for the purposes to which they are devoted." Boston's First Corps of Cadets, an elite unit that was once housed in the attic of Faneuil Hall, hired the third and fourth floors of 94 Tremont Street—though as the building had no drill hall, the Corps later leased the Massachusetts Institute of Technology gym for its drills. West of Boston, the Worcester Light Infantry had its quarters in Horticultural Hall, the company's eighth home since it was founded in 1803. The situation was much the same in St. Louis. The St. Louis Greys rented space above Thornton's stable. The Washington Guards leased rooms over Lee & Rucker's stable. And several German American units held meetings on the upper stories of Turner Hall, the basement of which was used as a saloon.[17]

Of the small group of militia units which had quarters of their own, only a few had exclusive use of them. The others had to share them, and not only with other military outfits. Four New York regiments took turns holding meetings and drills on the upper floor of the city's Centre Market. And several of their companies had to lease space elsewhere, because the rooms were not large enough to accommodate an entire regiment. Brooklyn's Thirteenth Regiment was housed in the Henry Street Armory, along with several of the city's other military outfits. And Brooklyn's Fourteenth Regiment had to share the Armory and Firemen's Hall with the fire commissioners, chief engineer, and other officials of the fire department. Not even New York's Seventh Regiment, whose Tompkins Market Armory was the most impressive in the country, had exclusive use of its building. The Seventh occupied the second and third floors of the armory, which consisted of eleven company rooms, a band room, two company drill rooms, and a regimental drill room that the New York *Times* called "the handsomest and largest" in the United States. But the first floor was a public market, crammed with butchers, greengrocers, fishmongers, and other shopkeepers.[18]

In light of how few armories were built before 1865, it is noteworthy that they did not have a distinctive architectural form that would have made clear what kind of buildings they were (and what kinds they were not). The Tompkins Market Armory was an Italianate building. With its long rows of fluted columns, it bore a close resemblance to A. T. Stewart's Uptown Store and many of New York's other commercial palaces. The Twenty-second Regiment Armory, by contrast, was an architectural hodgepodge, a French Empire structure that featured Romanesque windows and decorative medieval machicolations. Less elegant and more severe than the Tompkins Market Armory was Brooklyn's Henry Street Armory, an early Romanesque Revival building that could easily have been mistaken for a midcentury office building. Philadelphia's National Guards Hall, an imposing armory that was designed in the style of an Italian Renaissance villa, did not look much like the Tompkins Market Armory either. It did, however, bear a close resemblance to Tammany Hall, the meeting place of New York City's Democratic party. Philadelphia's First Troop Armory had little in common with the National Guards Hall (or, for that matter, with any of the other armories). Although erected by an elite unit, it was a small nondescript structure whose only distinctive feature was a one-story riding hall.

Thus by the end of the Civil War, more than two decades after the volunteer militia had evolved into a distinctive American institution, the armory had not yet emerged as a distinctive building type. Unlike the railroad station and state capitol, it had not yet acquired a characteristic architectural form that distinguished it from other kinds of civic and commercial structures. Speaking of the Tompkins Market Armory, probably the best known in the nation, the New York *World* remarked that at first sight "the country visitor inevitably mistakes [it] for the Astor Library," an imposing Italianate structure that was built by John Jacob Astor in the mid-1850s. Indeed, there were few signs that the armory might one day acquire a distinctive form before the mid-1870s, when the Philadelphia First Troop erected a new armory at Twenty-first and Chestnut streets. A squat three-story building, with a separate drill hall, it was designed, said the Philadelphia *Evening Bulletin,* to look like "an ancient fortress."[19] Not until the late 1870s, when New York's Seventh Regiment put up its new armory on the Upper East Side, was it clear that the day had arrived. Formidable yet elegant, easily identified as an armory (and only as an armory), the Seventh Regiment's widely admired quarters heralded the appearance of a new building type in America—a building type that tells us much about the fears and hopes of the American people in the late nineteenth and early twentieth centuries.

chapter one

Fears of Class Warfare

Shortly after the Civil War came to an end, George S. Batcheller, Inspector-General of the New York State National Guard, declared that the armories in New York and the state's other cities left much to be desired. While some regiments had adequate quarters, many others were housed in "miserable rooms and shanties," with barely enough space to store their weapons. It was time for the state legislature to supply suitable armories for its citizen-soldiers, Batcheller insisted. For without "an ample and well appointed armory," an armory that could serve as "the head-quarters of the regiment or company" and "the military home of the soldier," the militia could not carry out its mission.[1] Batcheller's remarks were the opening salvo in the postwar campaign for armories, a campaign that would go on for a decade or so, and not only in New York, but also in Boston, Cincinnati, and most of the nation's other big cities. Although this campaign made little headway, it laid the groundwork for the great wave of armory building that started after the railroad strike of 1877, a wave that grew out of the fears of class warfare that spread over the United States in the late nineteenth century.

Batcheller and those who agreed with him based their case on three principal points other than the militia's need for larger and better quarters. One was that the system of company armories was inefficient. Critics of the system contended that as long as the various companies were housed in separate quarters, "scattered without plan, wherever cheap accommodation can be found," it would be very hard for the militia to deal with riots and other disorders. Valuable time would be lost in bringing the members of the regiment together. The critics also argued that unless the companies were able to drill together as a regiment on a regular basis, which was impossible in the existing armories, it would be extremely difficult for the militia to develop a high degree of coordination. And without such coordination, it would be worth little as a military organization. Pointing to the defects of company armories, Samuel M. Quincy, a Boston alderman and chairman of the aldermen's Committee on Armories, said in 1873 that "the protection of the city, no less than the interests of the militia," demands "a concentration of the armories, or rallying points, of each regiment or battalion under the same roof." For small cities and towns, a company armory "may suffice," but "for the metropolis, which can hardly be supposed to call for less than a battalion, the regimental armory seems a necessity."[2]

The second point was that the policy of renting armories was uneconomical. Some cities had originally adopted the policy because it seemed the least expensive way to comply with state laws which required them to furnish quarters for the local militia. As the years went by, however, the rents increased so much that in a few cities they not only put a burden on the taxpayers but also created opportunities for skullduggery. A case in point is New York City, where the Tweed Ring obtained unoccupied buildings (or parts of them) and prevailed on the municipal authorities to rent them for military purposes at exorbitant rates. Thus when the city leased quarters for the militia in 1871, it paid about $280,000 for space worth at most $75,000. Of the total, $36,000 went for the top two floors of Tammany Hall, which would otherwise have rented for less than $3,000. Although no other city spent anything close to $280,000 a year for armories, Batcheller and others believed that it still made more sense to build armories than to lease them, that it would not be long before the annual savings more than offset the initial outlay. The Committee on Military Affairs of the Erie County Board of Supervisors reached much the same conclusion in the mid-1860s. Calling on the board to erect a regimental armory for the Buffalo militia, the committee claimed that the building would cost only $25,000 to $30,000, "the interest on which amount would be far less than the amount now allowed by law to be paid for rent for drill-rooms and armories."[3]

The third point was that the United States was on the verge of widespread civil disorder. Although this belief emerged in the antebellum period, it grew stronger in the aftermath of the Draft Riots of 1863, the worst disorders in the country's history; the postwar labor disputes, the harbingers of even more severe industrial strife; and the Paris Commune of 1871, the newspaper accounts of which stressed that anarchism, terrorism, and mob rule were rampant in the French capital. If riots and other disturbances erupted in American cities, Batcheller and others claimed that the authorities would have no alternative but to summon the volunteer militia. The municipal police may help keep order, he told the Military Association of the State of New York in 1867, "but they would be impotent, indeed, but for the moral presence of our armed Battalions, the consciousness of whose armed power is ever operating to restrain the restive spirits of license, and to maintain the public weal." Nor was this sentiment confined to military circles. Without the militia, the Cincinnati *Enquirer* wrote in 1869, "the city authorities would often find themselves powerless, in the presence of mobs, and the citizens placed at the mercy of the villainous rowdies that infest the city." The *Enquirer* urged Cincinnati to follow the lead of New York City—which, it said, "provides her militia regiments with handsome quarters in her iron market-houses"—and furnish the local militia "a suitable armory."[4]

The campaign for armories made some headway in a few cities. Early in the 1870s the New York State legislature appropriated $160,000 to build a new armory on Clermont Avenue for Brooklyn's Twenty-third Regiment, which had hitherto been housed in a commercial structure on Orange Street. Completed in 1873, the Twenty-third Regiment Armory was for a few years the largest armory in the country. The legislature also voted funds to erect a new armory for Brooklyn's Thirteenth Regiment, which had been quartered in the Henry Street Armory. The cornerstone of the building, which was located on Flatbush Avenue, was laid with great fanfare in 1874. Other armories went up in Philadelphia and Baltimore. In Philadelphia the First Troop decided to build a new armory in 1873, a scant nine years after its old armory was finished. Designed by the eminent architect Frank Furness, the armory cost

$30,000, most of which came from bequests by two former members and the rest from contributions by current members and other affluent Philadelphians. The building was completed in 1874. Baltimore's Fifth Regiment tried a different approach. Unhappy with its rooms in the Music Hall, it asked the local officials to erect an armory on top of the proposed new Richmond Market. Supported by prominent citizens, the request was granted in 1870. A year later the Fifth's new home was finished.[5]

The First Troop Armory was a monument to the loyalty (and timely demise) of two of the company's wealthy members. The other three armories were monuments to the largesse of the state and local officials. In each of these cases, the officials were swayed not only by the political influence of the volunteers, but also by their own feelings about the militia. They were convinced that citizen-soldiers were vital to American liberty. They were grateful to the volunteers for their service in the past and afraid that they might be needed in the future. The Reverend J. Halstead Carroll, chaplain of the Thirteenth Regiment, voiced these sentiments at the laying of the cornerstone of the Flatbush Avenue Armory. After praising the Thirteenth for its gallant record in the Civil War, Carroll said that it demanded "such a building as shall rise on this spot, one rivaling any, and excelled by none." And it deserved it too:

> Not merely or mainly because the old one is too small, too straight for our increasing numbers, [nor because it is unsafe], but as a proper and needed expression from State and city, of appreciation and regard for her citizen soldiers, ever present, rarely seen, quartered among us, not in camps and forts, but at the fireside, in the counting room, in the workshop. The man who sets himself to ridicule the National Guard, to exaggerate the defects of the system, to embarrass its administration, to bring it into discredit, wishes one of two things: He either wishes the country to be wholly exposed to insult from abroad and a prey at home to anarchy, to mob law and to club law, or he wishes to see cannon pointing down this avenue and to hold the exercise of his daily rights as a citizen at the discretion of a military commander.[6]

In most cities, however, the campaign for armories made little or no progress. Speaking on behalf of the Committee on Armories, Boston Alderman Quincy recommended in 1873 that the state should organize the Hub's militia into two regiments and that the city should provide quarters for both of them. But neither the state nor the city took action. Philadelphia's First Regiment, which had obtained a charter to build an armory in 1862 only to find that the community was so absorbed in the Civil War that it had no time for anything else, launched another effort in 1874. After looking at a few sites, each of which turned out to be unsuitable, impractical, or unavailable, the regiment abandoned the effort. The Milwaukee Light Guard made an attempt to erect an armory of its own in the late 1860s and even managed to persuade the citizens to subscribe to several thousand dollars of stock. But the scheme fell through before the company was able to do more than commission a local architect to draw up plans for the building. Even New York's Seventh Regiment, the city's favorite military unit, found the going very hard. Starting in the late 1860s, when it decided that the Tompkins Market Armory was no longer adequate, the Seventh put enormous pressure on the authorities to construct a new armory. But the authorities refused to do more than provide a site for it— and not even the site the regiment wanted.[7]

By the mid-1870s the volunteer militia had reason to be discouraged. Boston's First Corps of Cadets still rented quarters on Tremont Street and drilled at the Massachusetts Institute of Technology gym. For the Hub's other military companies, the city council leased space. New York's Twenty-second Regiment had an armory of its own, though its members were far from satisfied with it; but the city's other regiments met and drilled above public markets or in rented rooms. Philadelphia's First Troop was housed in its new armory, but the Second Regiment was quartered in the old National Guards Hall, and the First Regiment was still trying to secure a home of its own. Baltimore's Fifth Regiment occupied the upper floors of the Richmond Market Armory, and Buffalo's Sixty-fifth Regiment used the state arsenal on Broadway—one of a handful of such buildings erected by New York State to store arms and ammunition. Cleveland, Cincinnati, Detroit, and St. Louis had no armories to speak of. Neither did Milwaukee, which, as one prominent guardsman remarked, was "utterly defenseless. She has not the vestige of an arsenal or a defensible armory."[8] Of the nation's big cities, only Brooklyn came close to providing adequate quarters for the volunteer militia.

The campaign for armories labored under several handicaps, perhaps the most severe of which was that after the Civil War the volunteer militia was, as one scholar has written, "at its lowest ebb in our history." All but a few elite units had trouble attracting recruits, retaining members, and raising money. Between 1860 and 1868 Pennsylvania lost more than 90 percent of its citizen-soldiers. In 1871 Ohio's Adjutant-General reported that "the State has no militia organization worthy of the name." Only two of Milwaukee's companies survived the postwar years; and only a handful of the St. Louis units continued to meet and drill. The volunteer militia was on the wane in large part because most Americans were weary of war. "The people now regarded soldiering as a serious and bloody business," observed General George W. Wingate of New York's Twenty-second Regiment, "and were heartily sick of it." After five years of one of the bloodiest conflicts in history, many Americans found it hard to take the militia seriously. "To those who were daily accustomed to read of great battles and military manoeuvers upon a grand scale," wrote Wingate, "the idea of joining a National Guard regiment, to make street-parades and to drill in an armory, seemed like 'playing at soldiering.'"[9]

As memories of the war faded, interest in the militia revived. Before the revival gained much momentum, however, the United States was struck by the Depression of 1873, the worst yet in the nation's history. The depression, which lasted about five years, dealt a heavy blow to the campaign for armories. With many merchants, bankers, and manufacturers hard pressed to keep their businesses afloat and maintain their luxurious lifestyles, the private sector had little money to spare for armories. The public sector was even worse off. Even before 1873 many states and cities were suffering from what Clifton K. Yearley calls the breakdown of fiscal machinery, the symptoms of which were soaring expenditures, lagging revenues, and growing indebtedness. During the depression these financial problems grew so acute that many Americans held that the public could not afford to assume new obligations. Probably no one advocated this position with more fervor than Controller Andrew H. Green of New York City. Speaking out against the Seventh Regiment's demand for a new armory, Green based his case primarily on the city's grim fiscal plight. "Are not our taxes high enough!" he said in 1875. "Is not our debt large enough! Is this the time to put other demands upon us! Had we not better get rid of the monstrous claims now being urged upon the Treasury before we launch again into this sea of wasteful outlay!"[10]

Even as the economy picked up, the campaign for armories lagged because in the eyes of most Americans the volunteer militia was only one of many voluntary associations and not necessarily the most worthy of support. It was one thing for the volunteers to try to build armories on their own and quite another for them to solicit funds from private citizens and public officials. Convinced that the nation would not soon be drawn into foreign wars, most Americans were unimpressed by claims that the militia was crucial to national defense. Nor were they swayed by assertions that it was vital to public order. Troubled by the outbreak of industrial strife during and immediately after the Civil War, some Americans feared that the nation was on the verge of open warfare between labor and capital. These fears were heightened by the Paris Commune of 1871, the accounts of which stressed that the threats to society came not only from labor unions but also from socialists, communists, and the so-called dangerous classes. But through the mid-1870s, the historian James Ford Rhodes later wrote, most Americans held that such uprisings were European phenomena, inconceivable in "a free republic" like the United States. They remained confident that the country could solve its social problems by providing free schooling, abiding by its religious precepts, and making land available to those who needed it.[11]

The Reverend Henry Ward Beecher, a Brooklyn clergyman and probably the most famous preacher of his day, carried this position a step further. Although his remarks were made in 1858, they were still timely a decade and a half later. America is not Europe, Beecher said. It does not depend for its safety upon soldiers and fortresses. It already has armories—though these armories are not places "where the soldiery congregate to beat down the spirit of freedom and coerce obedience from unwilling citizens."

Our armories are all along the streets!—Wherever we shall find fathers educating their children, there are the best drill sergeants, the best soldiers. Vigorous, well-educated families are our armories. Wherever we shall find an intelligent laboring man, whose labor is not compulsory, enforced, back-scarred labor; wherever are the men who work with their hands or with brains, skilfully and cheerfully, are our armories. Our schools, where every man, no matter how poor in money, if rich in children, can have them educated; our schools that teach not alone the rich man's heir or the scholar's son, or the offspring of any favored class, but where the children of all religions, races and nationalities, and conditions are taught the common ideas of American citizenship—these are the truest armories, and the cities that have these are inexpugnable.[12]

So long as most Americans agreed with Beecher, the campaign for armories was stymied. And it remained stymied until the last quarter of the century, when a series of momentous events revealed that the United States might be as susceptible to class conflict as Western Europe, that the volunteer militia might be as vital to America as the standing army was to other countries, and that in the interest of public safety the United States might have to replace metaphorical armories with real ones.

Probably the most momentous of these events was the railroad strike of 1877, which began not long after most of the nation's carriers cut wages by 10 percent. The strike began in Martinsburg, a small town in West Virginia, and soon spread to Baltimore, Pittsburgh, Chicago, and St. Louis (where, under the leadership of the Workingmen's Party, it developed into a general strike). The strike closed down the Pennsylvania, the Baltimore and Ohio, and other railways, bringing traffic to a standstill just about everywhere east of the Mississippi except in the South and New England. Many Americans, fed up with the rapacious practices of the railroads, sided with the strikers. And many of them were enraged when the authorities ordered the police, the sheriffs, and, when they were overwhelmed, the militia to open up the rail lines. What started as a strike soon turned into a riot. The rioters tore up tracks, set fire to trains, yards, and depots, destroyed bridges, cut wires, and emptied water tanks. Thousands strong, many armed with guns, knives, and other weapons, they also fought with the militia. So fierce was the struggle, and so uncertain the outcome, that President Rutherford B. Hayes gave in to pressure from railway managers and state officials to send in soldiers to restore order and end the strike.[13] It was only the second time in American history that the army was used in a labor dispute.

The railroad strike was "the most extended and dangerous this country has yet seen," Congressman James A. Garfield of Ohio wrote in his diary. It was also the closest thing thus far to a national strike. For almost two weeks it shut down the greatest of the nation's industrial enterprises; at its peak it tied up roughly two-thirds of the country's seventy-five thousand miles of track. By the time the strike was broken, Baltimore and other cities had been turned into armed camps. The property damage was staggering. In Pittsburgh, site of the worst civil disorder since the New York City Draft Riots of 1863, the mobs destroyed the Pennsylvania Railroad's Union Depot and Hotel, thirty-nine other buildings, more than one hundred locomotives, and more than two thousand other cars. The devastation, which stretched for two miles, came to $5 to $10 million. In other cities, none of which was as hard hit as Pittsburgh, the damage reached another $5 to $10 million. Even worse was the loss of life. At least twenty and as many as forty died in Pittsburgh. Eight fell in Buffalo, at least a dozen in Baltimore, and from thirty to fifty in Chicago. Most of the victims were strikers, rioters, and bystanders, the great majority of whom were killed by the militia; but a few policemen, militiamen, and soldiers were also among the casualties. Hundreds more were seriously injured.[14]

The strike did a good deal of psychic damage as well. To a people who had long "hugged the delusion that such social uprisings belonged to Europe," the events of 1877 "came," in the words of James Ford Rhodes, "like a thunderbolt out of a clear sky, startling us rudely." They "seemed to threaten the chief strongholds of society." Calling the strike "a great national disgrace," Edwin L. Godkin, editor of the *Nation,* wrote that it had done much "to shake or destroy" the deep-seated faith that the United States was the one country that had "solved the problem of enabling capital and labor to live together in political harmony," the one country "in which there was no proletariat and no dangerous class." The strike also left many gravely concerned about the future. Shortly before the strike was broken, the New York *Times* declared that it was "very likely the beginning of a series of social problems—largely labor problems—which our country may next be called upon to solve." Thomas A. Scott, president of the mighty Pennsylvania Railroad, was even more pessimistic. Writing in the *North American Review,* he predicted that unless the United States was unique—and, as a result of the uprising, he no longer believed it was—"the late troubles may well be but the prelude to other manifestations of mob violence, with this added peril, that now, for the first time in American history, has an organized mob learned its power to terrorize the law-abiding citizens of great communities."[15]

Not all Americans agreed with Scott. The recent strike notwithstanding, some still believed that the United States was capable of solving its labor problem without violence—more capable than "any [other] country in the world," contended *Harper's Monthly*. This position gained some credibility in the early 1880s, a time of renewed prosperity, but lost much of it in the mid-1880s, a period of widespread industrial strife, militant radicalism, and, above all, the Haymarket Affair. The Haymarket Affair occurred in Chicago in 1886. In the midst of a protracted struggle over the eight-hour workday and a bitter strike against the McCormick Harvester Company, the International Working People's Association held a mass meeting to protest police brutality. When the police appeared suddenly and ordered the crowd to disperse, someone threw a bomb, killing seven officers, wounding scores more, and prompting the rest to charge and fire into the crowd. Haymarket not only generated a great outcry, it also triggered the first major "red scare" in American history. Haymarket, said *Harper's Weekly*, was "an outburst of anarchy; the deliberate crime of men who openly advocate massacre and the overthrow of intelligent and orderly society." The United States, the Washington *Critic* declared, "is not big enough for men who bring with them from foreign shores the pestilential doctrines of the Commune, and undertake socialistic revolutions in the sign of the red flag."[16]

Despite major strikes in the Pennsylvania coal fields and on a few large railway lines, industrial relations were relatively peaceful in the five years after the Haymarket Affair. But the peace was rudely shattered in the spring of 1892, when the Carnegie Steel Corporation, the nation's largest manufacturer, announced that it intended to reduce wages at its Homestead, Pennsylvania, plant. The Amalgamated Association of Iron and Steel Workers, one of the country's strongest unions, refused to go along. When the current agreement expired, Henry Clay Frick, Carnegie's manager, closed the plant and locked out the workers. Frick had already turned Homestead into a fort, popularly know as "Fort Frick." When he tried to infiltrate a body of Pinkertons into it, a step designed to enable the company to bring in nonunion labor, the workers resisted. Armed with carbines, rifles, and pistols, they fought a pitched battle with the Pinkertons along the banks of the Monongahela, a battle in which ten were killed and scores wounded. In the end the Pinkertons surrendered to the workers. But the victory was short-lived. Several days later Governor Robert E. Pattison sent in the Pennsylvania National Guard, which occupied Homestead and, openly siding with the company, helped break the strike and destroy the union. Along with the great strikes in the Coeur d'Alene, Idaho, silver mines, the Tennessee coal fields, and the Buffalo railroad yards, Homestead left the country reeling.[17]

If 1892 was bad, 1894 was worse. In the wake of the Depression of 1893, the worst downturn in twenty years, bands of jobless men, the most famous of which was "Coxey's Army," decided to march to Washington and ask Congress for aid. Although few marchers made it to the capital, where their leaders were promptly arrested, the march came as a great shock. Even more shocking was the Pullman strike, which erupted when the Pullman Palace Car Company, citing hard times, slashed wages 25 to 40 percent. When the newly formed American Railway Union refused to handle Pullman cars, the General Managers' Association, an alliance of midwestern railways, ordered the discharge of everyone who joined the boycott. By this order the Pullman strike was transformed into a national railway strike that tied up the entire Midwest and spread as far west as San Francisco. When Attorney-General Richard Olney swore in federal deputies to keep the trains running, violence erupted in Chicago. At the urging of the General Managers' Association, and over the opposition of Illinois Governor John P. Altgeld, President Grover Cleveland sent in federal troops to restore order. Under the combined weight of the presidency, courts, army, militia, and police, the strike collapsed.[18] Although much less violent than the 1877 strike, the 1894 strike was a fitting climax to nearly two decades of industrial strife and social upheaval unprecedented in American history.

Some Americans traced these problems to the giant corporations, ruthless and impersonal, concerned only about profits, indifferent to workers, hostile to unions, more than willing to buy judges and legislators. Many more blamed the so-called dangerous classes, the poor, the criminals, the immigrants, the "social dynamite," in the words of the Reverend Josiah Strong, and the demagogues, many of them socialists, anarchists, and communists, who inflamed them. But no matter whom they held responsible, most Americans believed that at the heart of the current crisis was the growing polarization of American society, a process that filled them with great concern for the future of the republic. Writing after the 1877 strike, the historian Francis Parkman observed, "Two enemies, unknown before, have risen like spirits of darkness on our social and political horizon—an ignorant proletariat and a half-taught plutocracy." A decade and a half later the Reverend William H. Garwardine, a minister who sided with labor in the 1894 strike, remarked that "we as a nation are dividing ourselves, like ancient Rome[,] into two classes, the rich and the poor, the oppressor and the oppressed."[19] Many people believed that, if the rich grew even richer, the poor even poorer, and the line between them even sharper, it would not be long before class warfare broke out in the United States.

Fears of class warfare had surfaced in the early 1870s, when the newspaper reports of the Paris Commune generated a good deal of anxiety about public order in the United States. Writing in 1872, Charles Loring Brace said that "in the judgment of one who has been familiar with our 'dangerous classes' for twenty years, there are just the same explosive social elements beneath the surface of New York as of Paris." Unless the civilizing influences of American life were extended to the dangerous classes, he foresaw an explosion that "might leave the city in ashes and blood." These fears grew stronger in the mid-1870s, a time of severe industrial strife in the Pennsylvania coal mines. And on the eve of the railroad strike of 1877, an English visitor found that many affluent Americans had "an uneasy feeling that they were living over a mine of social and industrial discontent, with which the power of Government, under American institutions, was wholly inadequate to deal: and that some day this mine would explode and blow society into the air." But it was only after the railroad strike, amid the widespread turbulence of the 1880s and 1890s, that fears of class warfare became commonplace in the United States, that "the volcano under the city" emerged as a popular metaphor of American life, and that many Americans concluded that the country was on the verge of a catastrophe that might well destroy its economy and society and topple its republican institutions.[20]

Fears of class warfare were especially strong among the wealthy, many of whom agreed with the railway magnate Jay Gould that the strike of 1877 was the start of "a great social revolution" that would lead to "the destruction of the republican form of government in this country." But the less well-off were also concerned. The Pittsburgh *Leader,* a labor newspaper, declared in 1877 that the railroad strike might be the beginning of "a great civil war in this country between capital and labor." Josiah Strong, who spoke for many middle-class Americans, wrote in 1886 that "the volcanic fires of deep discontent" would probably explode in the near future. And the Topeka *Advocate,* a Populist newspaper, said in 1894, "Conditions [now] are the same as preceded the French revolution, and unless a change is effected, and that very soon, the *result* will be the same." Nor were these fears confined to any one region. A few years after Homestead the Galveston *Press* wrote, "We are in danger. The final test of our republican instititions is probably at hand, and the prospect is no brighter for us than for many nations that have drifted rapidly from lawlessness and crime into the vortex of disastrous revolution." Two and a half years later the *Nation,* one of the leading journals of the Northeast, said that "Coxey's Army" and the other bands of jobless men had brought America "dangerously near the conditions of things at the time of the French Revolution."[21]

Fears of class warfare also showed up in the popular fiction of the late nineteenth century. They permeated John Hay's *The Bread-Winners* (1884), Joaquin Miller's *The Destruction of Gotham* (1886), and Paul Leicester Ford's *The Honorable Peter Stirling* (1894), each of which portrayed industrial strife, rioting, and social upheaval. These fears even appeared in two of the most famous utopian novels of the day, Edward Bellamy's *Looking Backward* (1888) and William Dean Howells' *A Traveler from Altruria* (1894). But nowhere were such fears expressed as powerfully as in Ignatius Donnelly's *Caesar's Column,* which was published in 1890. Donnelly was a former Congressman, part-time novelist, and Populist spokesman. His book, an attack on industrialization and urbanization and a lament for the passing of the yeoman, artisan, and small businessman, tells of the life-and-death struggle between the plutocracy, known as the "Oligarchy," and the proletariat, called the "Brotherhood." The struggle ends in widespread death and destruction, not only in the United States but all over the world. The column in the title consists of the bodies of a quarter million New Yorkers, the victims of the cataclysm, piled on top of one another to commemorate "the Death and Burial of Modern Civilization." *Caesar's Column* struck a responsive chord, selling sixty thousand copies in the first year and two hundred thousand more in the next fifteen.[22]

A product of the strikes and riots that racked the United States in the late nineteenth century, the fears of class warfare were heightened by the rhetoric of both the radicals and the elites. Besides attacking property, religion, the state, and the family, many radicals argued that there was "but one recourse—FORCE!" to quote the Pittsburgh Manifesto of the Revolutionary Socialist Party. One anarchist urged "the execution of all reactionaries and the confiscation of all capital by the people"; another, stressing the need to "meet fire with fire," demanded "death to the Vanderbilts, the Goulds, and the Chisholms." Some radicals favored dynamite, "the weapon of the son of toil." Others contended, "Whether one uses dynamite, a revolver, or a rope, is a matter of indifference." Indicative of the radical rhetoric was a socialist circular that was widely distributed in Cincinnati a day after the Haymarket Affair. After declaring that only revolution would bring relief to the working people, it called on them to "Form your battalions."

> Fling the police in the gutter, the militia in the river! Drag the venal politicians and corrupt judges from their seats; chase the capitalist hyenas from the town, the priests from the churches! . . . Blow up the infamous Legislature! Scourge the corruption of Congress from the capitol! . . . Why delay an instant? Are you not hundred thousands—millions? Who can withstand you if you choose? Into the street! Forward! Forward! *Allons, enfants de la patrie!*[23]

The elites were only slightly less belligerent. In the midst of the railroad strike of 1877, William W. Scranton, General Manager of the Lackawanna Iron and Coal Company, said, "I trust when the troops come,—if they ever get here,—that we may have a conflict, in which the mob shall be completely worsted. In no other way will the thing end with any security for property here in the future." Two decades later Theodore Roosevelt, already well known for his bellicosity, declared that the Populists were "plotting a social revolution and the subversion of the American Republic" and proposed that Populism be suppressed "as the Commune in Paris was suppressed, by taking ten or a dozen of their leaders out, standing them . . . against a wall and shooting them dead." Similar sentiments were often voiced by high-ranking national guard officers. Speaking at an annual convention of the Wisconsin National Guard in 1884, Colonel Charles King advised his fellow officers that in a riot, "Do not shoot until you have to, but when you shoot, shoot to kill"; he also spoke of the Milwaukee mobs, "on whom it might be a municipal blessing to fire." Seven years later Brigadier-General Albert Ordway of the Washington, D.C., National Guard wrote, "If you [the guardsmen] are ever brought in contact with a mob, let us hope that the anarchists will constitute the front ranks, if not the entire body of it. What otherwise might be a duty will then become a pleasure."[24]

The fears of class warfare were heightened not only by what the radicals and elites said, but also by what they did. Soon after the railroad strike of 1877, a group of St. Louis socialists held a meeting at which they urged workingmen to arm themselves and enrolled several hundred Civil War veterans in military units. Events in Chicago were even more ominous. As industrial conflict heated up in the mid-1880s, the Central Labor Union, an alliance of radical unions with about twelve thousand members, recommended that the workers use arms to defend themselves against the Pinkertons, police, and militia. At least one union, the metal workers, followed this recommendation. At the same time local anarchists decided to establish a school of chemistry "where the manufacture and use of explosives would be taught." Armed bands of radicals were also formed in other cities, among them the Detroit Rifles, the Cincinnati Rifle Union, and the New York International Guards Association. These developments produced so much anxiety in Illinois that the state legislature passed a law forbidding all armed bands except state militiamen and federal troops to drill or parade without a license from the governor. Upheld by the U.S. Supreme Court in 1886, the law drove these groups underground.[25]

The elites took similar, and even more drastic, measures. Afraid that the railroad strike might spread eastward and endanger life and property in New England, President Charles W. Eliot began drilling the Harvard College riflemen in 1877. A year later the Chicago Citizens' Association, a group of prominent businessmen, gave the city's police force one hundred handguns and rifles, four cannons, one Gatling gun, and thousands of rounds of ammunition, all of which were to be used only in the event of civil disorder. During the 1880s many businessmen and other community leaders formed vigilante groups, generally known as "Law and Order Leagues," to help maintain public order. To counter the armed bands of radicals, some Chicago businessmen set up military outfits for their employees. In one large wholesale house, for example, there was an organization of 150 young men who were armed with Remington rifles and drilled on a regular basis. Even more menacing were the private (or corporate) police forces, the most infamous of which were the Pennsylvania "Railroad Police" and "Coal and Iron Police." Authorized by the state legislature in 1865, these outfits grew rapidly after 1877. Although commissioned by the governor, they were accountable only to the corporations that employed them. Armed with handguns and rifles, these forces patrolled the state much like an occupying army.[26]

With hindsight, the fears of class war seem exaggerated, perhaps even a little paranoid. During the late nineteenth century capital and labor fought one battle after another, but civil war did not break out. Republican institutions swayed, but did not topple. There were riots, but no insurrection; upheavals, but no cataclysm. Well aware of this, some historians have put forth ingenious explanations for these fears. One has argued that some Americans viewed every challenge to their ideas as a threat to the nation—and "seemed always to sense revolution breathing down their necks, to smell the blood of martyrs, indeed, to anticipate the sharp edge of the guillotine"—because they lacked faith in the "natural laws" of political economy. Another has contended that urban elites felt particularly threatened because they were "preoccupied by their own physical and moral decay," seriously troubled by the decline of stamina, vigor, and the Spartan spirit, by the transformation of ruddy farm boys into sallow industrial men.[27] There is something to be said for these explanations. But they should not lead us to forget that for many Americans who read about the conflagration at Pittsburgh, the slaughter at Haymarket, and the bloody battle at Homestead, who heard the threats of the radicals and elites and watched them arm as if for Armageddon, there was ample evidence that the country was well along the road to class warfare.

During the late nineteenth century Americans came up with a wide range of schemes to head off class war. Some were designed to exclude immigrants, others to assimilate and uplift them. Some were proposed to disenfranchise the poor, others to improve their housing, schools, and neighborhoods. Some were intended to regulate railways and other giant corporations, others to emasculate labor unions and radical groups. But if Americans sharply disagreed about the long-term solutions to their current problems, they generally agreed on the short-term response. They believed that no matter how pressing the problem or great the grievances, order must be maintained at any cost. *Harper's Weekly* took this position shortly after the railroad strike of 1877, insisting that the moment a group resorts to violence, "all good citizens, whatever their sympathies, are of one mind and purpose, and combine to vindicate the law and preserve order at all hazards." The same point was made by George B. McClellan, a former Civil War general and one-time presidential candidate. "If any proper and practical thing is asked, it should be granted promptly and graciously," he wrote a few months before Haymarket; "but if any attempt is made to gain [something] by violence, it is absolutely necessary to meet force promptly with overwhelming force, and crush the outbreak at once and effectually."[28]

In the cause of maintaining order, most Americans were more than willing to use force. As the *Independent,* a religious periodical, put it after the railroad strike of 1877: "If the club of the policeman, knocking out the brains of the rioter, will answer, then well and good; but if it does not promptly meet the exigency, then bullets and bayonets, cannister and grape—with no sham or pretense, in order to frighten men, but with fearful and destructive reality—constitute the one remedy and the one duty of the hour . . . Napoleon was right when he said that the way to deal with a mob was to exterminate it." The same sanguinary spirit surfaced in the wake of the Haymarket Affair. *Harper's Weekly* called for "the most complete and summary methods of repression." The New York *Tribune* demanded "the sharpest and sternest application of force." And branding the anarchists "incendiary scum," the Washington *Sunday Herald* claimed that they "should be disposed of as quickly as possible." The Buffalo switchmen's strike of 1892 triggered a similar response. Summing up the prevailing view, *Railway World* argued:

> Peace and order must be preserved, even at the point of the bayonet. It was necessary to teach the lawless element of Homestead a lesson, and it is necessary to suppress the outbreaks at Buffalo and other points. Civilization and not savagism must control this Republic, and those who think otherwise must be conquered. It is not long since the red savage fought desperately for the control of several States of this Union, only to find that the logic of events was sharper than the arrow and stronger than the tomahawk. The white savage needs his lesson.[29]

Probably no one voiced this implacable attitude more forcefully than the Reverend A. J. F. Behrends, pastor of Brooklyn's Central Congregational Church. In January 1895 Brooklyn was the country's third largest city, a city that took great pride in its homes and churches. It was also a city in turmoil, caught up in a bitter streetcar strike that had tied up the transit system, provoked sporadic violence, and prompted the authorities to send in the First and Second divisions of the New York State National Guard. "Brooklyn is humiliated," Behrends said in his Sunday sermon on Janury 20. "Its authorities are defied . . . It is time for firmness and determination. I want to back up the authorities. I want this church to speak up for law and order. The time has come when our representatives in the City Hall should know that the people are prepared for vigorous action. If clubs will not do, the[n] bayonets; if bayonets will not do, then lead; if lead will not do, then Gatling guns. If we must have martial law and a state of siege, then let us have them, and if the worst comes to worst we will turn our churches into hospitals. We must have peace, and we will have it at any cost." According to a reporter, Behrends then asked his parishoners, "'Do we want anarchy? Do we want Brooklyn to show the white feather?' The worshippers jumped to their feet and shouted 'No! No!' 'Say it again,' cried the clergyman, and the response was given with a shout that could be heard outside the building."[30]

This implacable attitude was an outgrowth of two things besides the fears of class warfare. One was the prevailing perception of the strikers and rioters. With exceptions, Americans believed that the troublemakers were foreigners. "These people are not Americans," said one newspaper shortly after Haymarket, "but the very scum and offal of Europe." They are, claimed another, the "rag-tag and bob-tail cutthroats of Beelzebub from the Rhine, the Danube, the Vistula and the Elbe." They have no appreciation of American values and American institutions, argued a national guard officer. Even worse, a New Jersey educator pointed out, they know little or nothing about "any higher pleasures than beer-drinking and spirit-drinking, and the grossest sensual indulgence . . . They eat, drink, breed, work, and die." Speaking of the railroad strike of 1877, the *National Guardsman* declared that many of the leaders were refugees from the Paris Commune. The troublemakers were socialists, nihilists, and communists, insisted a Portland, Oregon, judge, "enemies of God and man," who were "swarming" to the United States to foment hostility to "the reign of law and the rights of property." Joining the chorus of condemnation that followed the Haymarket Affair, the Buffalo *Courier* contended that these people had "forfeit[ed] every title to consideration at the hands of society . . . and put themselves beyond the pale of mercy."[31]

Their uncompromising attitude was also an outgrowth of the prevailing perception of the strikes and riots. Most Americans thought these uprisings were not so much squabbles between capital and labor, about which people of good will could disagree, as out-and-out insurrections, which left no room for differences of opinion. Speaking of the railroad strike of 1877, the Philadelphia *Inquirer* remarked that the strikers "have declared war against society . . . They have practically raised the standard of the Commune in free America." The strike, wrote the Washington *National Republican,* was "nothing less than communism in its worst form." Discussing the strike at the Cleveland Rolling Mill Company in 1885, the local newspapers put the blame on "Communistic scoundrels," who were manipulating the Polish and Bohemian laborers, "the canaille of Europe," in their attempt to establish socialism and nihilism in the United States. The Haymarket Affair was even worse. "An outburst of anarchy," in the words of *Harper's Weekly,* it demonstrated that the radicals would do anything, even murder policemen in the street, to destroy American society. Although the railroad strike of 1894 set off less hysteria than Haymarket, many Americans agreed with the commander of the Michigan Grand Army of the Republic, who called it "a rebellious effort to overthrow constitutional government, to destroy the avenues of interstate commerce and to suppress individual liberty."[32]

Most Americans stressed that they had nothing against labor or labor unions. They acknowledged the right of workers to organize, even to strike. But when they force other workers to strike, the *Independent* argued, "the question ceases to be one of allowable conflict between capital and labor, and instantly becomes an issue between law and anarchy. Laborers are then criminals in intent and criminals in fact. They are rioters and public enemies, and worse than wild beasts turned loose upon society." *Harper's Weekly,* a strong advocate of the widely accepted principle of "freedom of contract," made much the same point: "Every man has a right to work for whomsoever he prefers, and upon terms acceptable to both sides. But no man or body of men has the right to interfere with the equal right of other men to make their own labor bargains and the moment they attempt to interfere forcibly, and others for the worst purposes join them, they invite anarchy and become the enemies of civilized society."[33] Organized labor claimed that "freedom of contract" was a sham, that in view of the great power of the employers and the abundance of scab labor, it was impossible for the workers to bargain effectively as individuals. But when the workers resorted to collective action, when they formed picket lines and engaged in violent protests, most Americans held that the issue was no longer wages or working conditions. It was the supremacy of law and preservation of order. And with law and order at stake, there could be no temporizing.

This implacable attitude towards violent protest was also a function of the profound changes in American ideas about public order that took place in the nineteenth century. Throughout the late eighteenth century, the historian Pauline Maier has pointed out, riots and rebellions "were often calmly accepted as a constant and even necessary element of free government." Popular uprisings, Americans believed, served as a check on the authorities, though they were to be employed only after the legal avenues of redress were exhausted. The mob was composed of most segments of the community and often led by its more prominent members. Provided that it exercised restraint and selected its targets with care, the mob was generally regarded as an extralegal arm of the community, a legitimate form of vigilante activity. These beliefs were put to a severe test in the early and mid-nineteenth century, a time of widespread rioting. Time and again the mob resorted to violence, usually to preserve the status quo. To restrain minority groups, whites lashed out at blacks and Protestants at Catholics. Consumers also rioted to stop predatory practices by local merchants. But the conventional wisdom retained much of its force. And the elected officials responded to these uprisings in what another historian has called a "lackadaisical" manner, normally calling on the volunteer militia only when the situation threatened to get out of hand.[34]

After independence, however, new ideas about public order surfaced. Some Americans came to believe that the mob was unnecessary in a society where the people governed themselves and could redress their grievances at the polls. Appropriate in a monarchy, riots and rebellions were out of place in a republic. For several decades the old and new ideas coexisted. But after the great riots of the 1830s and 1840s, which left many casualties and much destruction, many Americans found the new view more compelling. In the wake of the Draft Riots of 1863 and the railroad strike of 1877, which were far more violent than the earlier uprisings and much more of a challenge to the status quo, the new view superseded the old. At the laying of the cornerstone of the new Seventh Regiment Armory in 1879, George W. Curtis clearly stated this position: "In a State where the people govern, every wrong can be lawfully redressed, and no wrong is so great as anarchy. A riot is an insurrection against popular government. It is the unpardonable sin in a Republic." The same point was made, though less eloquently, by Colonel William S. Brackett, Inspector-General of the Illinois National Guard and a man much troubled by the prospect of war between capital and labor. "With the ballot in every man's hand," he wrote in the early 1890s, "there is no room for the sword and torch of revolution in this free land."[35]

Indicative of the power of this notion of public order was the response to the Cincinnati Courthouse Riots of 1884. The riots grew out of what was regarded as a travesty of justice, the acquittal of a man who was almost certainly guilty of murder. A protest meeting triggered an attempted lynching and widespread rioting. By the time the police and militia restored order, at least fifty people had been killed, twice as many wounded, and the local courthouse burned down. Although most Americans decried the verdict, they still condemned the riots. As the Reverend T. De Witt Talmadge of Brooklyn put it:

> If ever a mob had a right to gather it was in Cincinnati last week, at the failure of the Courts to establish justice, murderers slipping through the fingers of the law until crime was at a premium and trial by jury a farce. If ever a mob ought to have succeeded, this was the mob. But they failed, and have given new illustration of the fact that mobocracy is under no circumstances to be countenanced . . . There may be some difference as to what had better be done; but this Cincinnati riot shows what ought not to be done. If the ballot-box and Christian reform can not correct these evils without bloodshed, then Republican and democratic form of government is a failure.[36]

The New York *Times* agreed. The riots, it said, revealed "the inevitable tendency of a mob once started on its mad career. It had evidently swept into its current the reckless and dangerous element which had no appreciation of the original motive for popular excitement and knew none of the restraints of sober people." Such uprisings, the *Times* went on, "cannot be regarded with anything but condemnation, and should be sternly suppressed by the authorities at whatever cost."

To suppress them was easier said than done. The elected officials had at their disposal three principal forces, the local police, state militia, and federal troops. A paramilitary body that served as the first line of defense against crime and disorder, the local police had been organized in the second third of the nineteenth century. By the late 1870s most big cities had at least one hundred paid officers, nearly all of whom were armed with clubs and handguns, dressed in distinctive uniforms, and on call twenty-four hours a day. These officers helped put down dozens of serious disturbances in the mid-nineteenth century—sometimes, as in the case of the Draft Riots of 1863, at great personal risk. But as the railroad strike of 1877 revealed, the local police were not up to dealing with a large and unruly mob. For one thing, they were too small. As late as 1880 only New York and Philadelphia had more than one thousand policemen; and only four other cities had as many as five hundred.[37] No American city had a force large enough to subdue the tremendous mobs that filled the streets of Pittsburgh and Baltimore in 1877.

And many small cities—even important transport and industrial centers like Martinsburg, West Virginia, and Reading, Pennsylvania, both of which were racked by riots in 1877—had no police force to speak of at all.

For another thing, the local police were unreliable, especially in the case of industrial disputes. Although most police forces usually sided with management, sometimes even engaging in blatant strikebreaking, the Pittsburgh police sympathized with labor in 1877. So did the Chicago police in 1894 and the Brooklyn police a year later. More often than not, the reasons were personal. Asked to account for what Colonel David E. Austen of the Thirteenth Regiment called the "execrable" conduct of the Brooklyn police in the streetcar strike of 1895, Police Commissioner Leonard R. Welles stressed that most of the force was recruited "from the same ranks as the striking motormen and conductors." Even when the local police were willing to deal with riots and other civil disorders, they seldom had the necessary arms and skills. Most policemen carried no weapons other than clubs and handguns, which were not enough to quell a large mob; and they received no training in the use of rifles, cannons, and Gatling guns. Nor did they know much about street maneuvers, riot drills, and other crowd-control tactics. Most officers were patrolmen, who usually worked on their own and rarely operated as part of a team. They could be counted on to check what the Reverend Howard Crosby termed "the sporadic ebullitions of crime," but to suppress a dangerous mob, a larger, more reliable, and more martial force was required.[38]

The federal troops were one such force. Although the regulars had rarely been used in domestic upheavals in the antebellum period, they conducted themselves with distinction in the railroad strike of 1877. Brave, steady, and well disciplined, they managed to intimidate the rioters without shedding much blood. The troops made so favorable an impression that Thomas A. Scott and other influential citizens argued that the army should be turned into an internal peacekeeping force and quartered near large cities and other business centers. To be effective, it should be expanded from about twenty-five thousand men, most of whom were scattered along the coast and on the frontier, to at least fifty thousand. Congressman James A. Garfield and other backers of this proposal stressed that public order was paramount and should be entrusted to whichever force would be best able to maintain it. The regulars, the Reverend Henry Ward Beecher claimed, "are in every way better than [the] militia, be they ever so good," more skillful, more efficient, even more humane. The railroad strike, wrote the journalist Edwin L. Godkin, proved "that the rioters had more respect for one Federal bayonet than for a whole company of militia." The proposal to enlarge the army won the support of many Americans, not the least of whom were military leaders looking for a new mission in the aftermath of the Civil War and Reconstruction.[39]

This proposal ran into a great deal of opposition, however. Some Americans objected on the grounds that the Civil War was over and a foreign war was highly unlikely. Instead of expanding the army, Congress should cut it back to about ten thousand men, who would serve as a nucleus around which militiamen and volunteers would rally in the event of emergency. Also opposed were many Southerners, who were angered by the army's role in Reconstruction and especially its support of carpetbaggers. New York Congressman Abram S. Hewitt and other opponents argued that the preservation of order was the responsibility of the towns and cities, and if need be the states, not the federal government. What with defending the coastline and frontier, the army had plenty to do without breaking strikes and quelling insurrections. An army of fifty thousand or more would also be a great expense, Hewitt pointed out, an expense that the taxpayers could ill afford.[40] By far the most important source of opposition stemmed from the longtime objections to a standing army, the deep-seated fears that such a body would undermine the republic and inevitably bring about despotism. In the face of such strong opposition, Congress refused to enlarge the army, leaving it with only twenty-five thousand men and thereby thwarting the attempt to turn the federal troops into a domestic peacekeeping force.

The only other force available was the state militia (or citizen-soldiers). In the absence of a large standing army, it was, as the Providence *Journal* put it in 1877, the country's "only defence against internal disorders." It was an adequate defense, many Americans insisted. Although the members were volunteers, their companies and regiments were a powerful force, the Reverend Mr. Crosby wrote. "Made up of citizens interested in the city's welfare and taking pride in its order, they form an army in themselves with the full apparatus of war, the knowledge of whose existence is an effectual curb to the vile and violent passions of the lawless." Besides stressing the volunteers' long and distinguished record, supporters pointed out that the militia was an extremely economical force. At very little cost, it served as backup to both the local police, in the case of domestic turmoil, and the federal troops, in the event of foreign warfare. Without the volunteer militia, both these forces would have to be substantially increased—at great cost to the taxpayers. Supporters also argued that it was far wiser to entrust the preservation of order to citizen-soldiers, who were citizens first and soldiers second, than to professional soldiers, who were little better than mercenaries. As Congressman William Kimmel of Maryland argued in 1878, one was part of the country, the other separate from it; one produced wealth, the other consumed it; one thrived on peace, the other on war.[41]

From 1877 on the volunteers and their backers stressed that "in its militia [the community] has an arm to reinforce its police—[and] that this arm is the last resort for the public peace if the police give way." During the 1880s and 1890s they also emphasized that the militia served the nation in other important ways as well. The militia, said Judge George H. Williams of Portland, Oregon, keeps alive the military spirit, a spirit that fosters patriotism, loyalty, strength, and honor—the virtues that made the United States a great nation. The militia is "the nation's great school," wrote Lieutenant-Colonel Henry L. Turner of Chicago's First Regiment. Besides "love of country," it teaches courage, steadiness, and self-reliance. To this list Governor William E. Russell of Massachusetts added obedience, discipline, and self-control. The militia turns out good employees as well as good citizens, declared Colonel William McMichael of Philadelphia's First Regiment. "The punctuality, obedience, and manly bearing taught to the young men are reflected in the precision of their business habits, for he who serves well his [military] company will be found prompt and faithful to his employer."[42]

In the aftermath of the railroad strike, however, many citizens were skeptical about the militia. The New York *Times,* ordinarily an ally of the volunteers, said that it was no longer clear that "our Militia system, as now constituted, can hereafter be relied upon to restore law and order in any formidable riot." The Chicago *Tribune* went further, arguing that it was evident that "people who play soldiers under the name of militia or independent military organizations are rather worse than no soldiers at all for the purpose of quelling insurrection." The skeptics held that in many states the militia was an effective force only in the large cities and that in many others it was a military force in name only. They also argued that the militia was badly organized and poorly trained, that the companies and regiments functioned more like social clubs than military units, spending the bulk of their time at dinners and parades rather than at target practice and riot drill. A more serious charge was that a volunteer force was inherently defective. To be effective, the *Nation* said, a volunteer must be "a businessman, a skilled artisan, a property-holder, somebody having a stake in the country." Yet if called upon, he must leave his home and work "to perform duties with which he is unfamiliar and which are distasteful to him." By its very nature, a volunteer force is "a clumsy substitute either for a military or a police establishment."[43]

The widespread skepticism about the volunteer militia was based largely on its showing in the railroad strike, which even its staunchest supporters conceded left much to be desired. The militia was probably at its best in New York State. Yet in New York City half of the volunteers failed to report for duty. As a militia officer admitted, one of the city's leading regiments consisted largely of "Irish workingmen in perfect sympathy with their oppressed fellow workmen." One upstate regiment had so low a turnout that the brigade commander declared it "unfit to bear arms" and recommended it be disbanded. One upstate company allowed a mob to board its train; whereupon the mob attacked the volunteers, took away most of their weapons, and forced them to flee from the scene. The story was much the same elsewhere. The militia did not turn out in Indiana. And in Ohio, Illinois, and West Virginia, it did not obey orders. Many volunteers refused to fire on workers fighting wage cuts and on crowds of friends and relatives. Instead, they mingled, even fraternized, with the mob. In Baltimore most volunteers reported for duty, but were later overwhelmed by the rioters. When the Sixth Regiment made an attempt to restore order, a ferocious mob drove many of its members back into their armory.[44]

The militia was probably at its worst in Pennsylvania. Its conduct, said the New York *Times,* ranged from "disgraceful" to "pitiable." In Pittsburgh, where most residents sympathized with the strikers and loathed the Pennsylvania Railroad, the Fourteenth and Nineteenth regiments were completely ineffective. Many of their members stayed home; others mingled with the strikers, even "giving them muskets" and "eating hard-tack with them," one observer testified. Norristown's Sixteenth Regiment fraternized with the rioters in Reading and, according to an official investigation, "declared [its] intention, in case of further trouble, of siding with them." It even gave the rioters ammunition. Several companies of the Sixteenth were subsequently disbanded for insubordination and mutinous conduct. The militia was so ineffective in western and central Pennsylvania that the authorities sent in supposedly crack units from Philadelphia. These units were more formidable and less sympathetic. Even so, a detachment of the Philadelphia First Troop was captured near Harrisburg, stripped of its weapons, and, in what the state adjutant-general called "a humiliating spectacle," paraded through the streets. The mob handed the arms and ammunition over to the mayor on the condition that they would not be used against the strikers. It also freed the prisoners, who "drifted, demoralized, piecemeal back to Philadelphia," wrote the *Times.* "The revelation of their helplessness is startling."[45]

Although severely troubled by the militia's conduct in the railroad strike, most Americans still believed it could be relied upon to preserve order. They rejected arguments that a volunteer force was a poor substitute for a professional force, contending that citizen-soldiers were the proper military force in a republic and that the United States did not have a standing army large enough to deal with widespread disorder. They also bridled at charges that the militia would inevitably side with the mob. "I do not believe so ill of my countrymen," declared Congressman Hewitt. "I do not believe they are so ignorant of the rights and duties of citizenship. If they are, then this whole government is founded on a delusion and a snare."[46] So far as most citizens were concerned, the militia should be revitalized, not replaced. To achieve this goal, militia leaders argued, the states would have to provide more money; this would make it possible to increase the number of volunteers and improve their facilities. Even more important, the militia would have to be completely overhauled, its structure tightened, its personnel better trained and better disciplined, and its mission focused on crowd control. Starting soon after 1877, militia leaders and public officials launched a nationwide campaign to transform the citizen-soldiery along these lines.

The campaign made much progress in most states. A good example is Pennsylvania, where the volunteers had been disgraced in 1877. The militia—or, as it was now referred to, the national guard—was centralized along military lines. The companies were formed into regiments, the regiments into brigades, and the brigades into a division. A tight chain of command extended from the adjutant-general down to the rank and file; and though the guardsmen could still choose their officers, their choice would now be reviewed by a military board. To encourage enlistment, the state reduced the term of service from five to three years and increased the stipends for active duty. To tighten discipline, it created a system of military justice, under which errant guardsmen could be court-martialed and drummed out of the service. At great expense, the state set up a summer camp where guardsmen spent as many as fourteen days a year on field maneuvers and other military tasks. It also provided new weapons and new uniforms, replacing the swallow-tailed coats and plumed shakos with combat fatigues. Other states, of which New York was the most prominent, adhered less closely to the military model than Pennsylvania, abandoning fewer of the traditions of the volunteer militia.[47] But without exception they too turned their national guards into more centralized and professional military organizations after 1877.

Closely related to these reforms were the efforts to develop tactics to deal with riots and other civil disorders. Here the lead was taken by two New Yorkers, E. L. Molineux, commander of the Twenty-third Regiment and later of the Second Division, and William Brownell, head of the Forty-seventh Regiment and later of the Fourth Brigade. Their writings described how to maneuver in streets, maintain communications, remove barricades, and safeguard vital points. Underlying the tactics was Molineux's principle that "promptness, rapidity of movement, iron decision, crushing power exercised relentlessly and without hesitation, is really the merciful, as it is the necessary, course to be pursued." Spread via journals of martial affairs and conventions of state guardsmen, these tactics were soon adopted by most national guard organizations and incorporated into their training manuals. On occasion they were even tried. In May 1889 New York's Seventh Regiment performed one of Brownell's riot drills on the streets of the Upper East Side. In November 1890 the Massachusetts Volunteer Militia conducted a sham battle in which one regiment captured Lawrence and another took New Bedford. Besides providing the national guard the opportunity to perfect its skills, the riot drills and sham battles sent a not-so-subtle warning that the states were prepared to use whatever force necessary to suppress riots and other uprisings.[48]

By the mid-1890s, at the latest, the national guard had been transformed. As one of its boosters put it:

Time was, and not so many years ago, when the militia of our various States served only as the never-failing topic of ridicule and jest, useful only on holiday occasions to add to the brilliant pageantry of the scene. But, happily for the dignity and safety of the State, and by reason of the introduction in recent years of a thorough system of drill and other practical methods of military instruction, we have now in almost every State, large bodies of educated and skillfully trained men who, in their discipline and fitness for the field, rival even the regulars of the national government.[49]

The guard now consisted of 112,000 men (of whom 9,000 were officers), or roughly four times as many as the U.S. Army. New York had 12,800, by far the largest force; Pennsylvania had 8,600, Ohio 6,100, and Massachusetts 5,700. Even more were eager to enlist. As early as 1885 there was a long waiting list in Pennsylvania; and in 1893, a Wisconsin guardsman remarked with envy, there were regiments in New York "to which admission is as difficult as to some exclusive clubs." Moreover, the guardsmen were committed to maintaining order no matter who was disrupting it or how well founded their grievances. Their attitude was nicely summed up by a mill worker who belonged to Pennsylvania's once infamous Nineteenth Regiment. "It'll be a hard thing for me to shoot into a crowd of men who are bound to me by all the ties of human interest and friendship," he said in 1892, "but when I have my uniform on and the command of 'Fire!' is given, I will shoot."

Thus unlike the militia, which had served as a check on the state, a means of helping to preserve liberty, the guard was an agency of the state, a means of maintaining order and protecting property.

This change was a mixed blessing. On the one hand, the guard developed into an effective peacekeeping force. During the 1880s and 1890s it was repeatedly called upon to put down riots and other civil disorders. Although the guardsmen sometimes let the situation get out of hand, their performance on the whole was impressive, much more impressive than their showing in the railroad strike of 1877. Turnout was high, and discipline tight. Few guardsmen mingled or fraternized with the rioters, and fewer were overpowered and captured by the mobs. Impressed by the guardsmen's strength, reliability, and willingness to shoot to kill, even critics admitted that the national guard was a strong repressive force. Spokesmen claimed that the guard was an effective preventive force too. As New York Adjutant-General J. G. Farnsworth wrote, it had "a moral effect upon the disturbing element" that prevented many outbreaks. Many ordinary citizens shared this view. "The mere fact," said one of them, "that there is a compact body of armed men, always ready to assist the civil officers in the preservation of the peace, is in itself one of the surest guarantees against the necessity for its ever being called into the field."[50]

On the other hand, the guard also developed into a powerful strikebreaking force—into, in one historian's words, the "policeman of industry." After 1877 it was often called up to deal with disorders that grew out of labor disputes; indeed, it was called up more often to deal with this type of disorder than with any other. Some of the call-ups involved only one or two companies and lasted only a day or two; others, among them the Homestead lockout and Buffalo switchmen's strike, involved several regiments and dragged on for a week or longer. In some cases the guard used minimum force to maintain order; in others, among them the Colorado militia's war on the Western Federation of Miners, it acted ruthlessly and illegally. Spokesmen contended that the national guard was strictly neutral, committed not to capital or to labor but to public order. But given the assumption of "freedom of contract," and the corollary that the state had an obligation to defend anyone who wanted to cross a picket line, the guardsmen invariably sided against organized labor and thereby strengthened the already commanding position of management. As another historian has pointed out, "One searches United States labor history in vain for a single case where the introduction of troops operated to the strikers' advantage."[51]

Once established as the "policeman of industry," some state guards weeded out officers and units which were allegedly sympathetic to organized labor. Others also screened out union members. Brooklyn's Forty-seventh Regiment asked each applicant, "Are you connected in any way with any labor organization?" If he said yes, he was rejected. Brooklyn's Thirteenth Regiment followed a similar policy. Asked if it inquired about membership in the bar association and stock exchange as well, Colonel David E. Austen replied, "No. We don't inquire into any thing else than labor organizations." Asked why, he answered that it was obvious. "All the disturbances of the peace of recent years have been made by the workingmen." These practices had no impact on the elite units, which had normally recruited only upper-middle- and upper-class men who, in Colonel Thomas F. Edmands' words, had a "good education and the instincts of a gentleman." But they had a great impact on the rest of the national guard. Because some workingmen were turned down and others discouraged from applying, the guard became a much more homogeneous force, whose rank and file came mainly from the middle class and whose commanding officers belonged largely to the upper-middle and upper classes. Some workingmen, even some with strong ethnic ties, were admitted into the national guard, but they had to give up their prolabor views, act in spite of them, or eventually drop out of the service.[52]

These changes infuriated organized labor. At the annual convention of the American Federation of Labor in 1892, Samuel Gompers protested that the militia had been transformed from an organization to defend the people into a machine to oppress the workingmen. A special committee appointed to study the problem recommended to the convention that unless the authorities took steps to curtail the use of the national guard in labor disputes, the Federation and its affiliates should forbid their members to join the militia. Four years later the Federation adopted a resolution along these lines, though only after a heated debate; and several of its affiliates subsequently amended their constitutions to prohibit membership in the guard. The AFL was not the only source of animosity. In the wake of Homestead, an Ohio labor organization sent circulars to workers who belonged to the guard charging that the militia was the friend of capital and foe of labor. A year later the AFL's rival, the Knights of Labor, called for the abolition of the guard. And not long after the railroad strike of 1894, the Cleveland Central Labor Union boycotted local firms which employed guardsmen. This hostility sorely troubled guard leaders, one of whom complained in 1895 that "we have today every labor organization against us."[53]

Opposition to the national guard also came from other groups. Among them were the Populists, many of whom believed that the guard was, in the words of the Topeka *Advocate,* "a private army directly under the command of the capitalists" and ready, at their order, "to suppress any uprising of the common herd." Also opposed were the socialists, who viewed the guard as a capitalist tool and insisted that it should either be abolished or turned back into a popular force. Still other Americans objected to the national guard on the grounds that its heavy-handed practices increased the likelihood of class warfare in the United States.[54] The opposition did not, however, have much impact on the guard, at least not before 1900. One reason is that the opposition had much less power than the upper-middle- and upper-class allies of the national guard. Another was that the fears of class warfare served to insulate the guard from criticism. Still another reason was that its opponents were hard pressed to offer a plausible alternative to the national guard. However much they detested the guard, they detested the Pinkertons and Coal and Iron Police even more; however much they feared the guardsmen, they feared even more the regular troops. Even Americans who sympathized with organized labor believed that though the guard might be bad, the alternatives might well be worse.

The emergence of the national guard as the country's chief peace-keeping force, its principal protection in the event of civil disorder, did not change the purposes of the armory. It remained the home of the guardsmen—the place where they stored their equipment and uniforms and where they drilled, socialized, held meetings, and assembled when summoned by the elected officials. But the transformation of the guard greatly enhanced the importance of the armory. It was now commonly regarded as an integral part of the guard, an essential element, as an Ohio judge wrote in 1893, of "a complete and perfect state militia." From this point of view, the national guard would not be a fully effective military force until spacious and comfortable armories were built for all the troops.

Perhaps no one expressed this position more forcefully than New York State Adjutant-General Josiah Porter, who wrote in 1888:

> The armory lies at the basis of our State system in military matters. In establishing a National Guard organization, almost the first thing to be considered is how to get a drill-room. The men, except on rare occasions, can only be assembled for drill and instruction in the evening, and necessarily, therefore, there must be a drill-room capable of being well lighted and heated, and there must also be a place where their arms, equipments, ammunition and uniforms can be safely kept while they are engaged in their occupations as citizens. *In other words, there must be an armory or there will be no soldiers.*[55]

Spokesmen for the guard hammered away at this point, insisting that a first-rate armory was essential in order to attract qualified recruits. The guard was made up not of professionals or conscripts but of ordinary citizens, who were under no compulsion to join. As General James McLeer, commanding officer of New York State's Second Division, remarked in 1891, "The only chance of getting good men to volunteer for the guard work lies in making that work as attractive as possible. Comfortable quarters and pleasant surroundings and a little amusement now and then all do their share toward keeping the guard recruited with desirable men." Pointing to New York's Seventh Regiment, Colonel William E. Seward, head of the city's Ninth Regiment, claimed in 1887 that its great popularity was largely a consequence of its splendid armory. Much the same point was made by Colonel Thomas F. Edmands, commanding officer of Boston's First Corps of Cadets. For years he contended that his troops sorely needed a place not only where they could keep their weapons and practice their drills, but also where they could "drop in, as they would at a club, and find comforts and conveniences which will be in a degree some compensation for the work they are called upon to do in a Military way." "Could we have such a place," he wrote in 1890, "it would certainly assist us to increase our numbers to a strength commensurate with the dignity and reputation of our organization and thus increase our true Military efficiency."[56]

Spokesmen for the guard also insisted that a first-rate armory was essential in order to turn the recruits into capable soldiers. The guardsmen received valuable instruction and training at their summer camps, but they spent only a couple of weeks a year there. To train a soldier—to teach him how to use a rifle and drill with precision and to inculcate in him the discipline and esprit de corps which are the hallmarks of an effective military unit—took more time. It could only be done in an armory. Speaking at the laying of the cornerstone of Brooklyn's new Fourteenth Regiment Armory in 1883, Mayor Seth Low told the troops that he was delighted with the building not so much because it would provide a pleasant place to drill and socialize as because "it will make of you a better regiment and better soldiers." Addressing the National Guard Association of the State of New York, its chaplain, the Reverend Newland Maynard, said in 1890 that handsome armories would foster both the military and the social sides of the guard. General Charles R. Dennis, Rhode Island Quartermaster General, went even further. Nothing the state could do, he declared in 1891, would "so much enhance the value of its militia, make it self-respecting and respected, ensure enlistments from good, reliable and proper men, or make it more honorable to wear the insignia of an officer [as supplying] good drill halls and rooms for its work."[57]

Spokesmen for the guard stressed that a proper armory served the citizen-soldiery in two other vital ways. One was as a place for storage. It made no sense for the state to give the guardsmen new weapons, more ammunition, new uniforms, and more equipment without providing safe places to store them. The existing facilities were far from satisfactory in most cities. In some they were completely inadequate. A case in point is Boston. In the late 1880s a special committee of the state legislature found that the city had roughly "1,300 stand of arms, four field-pieces, two gatling guns, sabres, carbines and ammunition distributed at twenty-two different isolated points, unprotected, ready [to fall into] the hands of the first comers in case of any disturbance."[58] As both the Draft Riots of 1863 and the railroad strike of 1877 revealed, the mob knew where the militia kept its arms and ammunition. If another serious uprising occurred, many people believed that these places would be prime targets. In the event of an attack, it would have been bad if the arms and ammunition were destroyed and even worse if they fell into the hands of the groups from whom the guard was supposed to defend the country.

The other vital way in which a proper armory served the citizen-soldiery was as a means of defense. It made no sense, argued spokesmen for the guard, for the state to entrust the life and property of its citizens to the guardsmen without providing them secure quarters of their own. Again, the existing facilities were barely satisfactory in some cities and hopelessly inadequate in others. After looking into the situation in Boston, the special committee of the state legislature pointed out the dangers of small, isolated, defenseless armories located on upper stories of combustible buildings. "In case of a riot extending over the whole city the individual members of the militia would be overpowered and prevented from assembling in the first instance, or, even having assembled in companies of fifty or sixty, could be cut off, surrounded, smoked out in their attics and extinguished in detail by the mob." As the Draft Riots and the railroad strike revealed, the guardsmen needed a safe place to assemble and, if worst came to worst, as it did for Baltimore's Sixth Regiment in 1877, a safe place to retreat and regroup. They needed fortresses, declared Colonel Thomas F. Edmands, strong, defensible structures, "impregnable to mobs."[59]

Spokesmen for the guard contended that the revitalization of the militia could not be completed as long as most guardsmen lacked suitable armories. "The best armory in the State will not of itself make a good regiment," declared New York State Adjutant-General Josiah Porter in 1888, "but the best officers in the State will find it difficult, under the conditions of National Guard service, to make a regiment in a barn." To a generation that was filled with deep-seated fears of class warfare, such a prospect was intolerable. Now that the nation intended to uphold order not, in the words of an antebellum jurist, by "the moral sense of the community," but by "the strong arm of authority," the belief spread that the revitalization of the national guard had to be completed whatever the cost. And if part of the price of an effective guard was what Reverend Maynard called "handsome and commodious" armories, most Americans were ready to pay it.[60]

chapter two

The Building of the Armories

To build a "handsome and commodious" armory cost a good deal more money than even the wealthiest regiments could afford. To raise it the guardsmen had to appeal to private citizens, public officials, or both. In short, they needed good friends and good connections. Probably no military unit had more of both than New York's Seventh Regiment, the first unit to erect an imposing and fully equipped armory of its own. The Seventh decided to mount a campaign for a new armory in 1868, less than a decade before the great railroad strike. Its leaders knew that many New Yorkers would be unsympathetic, if only because the Tompkins Market Armory was by far the largest and most elegant in the city, but they believed they had a good case. The job of making it fell to Colonel Emmons Clark. A Hamilton College graduate, a successful New York businessman, and, like many other militia leaders, a veteran of the Civil War, Clark had enlisted in the Seventh in 1857 and was elected its commanding officer seven years later. The Tompkins Market Armory lacked an adequate drill hall, Clark argued; the ground floor, the best place for a drill hall, was occupied by local shopkeepers, and the top floor, where the drill hall was located, could not bear the weight of the entire regiment. The Tompkins Market Armory was also in need of repair. Worst of all, it was located too far south. As the Seventh's upper-middle- and upper-class members moved uptown, they found it a burden to make the long trip downtown for

regimental affairs. Unless the Seventh obtained a new armory uptown, Clark said, "not only the prosperity and efficiency, but the
very existence of this Regiment is endangered."[1]

From 1868 to 1874 the Seventh's campaign for a new armory
was bogged down in a controversy over the site, a controversy that
will be discussed in Chapter 3. In the end the city leased to the
regiment, at no cost, a two-acre parcel on the Upper East Side.
Originally the Seventh had planned to finance the armory on its
own, relying on subscriptions by members and friends. But as the
Depression of 1873 fastened its grip on the nation, the regiment's
leaders changed their minds. They now insisted that it was unfair
to expect them to erect what was essentially a public building at
their own expense, especially when they already gave so much time,
energy, and money to the regiment. General Alexander Shaler,
commander of the First Division, agreed, arguing that it was as
unreasonable to ask militiamen to build their own armories as it
was to ask policemen "to build their own station houses." The
Seventh therefore began to press the authorities to appropriate an
estimated $350,000 for the building. Besides repeating the argu-
ments put forth by Colonel Clark, the Seventh claimed that the
outlay would not materially increase taxes and pointed out that
twenty thousand of the city's largest taxpayers had signed a petition
urging the municipal authorities to erect a new armory for the
regiment.[2]

For a while it looked as if the Seventh might succeed. In the
middle of 1875 the city council voted to appropriate $350,000 for
a new Seventh Regiment armory. The appropriation, however, had
to be approved by the Board of Estimate, which had strong reservations about the proposal. An outgrowth of the notion that the city
had already spent more than enough money to provide adequate
quarters for its militia, these reservations first appeared shortly after
the depression struck. As the depression grew stronger, so did the
reservations. The Seventh's chief opponent on the board was the
redoubtable Controller Andrew H. Green, who argued against the
proposal on two grounds other than the city's high taxes and large
debt. One was that the city had given the Seventh Regiment a site
for its new armory with the clear understanding that the regiment
would pay for the building. The Seventh should stand by its commitment. The other ground was that the city could not afford it. If

it gave in to the Seventh's demands, each of its twenty other military units would ask for a new armory, and the point would soon be reached where "we shall have no property to protect, and armories and regiments will alike be unnecessary."[3]

Colonel Clark did his best to blunt the controller's attack. He denied that the regiment had accepted the site on the condition that it would build the armory, ignored the issue of the city's fiscal problems, and restated the then familiar arguments in favor of the new armory. The mayor and president of the board of aldermen were persuaded, but the controller and commissioner of public works, the other members of the Board of Estimate, were not. With the board deadlocked, the appropriation was blocked. The regiment brought a lawsuit, charging that the board had acted illegally in blocking the appropriation, but the court ruled against it. The regiment then filed an appeal. As the months passed, however, Colonel Clark and his fellow officers saw that by pursuing the issue through the courts they were antagonizing many prominent New Yorkers who agreed with Controller Green. Thus in January 1876 the regiment reversed itself again and decided to make an attempt to finance the armory privately.[4] Other military groups had done so in the recent past. New York's Twenty-second Regiment had raised $20,000 for an armory in the early 1860s, and Philadelphia's First Troop had raised $30,000 for an armory in the mid-1870s. But no military group had ever attempted to raise as much as $350,000 to erect an armory, much less to raise it in the midst of the worst depression in the nation's history.

Shortly afterwards the Seventh Regiment organized a general committee, chaired by Colonel Clark, to solicit money from members and friends. In mid-February it requested contributions from the general public as well. To instill popular confidence in the enterprise, it asked three extremely wealthy and well-respected New Yorkers to serve as trustees of the fund. In both private and public appeals, advocates emphasized that the Tompkins Market Armory was inadequate and inconvenient, that the time was inopportune to build an armory with public money, and, above all, that the Seventh played a vital role in maintaining order in New York City. As one of the regiments's circulars put it:

The Seventh Regiment, since its organization in 1824, has always been called upon to aid the civil authorities whenever the peace of the City, or the lives and property of its people were in danger, and from its reputation for drill and discipline, and from the fact that its officers and members, directly or indirectly, represent the friends of law and order and that part of the community which has large financial interests that are often imperilled by the riotous and disorderly, has always been relied upon for assistance on occasions of local disturbance. *It has never failed to promptly respond when called upon, or to perform its duties to the entire satisfaction of the civil authorities and of the people.*[5]

"If history repeats itself," the circular warned, "the time when the services of this regiment may be needed again may not be far distant, and it is the interest of every citizen to spare no effort or expense to keep it in the highest state of military efficiency."

The response was favorable, if less than enthusiastic. Calling the regiment's decision commendable, the New York *Herald* observed that the armory would be useful in the event of a serious disturbance in the city. "Property should think of this when it sees the subscription list." The New York *Tribune* remarked that "the banks, insurance and trust companies, in fact all the large corporations of every kind, owe to themselves as well as to the regiment, ample aid in this matter." The drive got off to a good start. By the end of February, about $55,000 had been raised, and by the beginning of May roughly $80,000. Half came from current or former members of the regiment, scions of such prominent New York families as Phelps, Lenox, and Vermilye, the rest from New York's wealthiest residents and businesses. Alexander T. Stewart, the department store magnate, gave $2,500. John Jacob Astor, the real estate tycoon, donated $1,000, as did William H. Vanderbilt, the railroad baron, Drexel, Morgan & Company, the investment bankers, Harper Brothers, the publishers, and Singer Manufacturing Company, the maker of sewing machines. In the summer and fall, however, the drive slowed; by November it came to a complete stop. With the nation preoccupied with the presidential election, the Seventh suspended its efforts to raise additional money—though as a sign of its determination to go ahead, it proceeded to let the contracts for the excavation and foundation of the new armory.[6]

These efforts stayed suspended through July 1877, when the railroad strike got under way. New Yorkers expected the worst. An important railroad center, the city had a great many workers and radicals, most of whom sympathized with the strikers. Yet New

York was spared the sort of violence that racked Pittsburgh and Baltimore. Not even a mass meeting at Tompkins Square, the site of pitched battles between policemen and workers only three years earlier, triggered a serious riot. "What was generally supposed to be the worst-governed city on the continent," the New York *Tribune* wrote, "turned out to be the only one in which a mob durst not raise its hand." Many New Yorkers attributed the city's good fortune to the rapid mobilization of both the police force and the volunteer militia, which was either held on reserve in its armories or sent out to the trouble spots. And it was widely believed that not only the city but the entire nation was deeply indebted to the militia. As the *Journal of Commerce* wrote shortly after the strike:

> There is not a property owner or lover of peace and order in the country who does not owe the citizen soldiers of this city at least his hearty thanks. If the riotous elements in this city and State had not been overawed by the brave and determined attitude of our militia . . . the mobs, now dispersed or checked in nearly every State of the Union, would have done far more damage than they have inflicted. A successful rising of the roughs and thieves of the metropolis would have been the signal for more desperate resistance to the laws in all parts of the land.[7]

By highlighting the city's dependence on the volunteers, the railroad strike offered the Seventh Regiment a wonderful opportunity, which it lost little time in seizing. A week or so after the strike came to an end, Colonel Clark resumed the dormant campaign by making a public appeal for funds, an appeal that stressed the regiment's prior service in preserving order and protecting property. He did not refer specifically to the recent strike, but as it was on everyone's mind, there was no need to. This time the response was extremely enthusiastic and virtually unanimous. Colonel Clark's appeal, wrote the New York *Commercial,* "ought to meet with a prompt response from our wealthy citizens, who, now, more than ever, appreciate the value of reliable military organizations in the preservation of order and protection of life and property." The New York *World* made the same point. "There should be no question of the results of such an appeal at this moment, when the remembrance of the invaluable services rendered by the citizen soldiery of New York to the community is still so fresh and so vivid." "That this gratitude should take on the monumental and expressive form of a new armory, given out and out by appreciative citizens to their brave defenders is preeminently fitting," wrote the New York *Evening Mail*.[8]

The results of the appeal were impressive. By November 1878, about a year after the regiment laid the cornerstone of the new armory, another $110,000 had been subscribed. It came not so much from a few regimental officers and very wealthy New Yorkers as from many upper-middle- and upper-class individuals and institutions with a tremendous stake in the status quo. Colonel Clark explained the regiment's success as follows:

> Although it was a period of financial and business depression many merchants, bankers, manufacturers and taxpayers contributed to the fund, when solicited, for the reason that they believed that a well drilled and disciplined military organization must be sustained and is necessary in a large city as the right arm of the civil power. Finally the banks, insurance and trust companies and other corporations were appealed to for aid to the New Armory Fund and several thousands of dollars were contributed by these conservative institutions for the reason solely that, in the opinion of the officers and directors, such appropriations afforded additional security and insurance to the property of their stockholders and customers.[9]

The elites were more generous to the Seventh after 1877 than before mainly because of the railroad strike, though a gradual upturn in the economy may have helped. The strike confirmed the regiment's claims that the nation was prone to civil disorder and that the militia was its principal safeguard. For the elites it was now hard to say no to a proposal that was supposed to promote the volunteers' military efficiency and increase their repressive force.

Although the regiment had raised $190,000, it was still short of its goal. Late in 1878 Colonel Clark therefore issued yet another appeal. He urged businessmen and taxpayers to subscribe, warning that unless more money came in work on the armory would be suspended. Despite support from the press, this appeal brought in only $20,000, leading the regiment to look for other ways to raise the rest of the money. In 1879 it found them. At the regiment's behest, the state legislature authorized it to issue $150,000 worth of bonds, the site and building to serve as security. The legislature also mandated the city to pay the regiment $15,000 a year for fifteen years (in lieu of rent for an armory), a sum that would be used to pay principal and interest on the bonds. Sold at a premium—and, as a favor to the regiment, handled at no charge by New York Life and Trust Company—the bond issue realized close to $151,000. Also at the regiment's behest, the legislature directed the Board of Estimate to pay for the heating and lighting systems in the new armory and for the sidewalks around it, which brought in another $31,000. And it required the city controller to purchase from the regiment the furniture and fixtures in the Tompkins Market Armory, which came to $24,000.[10] The state's largesse—with the city's money—was testimony not only to the clout of the Seventh Regiment but also to the fears of class warfare.

By April 1879 the administration building was standing, and the drill shed under construction. But to complete the interior and furnish the rooms, the Seventh needed even more money. To raise it, the regiment held a gala fair inside the new armory. After several months of work, the fair opened in mid-November. It was a spectacular sight; the armory was filled with lights, flowers, and booths that resembled a Chinese gateway, a Persian pavilion, and a Venetian tent. It was a high-spirited celebration of the Seventh Regiment, the volunteer militia, the city of New York, and the city's upper-middle and upper classes. Above all, the fair was a terrific fund-raiser. Tens of thousands attended—admission was fifty cents for a day and three dollars for all three weeks—and most of them came to spend. They bought raffle tickets and subscription drawings, played grab bag and wheel of fortune, and purchased food, books, candy, tobacco, pianos, carriages, and even a yacht. The fair earned a whopping $159,000. As just about all the work was done by the officers and their wives and nearly all the goods were donated by local merchants (and military units from other cities), the expenses came to less than $18,000, leaving a surplus of about $141,000. Of this, $91,000 was earmarked for the armory, $30,000 for the company rooms, and $20,000 for the veterans' room.[11]

Shortly after the armory was completed in 1880, the Seventh reported that it had raised more than $589,000—or about twice as much as was raised for the Statue of Liberty. About $90,000 came from the regiment's members, $27,000 from its veterans, and $5,000 from "the ladies." Citizens gave $81,000, corporations an

additional $33,000. The bond issue produced $151,000, th\
$141,000, and miscellaneous receipts close to $61,000. Excep\
the funds given by the city, virtually all the money came in \
way or another from the upper-middle and upper classes, who sa\
the militia as the main bulwark of public order. With this money,
the regiment built by far the largest, most impressive, most elegant
armory in the country (as well as one of the most expensive structures in the city). With its huge drill shed and imposing administration building—which provided rooms for the commander, the other
officers, the veterans, the band, and each of the ten companies and
which held a gymnasium, a library, a rifle range, and several small
drill rooms—the new Seventh Regiment Armory was, one New
Yorker later wrote, "the last word in armories in those days."[12] The
Seventh Regiment did more than build an armory. It did even more
than build an armory that profoundly influenced the structure and
style of later armories, a point that will be discussed in Chapter 4.
The Seventh also inspired other militia units, in New York and
other cities, to build new armories of their own. By showing these
units how to do it, the Seventh helped build many other armories
as well.

After the railroad strike of 1877, Philadelphia's First Regiment,
Boston's First Corps of Cadets, and several other militia units
mounted campaigns for new armories. For most it was their first
effort. Some had no quarters of their own; others had inadequate
quarters. But each thought it was entitled to a spacious and handsome armory; and in light of the success of New York's Seventh
Regiment, each believed it stood a good chance of obtaining one.
A few of these units appealed to the elected officials for help, an
appeal that was ordinarily supported by the adjutants general, most
of whom held that the states should pay for the armories. With the
exception of New York's Eighth Regiment, however, none of them
had much success. Even the Eighth, which prevailed on the state
legislature to appropriate $100,000 for a new armory in 1879, lost
out when the local officials failed to provide a suitable site. Some
elected officials opposed the requests for help on the grounds that
the state's taxes were too high or its debt too large. Other officials,
especially representatives of rural communities in the Midwest,

objected on the grounds that the armories were exclusively for the benefit of big cities.[13] In the face of this opposition, a good many militia units opted to follow the example of the Seventh Regiment and build new armories on their own.

Most of these units modeled their campaign on the Seventh Regiment's. They set up special committees to solicit funds from members, friends, affluent citizens, and large corporations. To assure potential benefactors that the money would be used properly, they invited people of great wealth and standing to serve as members of the committees and as trustees of the funds. A case in point is Chicago's First Regiment. It appointed as trustees of its armory association A. G. Van Schaick and C. L. Hutchinson, "each," wrote one of its officers, "with his fifteen or twenty directorships," J. J. Mitchell, "with the burden of his great bank," and H. H. Kohlsaat, "with his prosperous business and varied investments." In addition to soliciting contributions directly, the units also raised money indirectly from the upper-middle and upper classes. Philadelphia's First Regiment held two fairs, one in 1880 and another in 1884; they were managed, wrote former Adjutant-General Joseph A. Latta, by the "best of society's best women." The Pennsylvania State Fencibles also held a fair, as did the Ninth (Wilkes-Barre) and Thirteenth (Scranton) regiments. Boston's First Corps of Cadets tried a slightly different, but extremely lucrative, device. Instead of holding a fair, it produced a series of popular theatricals accompanied by souvenir programs full of advertising.[14]

Most of these units based their appeals on more or less the same grounds as the Seventh Regiment. Pointing to the railroad strike and other uprisings, they stressed the precarious nature of American society. "The skies may be clear to-day, and the functions of government may run smoothly and peacefully, and no enemy may seem to be lurking at home or abroad," warned Boston's First Corps of Cadets, "but no man knows when the storm may burst." The militia had quelled such uprisings in the past and could be counted on to quell them in the future. Support for the militia was more than an expression of gratitude; it was a form of insurance as well. As Colonel Thomas F. Edmands of the First Corps remarked, "It is the duty of every citizen to interest himself in the militia just as he would look after the security of the lock on his safe." To ensure an efficient militia, a militia that attracted qualified recruits and turned them into capable soldiers, it was essential to provide large and comfortable armories. "Armories," declared the First Corps, "are public necessities, because public safety demands them for the proper maintenance of the militia, which is the last resort, in time of public danger, as an auxiliary to the police."[15]

The response to these appeals was as a rule quite favorable. After praising Philadelphia's First Regiment for its "splendid work" in 1877, the *North American* urged the citizens to give to the campaign for a new armory. Although it was unlikely that the regiment would be needed again in the near future, one could not be sure. To protect the community against "any possible outbreak of lawless violence," the newspaper said, it was vital to support the First: "Every large holder of property should, for his own sake, make a regular contribution for its maintenance. Corporations especially, which have the most to lose and are the first to be attacked when the public peace is broken, ought to make generous and regular donations for its support. They may be sure of getting full value for their money."[16] In Boston the newspapers strongly endorsed the First Corps' campaign. Calling units like the Corps "the last resort in disturbances of the peace, and in the protection of life and property," the *Daily Advertiser* declared that the new armory "will prove one of the best investments that our citizens can make." The *Journal* insisted that the First Corps was "just as necessary as our police and our fire department" and urged the citizens to look upon the new armory as a form of insurance. Showing a high degree of urban chauvinism, some Boston newspapers took the position that Bostonians should do at least as much for the First Corps as New Yorkers had done for the Seventh Regiment.

Philadelphia's First Regiment, which had tried without success to build an armory of its own in the mid-1870s, renewed its efforts in 1878. It started out with $26,000, the bulk of which was left over from the prior campaign, and in only a few years raised another $174,000. Of this roughly $90,000 came from private subscriptions. The Pennsylvania Railroad, the largest corporation in the state, gave $5,000. The principal target in the railroad strike, the Pennsylvania was headed by Thomas A. Scott, who had urged President Hayes to send in the troops in 1877 and a year later proposed that the army be turned into a domestic peacekeeping force. Another $5,000 was given by Major Edwin N. Benson. A wealthy Philadelphia businessman from a prominent Philadelphia family, Benson had joined the First in 1861, the year it was organized, served with distinction in the Union Army, and in 1875 founded the regiment's Veterans Corps. Other affluent Philadelphians made generous contributions, ranging from $500 to $1,000, as did several banks, insurance companies, investment houses, and railroad companies. Another benefactor was John Wanamaker, one of the city's leading merchants, who sold the First the site for the new armory for $80,000—which was $20,000 less than fair market value, according to real estate dealers. The regiment raised $40,000 by holding fairs, benefits, and a circus and picked up another $40,000 by taking a mortgage on the property.[17] The fund raising went so well that the regiment was able to lay the cornerstone in 1882 and move into what was perhaps the finest armory outside of New York two years later.

Boston's First Corps of Cadets began to think about building an armory of its own in 1878, when it was renting quarters on Tremont Street and holding its drills in the nearby MIT gymnasium. In 1880, when it saw that it could not count on help from the public sector, the Corps solicited funds from private sources. In charge of the campaign was Colonel Thomas F. Edmands, a Civil War veteran and successful Boston businessman who had assumed command of the Corps in 1868. The campaign got off to a good start, but came to a standstill after President James A. Garfield was assassinated in 1881. Edmands, who was deeply concerned about the prospect of civil disorder, then decided to look for twenty wealthy Bostonians to contribute $2,500 apiece. He found them, though it took a while. Among the benefactors were Kidder, Peabody & Company and Lee, Higginson & Company, the investment bankers, and members of the Forbes, Sears, Ames, Weld, Nickerson, and Hunnewell families, the same Bostonians who went to Harvard College, worked on State Street, and were buried in Mount Auburn Cemetery. In the end the Corps raised $269,000 through direct contributions. Its fifteen theatricals, the first of which was produced in 1884, earned another $236,000. A mortgage on the property, plus miscellaneous revenues, brought the total to a whopping $688,000.[18] It took two decades to raise all the money, but when the drill shed was finished in 1897, two years after the administration building was completed, the Corps had by far the most impressive armory in New England.

Chicago's First Regiment, which had taken a ten-year lease on a small armory erected by the Union Mutual Insurance Company in 1878, began to feel cramped for space in the mid-1880s. Shortly after the Haymarket Affair it launched a campaign to build a new armory of its own. Outraged by Haymarket, the city's commercial and civic elites strongly supported the regiment's efforts. The principal benefactor was Marshall Field, the department store magnate and one of the local merchants who had put his delivery wagons at the disposal of the police force in 1877. Field leased to the regiment a large site on Michigan Avenue for ninety-nine years at $4,000 per year—a site for which he had been offered $8,000 per year with a revaluation every ten years. The lease, observed the Chicago *Tribune*, "is a virtual gift to the First Regiment of $400,000." As the value of the site was bound to rise, the lease was worth even more. Although Mayor De Witt Clinton Cregier deplored the policy of "passing around the hat" to build armories for the militia, neither the state nor the city gave the First any money. But with the help of some prominent bankers and the backing of the Citizens' Association, the businessmen's organization that had furnished the police force with arms and ammunition in the aftermath of the railroad strike, the regiment had little trouble raising $150,000 for the building. With much fanfare, it laid the cornerstone in 1890.[19] When the armory was completed two years later, it stood out as one of the most formidable structures in the Midwest.

The Detroit Light Guard, one of Michigan's oldest military organizations, began its campaign to build a new armory of its own in 1895. Given the opposition of rural interests to using state funds to erect armories, the Guard had no alternative but to rely on private sources. To acquire a site, which cost $40,000, and construct a building, which cost another $60,000, the Guard adopted an unusual strategy. It first took $2,000 life insurance policies on more than forty of its members, the premiums on which came to $5,600 a year. Using these policies and a first mortgage on the armory as security, it arranged a loan of $35,000 from the Provident Life Insurance Company—though as it allowed these policies to lapse in 1898, it only received $25,000 from the company. The Guard then issued $60,000 (and later another $20,000) in bonds, which were secured by a second mortgage on the armory. At the prompting of Mayor W. C. Maybury and other civic leaders, local businessmen subscribed to most of the bonds. Among the chief benefactors were William A. Butler, a wealthy businessman with interests in banking, insurance, and real estate, and Henry M. Duffield, a graduate of Williams College and a general in the Union Army who later served as head of the Light Guard and first president of the Michigan State Bar Association.[20] The Guard made such rapid progress that it was able to lay the cornerstone in 1897 and finish the armory a year later.

For many militiamen, especially members of the elite units, a contribution to the armory fund was a way of expressing loyalty to their military organization, improving its facilities, and enhancing its prestige. It was also a means of affirming their own values. The Hunnewells, Peabodys, and Welds regarded a gift to Boston's First Corps in much the same way as a gift to Harvard College, the Boston Athenaeum, Massachusetts General Hospital, and other Brahmin institutions. For many other Americans, most of whom had no formal ties to a military unit, a contribution to an armory fund served other purposes. Some believed that the national guard helped keep alive patriotism and nationalism and foster obedience, discipline, self-control, and other middle-class values. They gave money for armories in much the same spirit as they made gifts to YMCAs and other institutions which were supposed to turn young men into good citizens and good employees. Many prominent businessmen also saw the national guard as the chief defense against civil disorders—a means of protecting life and property and upholding the status quo. For them a donation to an armory fund was a way to reward the militia for its previous service and to ensure its readiness and reliability in the event of future trouble.[21] In other words, it was a form of insurance, a quid pro quo that was agreeable to businessmen and guardsmen alike.

Perhaps nowhere was this quid pro quo so explicit as in Scranton, Pennsylvania, the center of a great coal and iron mining region that suffered some of the country's worst industrial strife in the late nineteenth century. In 1899 the Thirteenth Regiment decided to replace its old armory, a small structure built by the Scranton City Guard with the help of local coal, iron, and railroad companies shortly after the railroad strike of 1877. To raise a large part of the $250,000 that was needed, the regiment asked the major coal companies to contribute 1 per cent of the cost of each ton of coal mined in 1898. A committee of industrialists turned down this request and proposed instead that the Thirteenth finance the armory by issuing no-interest bonds. The companies would buy the bonds and, provided the regiment remained an effective force in the community, hold them indefinitely. Although this arrangement put the Thirteenth at the mercy of the companies—which, if dissatisfied with its conduct, could demand that the bonds be redeemed—the regiment went along. The Delaware, Lackawanna and Western Railroad Company and three other powerful corporations promptly purchased $91,000 worth of bonds. Following their lead, other coal and iron companies, railroads, banks, and wealthy citizens bought the rest.[22] The fund raising went so well that the new Thirteenth Regiment Armory, a large armory for so small a city, was completed in 1900.

The elites supported the national guard in a number of ways other than by making contributions to the armory funds. In 1881 the Pennsylvania Railroad carried the entire state guard without charge to Washington, D.C., to celebrate the inauguration of President Garfield. In 1897 the Pennsylvania and other railroads transported the guardsmen to Philadelphia, again at no charge, to attend the dedication of the Washington Monument. The Delaware, Lackawanna and Western Railroad gave Scranton guardsmen free trips to and from their summer camp, the cost of which was covered in part by Scranton businessmen. The Lackawanna Iron and Coal Company provided the troops with a rifle range, and the Dickson Manufacturing Company donated iron targets. Things were much the same elsewhere. Baltimore merchants and manufacturers raised money to send Maryland's Fifth Regiment to the Inter-state Fair in Raleigh in 1891 and the Cotton States and International Exposition in Atlanta four years later. In Indiana the railroads carried the guardsmen to and from their summer camp at no charge; and the cost of the encampments was covered in part by Indianapolis civic leaders. In St. Louis and Kansas City wealthy residents helped finance the guardsmen's day-to-day activities as well as their summer camps.[23] In much of the country businessmen also supported the national guard by allowing employees time off to attend summer camps and engage in other military matters.

With the help of the elites, other militia units built armories of their own after 1877. The St. Louis militia erected an armory in

1882, the money for which was raised by a committee of affluent merchants and other prominent citizens. St. Louis' Battery A financed an armory with private subscriptions in 1898, as did Kansas City's Battery B a decade later. In 1882 Chicago's First Cavalry built a new armory with the proceeds of a bond issue. And a decade later the Cleveland Grays raised the money to put up an imposing armory of its own. Perhaps nowhere were private efforts more successful than in Pennsylvania. During the 1880s and 1890s the guardsmen built dozens of armories, almost all of which were paid for with private funds. In the late 1890s, for example, Philadelphia's Second Regiment built a new armory with money supplied by what one scholar has called "a 'who's who' of Philadelphia's financial, industrial, and social elite." And shortly thereafter Philadelphia's First Troop—which had been one of the first military groups to use private funds to build an armory, putting up its first in 1864 and its second in 1874—prevailed upon its members and friends to finance its third (and, as it turned out, its last) armory.[24]

Not all the military units that attempted to emulate New York's Seventh Regiment were successful. A case in point is New York's Twenty-second Regiment. Early in the 1880s the regiment decided to build a new armory, one that would replace its old armory on Fourteenth Street, a small building in need of major repair. Following the example of the Seventh Regiment, the Twenty-second formed a committee to solicit contributions. But as one of the regiment's officers later wrote, the members found that "the Seventh Regiment had been over the ground before them and had practically exhausted the field."[25] Despite a strong effort, the committee raised barely enough money to cover expenses. The regiment felt it had no option but to ask state and local authorities for funds. Many other military units ran into the same problem and reached a similar conclusion: in order to obtain a new armory, they had to seek help from public officials, and especially from the state legislature.

In their appeals for public funds, these units made several points other than that the country was in grave danger of social upheaval, that the national guard was the chief bulwark of public order, and that adequate armories were essential for an effective force. One of these points was that the existing armories were woefully inadequate (and very expensive to boot). The guardsmen claimed that their quarters were small and dangerous. They did not have enough room to store arms and equipment, much less to hold regimental drills; they were unsafe in the event of a fire and could not be defended in the face of a mob. Speaking in 1897 at the opening of the campaign for a new armory for Baltimore's Fifth Regiment, Captain C. Baker Clothworthy said of the old Richmond Market armory: "To have a first-class regiment quartered in a barn like this is a disgrace as well as a peril to the State." Other guard leaders insisted that for the same money the elected officials spent to rent inadequate quarters they could build spacious and attractive armories. Typical were the comments of Colonel John F. Jones, commanding officer of New York's Twelfth Regiment, which was housed on the second and third floors of a building on West Forty-fifth Street. "I am of [the] opinion," Jones stated in 1884, "that land could be bought and a suitable building erected at a cost the interest on which will amount to less than the rent now paid."[26]

A second point that the guardsmen made was that armories should be built by public authorities and not by private individuals. To erect suitable armories was an integral part of the state's responsibility to maintain public order. It was unfair to expect the troops to pay for what were public buildings, especially when they gave so much of their time and energy to the service. The guardsmen also contended that it was up to the states, not the cities, to build the armories. As soldiers of the state, they were sworn to serve everywhere within its borders. They carried the state's weapons and wore its uniforms. They were regulated by the legislature and accountable to the governor. Arguing in favor of a new armory for the Fifth Regiment, one-time Attorney-General John P. Roe emphasized that "this is not a Baltimore affair, it is a Maryland affair." Supporters dismissed objections that the states should not build armories because they served only the big cities. "It will not do for the people of localities where riots are not likely to occur to object to this item of taxation," said Lieutenant-Colonel David Williamson, president of the National Guard Association of the State of New York. "Disturbances begun in one portion of the State may rapidly reach another and endanger the lives and property of its citizens."[27]

A third point that the guardsmen made was what might be called state pride. In 1888 the Rhode Island Quartermaster-General proposed that Rhode Island build armories for its militia in order to keep up with New York and other states. Pointing out that New York and New Jersey had already built several new armories, the Pennsylvania Adjutant-General argued in 1896 that "there seems to be no good reason why Pennsylvania, not usually behind in the treatment of its Guard, should not emulate their example." The Maryland Adjutant-General wrote in 1891 that New York and other cities had left nothing "undone to promote the comfort of the troops." And a former Maryland governor later indicated that state pride played no small part in the decision to finance Baltimore's new Fifth Regiment Armory.[28] Moreover, the regiments cited a decision to build an armory for one unit as a reason to build one for the others. In its request for public funds, New York's Ninth Regiment declared that the city had recently erected imposing armories for the Eighth, Twelfth, and Twenty-second regiments; and Buffalo's Sixty-fifth Regiment stressed that the state had previously constructed an enormous armory for its rival, Buffalo's Seventy-fourth Regiment.

The guardsmen had a strong case. Most of the armories were inadequate, and many were dilapidated. To pay high rent for such deplorable quarters was "exceeding[ly] extravagant and wasteful," a special committee of the Massachusetts legislature pointed out in 1887. Now that the states supplied the troops with arms, ammunition, equipment, uniforms, and even summer camps, it seemed appropriate for them to provide suitable armories as well. The guardsmen worked hard to make their case. They drafted bills, testified before legislative committees, lobbied legislators, and, in some instances, brought pressure on governors.[29] By using their political connections, mobilizing influential veterans and friends, and organizing state, regional, and national associations, the guardsmen became a pressure group to be reckoned with in most state capitals. But in view of the experience of New York's Seventh Regiment, which had been unsuccessful in its efforts to obtain public funds for a new armory in the mid-1870s, it is clear that a strong case and a great deal of clout were not enough. And it is unlikely that other military units, most of them much less influential than the Seventh Regiment, would have been successful in their efforts save for two other developments in the late nineteenth century.

By far the more important was the fears of class warfare that swept the nation after the railroad strike of 1877. These fears did more than just prompt the elected officials to designate the national guard as the principal defense against civil disorder and to transform its structure, personnel, and function accordingly. They also deepened the authorities' gratitude to the guard for its previous service and strengthened their determination to ensure its effectiveness in future riots. The elected officials were therefore in no position to withstand the guardsmen's arguments that adequate armories were essential to attract qualified recruits and turn them into capable officers. As the fears of class warfare grew, many public officials also concluded that if a serious riot erupted a system of small, isolated, and unprotected armories was, in the words of the special committee of the Massachusetts legislature, "simply deplorable." These armories were not a safe place for the troops. In the event of a riot, they would be at the mercy of the mob. Nor were these armories a safe place for the arms and ammunition, said Boston Alderman John A. McLaughlin in 1887. In most of them "there is nothing between the mob and the muskets . . . but a door."[30] A few large, defensible regimental armories would be much better.

The other development was the spirit of nationalism, patriotism, and militarism that spread in the United States in the 1880s and 1890s. These sentiments were reflected in the proliferation of hereditary and veterans' societies, the adulation of the flag and agitation to prohibit its desecration, and the campaigns to mark the graves of American soldiers and preserve historic landmarks and national records. Closely related were the formation of military outfits for youths, including a nationwide "Boys' Brigade," the attempt to introduce military instruction into the public schools, a passion for the strenuous life, and an enthusiasm for military values and overseas adventures. One historian has traced the growth of these feelings to an attempt to stave off moral decay, attributed to radical ideologies by some Americans and to unbridled materialism by others. Another historian has linked it to the elite's yearning for class revitalization, a yearning stimulated as much by concerns about its own enervation as by fears of lower-class upheaval. Whatever the reasons, this surge of nationalism, patriotism, and militarism generated support for the national guard, which embodied these views and the values underlying them.[31] It helped to create an environment in which elected officials would have to give requests from guardsmen a sympathetic hearing.

Influenced by the fears of class warfare and the rise of nationalism, patriotism, and militarism, the elected officials appropriated
funds for a few armories and then for a few more. Before long
armory construction turned into a form of pork barrel legislation—
which, given the nature of state politics, was perhaps inevitable. As
one scholar has argued (with some exaggeration), armory bills were
to the state legislature "what river and harbor bills were to Congress." New York State is a good example. Once the state legislature
started to appropriate funds for armories, local officials realized that
these funds provided business for local contractors, jobs for local
workers, possibly commissions for local architects, and certainly
patronage for local politicians. Determined to get a fair share of
these funds for their communities, these officials joined with the
guardsmen to pressure the state to erect armories just about everywhere in New York. The legislature responded liberally. Between
1886 and 1900 it voted funds for roughly twenty-five armories.
While a few were built in Brooklyn and Buffalo, most were erected
in Mohawk, Tonawanda, Hoosick Falls, and other upstate villages
in little danger of civil disorder. Watching the legislature appropriate
funds for one upstate armory after another, the Brooklyn *Eagle*
snidely remarked in 1895 that "the country companies have sunk
their grappling irons in the public pork barrel with good results."[32]

Although the authorities had built a few armories before 1877,
the breakthrough occurred in 1884, when the New York State
legislature gave in to pressure from the Twenty-second and other
regiments and established the New York City Armory Board. The
board was empowered to erect armories for the city's regiments at
the city's expense. From the start the board was besieged by local
guardsmen. Between 1884 and 1911 it approved the construction
of new armories for the Eighth, Ninth, Twelfth, Twenty-second,
Sixty-ninth, and Seventy-first regiments (as well as for Troops A
and C and the First and Second batteries). Most of them were
located in Manhattan, a few in Brooklyn and the Bronx—among
them the Eighth Coastal Artillery Armory (popularly known as the
Kingsbridge Armory), the largest in the country. The cost came to
more than $13 million. The state legislature also approved the
construction of armories outside New York City, many of which
were erected by the State Armory Commission. The state funded
armories for Brooklyn's Twenty-third and Forty-seventh regiments

and authorized Kings County to build armories for the city's Thirteenth and Fourteenth regiments. The state also appropriated funds for Buffalo's Seventy-fourth Regiment Armory and later its Sixty-fifth Regiment Armory, which cost $1.4 million and, according to *Harper's Weekly,* was the finest armory in the world. The state erected armories in Albany, Rochester, and other cities as well, though they were dwarfed by the huge New York, Brooklyn, and Buffalo armories, which served as models for the entire nation.[33]

Other states followed New York's lead. At the behest of the guardsmen, the Massachusetts legislature established the State Armory Commission in 1888. It was authorized to build armories in the commonwealth, but only with the community's agreement and at its expense. During the next two decades the commission erected two large armories in Boston, the East Newton Street Armory and the Irvington Street Armory, and smaller ones in Worcester, Lowell, and other cities. The cost came to over $2 million. In Rhode Island the Providence Armory Commission, set up by the state legislature in the mid-1890s, built the Cranston Street Armory. An impressive building, it took ten years to complete and, exclusive of the site, cost $500,000. At about the same time the Connecticut Arsenal and Armory Commission, also established by the state legislature, began work on an armory in Hartford. Finished in 1909, it was the largest armory in New England and one of the largest in the United States. New Jersey launched its campaign in the early 1890s; and in about a decade it built new armories in Newark, Trenton, Camden, Jersey City, and Paterson. Even Pennsylvania, which had hitherto relied almost exclusively on private funding, fell into line in 1905, when the state legislature established the Pennsylvania Armory Board.[34]

Although some guardsmen complained that the West lagged well behind the East, the authorities built armories in many western cities too, especially after 1886. The Ohio legislature provided funds for Cincinnati's First Regiment Armory, which was completed in 1889 at a cost of $115,000. Four years later Cuyahoga County erected Cleveland's enormous Central Armory, which housed several of the city's national guard units. Under pressure from Minneapolis guardsmen, the Minnesota legislature authorized the city to put up a new armory in 1903, which was financed by municipal bonds and finished in 1907. A few armories went up in the Far West as well. In the wake of anti-Chinese rioting in the late 1880s,

Multnomah County put up a medium-sized armory for Portland's two militia companies. It later housed Portland's First Regiment. Early in the 1900s Seattle, Kings County, and the state of Washington joined forces to build an armory to serve as quarters for the Seattle guardsmen and headquarters for the state guard. An impressive structure, it was completed in 1909 for $200,000. Four years after the earthquake of 1906, which left the San Francisco militia homeless, the city's guardsmen prevailed upon the California legislature to provide funds for one of the most imposing armories west of Chicago.[35]

Guided by the logic of pork barrel politics rather than the fears of class warfare, the authorities erected armories not only in big cities, where the so-called dangerous classes were congregated, but also in small cities (and even towns and villages). New York State built armories in Kingston, Poughkeepsie, and Hoosick Falls as well as in Brooklyn and Buffalo. The Massachusetts Armory Commission erected them in Brockton, Marlborough, and Fitchburg as well as in Boston and Worcester. Rhode Island appropriated funds not only for the Providence armory, but also for armories in Pawtucket, Bristol, and Newport, the summer resort of many of the nation's wealthiest families and an unlikely place for a social uprising. Included in the legislation that created the Pennsylvania Armory Board were restrictions that prevented it from building anything as costly as a regimental armory. During its early years the board therefore erected armories only in small towns such as Easton, Pottstown, and Pine Grove. Not until the restrictions were eased was it able to help underwrite the construction of Pittsburgh's Eighteenth Regiment Armory and other big-city armories.[36] With few exceptions, the small-town armories were one- or, at most, two-company armories, much smaller and less expensive than the regimental armories in which New York and other big cities took so much pride.

The erection of so many armories (and the proposals for so many more) sorely troubled two groups, which otherwise had very little in common. One group, which consisted mainly of ordinary upper-middle-class Americans, objected to them on fiscal grounds. Although they feared social upheaval and favored a strong national guard, these Americans held that many armories were too large, too luxurious, and too extravagant for the purposes they were supposed to serve. It was appropriate for the guardsmen to solicit money from individuals and corporations. But it was not appropriate for them to demand funds from states and cities, most of which were already burdened by high taxes and large debts and had more pressing claims on their limited resources. These views prompted the New York *Tribune,* ordinarily a strong supporter of armories, to urge the state legislature in 1890 to defer appropriations for armories, wherever possible, until 1891—or perhaps even later. So far as armories go, the *Tribune* said, "'Make haste slowly' is a good motto for those who are charged with the responsibility of handling the common purse."[37]

A look at Brooklyn in the late 1880s and early 1890s reveals a good deal about the opposition to armories on fiscal grounds. At the time the city's Thirteenth, Fourteenth, and Twenty-third regiments were housed in armories on Flatbush, North Portland, and Clermont avenues, respectively. Although these armories were large, solid structures, the oldest of which had gone up only fifteen years earlier, the regiments were no longer satisfied with them. Following the example of the Forty-seventh Regiment, which had obtained a new armory in the mid-1880s, the Thirteenth, Fourteenth, and Twenty-third began to lobby for new quarters. Shortly thereafter the elected officials appropriated $300,000 apiece for new armories for each regiment. Although the guardsmen had assured the officials that $300,000 was enough to build a first-rate armory, two years later, after the plans were drawn and the work under way, they announced that more money would be needed. The Fourteenth and Twenty-third asked for another $100,000, the Thirteenth for an additional $200,000. What should have cost about $900,000 would now cost at least $1.2 million and perhaps as much as $1.5 million, reported the New York *Times.* Castigating the regiments and their supporters for engaging in "a species of bunko steering," the *Times* charged that the guardsmen had knowingly accepted plans for buildings which could not possibly have been erected with the funds available.[38]

Even more irate than the *Times* was the *Eagle,* Brooklyn's most influential newspaper. A strong advocate of good government, the *Eagle* blamed the overruns on a complete disregard of business principles. It insisted that these principles applied as much to armories as to other projects. "To apprehend this it is not necessary to distinguish a cartridge from a canteen or ever to have seen a drill or a parade." The *Eagle* labeled the Thirteenth Regiment's request for an additional $200,000 "a scandal of no common dimensions." And it quoted a former guardsman who lambasted "the insatiable greed of the military-political element which has already bamboozled the public to a disgraceful extent." The newspaper grew more irate one year later, when the Fourteenth Regiment reported that it would need another $200,000, not $100,000, to complete its armory. Fed up with these endless demands, the *Eagle* wrote:

> Given a regiment, and you have a new armory about every twenty years. Given an old armory or a new one and you have a perennial fountain of "repairs" which the average committee of the average board of supervisors finds as useful for working as a gold mine. Given a new armory to one regiment and you have the claim of a new one by every other regiment, merely *because* the first regiment has obtained one. A long and close acquaintance with the subject has convinced the EAGLE that the armory account is the most lucrative one in this county—the jail and the St. Johnland plant [a Kings County asylum for paupers and the insane that was built in the 1880s and plagued by cost overruns] always excepted.[39]

"If in the future any regiment outgrows its armory, then there should not be more armory but less regiment."

Some of the *Eagle*'s readers were also disturbed by the cost of the new armories. After reading the *Eagle*'s description of the plans for the new Thirteenth Regiment Armory, one Brooklyn resident wrote in 1890:

> Can any military gentleman of the National Guard inform the tax payers what services they have rendered to the city and State that they should be provided with such expensive and luxurious accommodations, such grand halls for drill and dancing, gymnasiums for exercise, kitchens and mess rooms? Why kitchens and mess rooms? Are the Thirteenth going to live in the armory? . . . Is it intended for a military hotel, or what? Will the tax payers have to settle the mess bills also? . . . The officers may be wealthy and may expect luxurious accommodations, but why the tax payers should be called upon to foot the bill, as I said before, beats my time.

A few years later another Brooklynite wrote an even more caustic letter. He began by quoting Sir Walter Scott on the English militia:

Mouths without hands, maintained at vast expense,
In peace a charge, in war a weak defense;
Stout once a month they march, a blustering band,
And ever, but in time of need, at hand.

Then turning to the Brooklyn guard, he went on to say: "Why should a body of uniformed young clerks be furnished with such magnificent quarters in which to hold balls, rackets and athletic tournaments at the expense of the business community? They can point to no achievement in war or peace that entitles them to be considered a valuable addition to our municipal force. The police are our best protection and are always ready."[40]

The Brooklyn guardsmen ignored the charges that they had deliberately underestimated the cost of the armories in order to obtain the appropriations and knowingly approved plans for buildings that could not have been put up with the funds available. But they responded to the charges that the armories were too large and too luxurious and that the regiments had done nothing to justify imposing such heavy burdens on the taxpayers. Referring to the criticism as "ballroom talk," General James McLeer, commander of the Second Brigade, declared in 1891 that, far from being luxurious, "the new armories will be simply commodious, attractive structures, suited to the demands of the regiments for which they are being built." A more forceful response was made by a member of the Thirteenth Regiment, who wrote to the *Eagle* in 1893:

Take away our police force and what safety would the community have from thieves, thugs and other lawless creatures? On a larger scale what safety in greater communities would there be in times of excitement if it were not known that the law was backed up by the stronger arm of the militia? Mobs have no chance, law breakers bow before a musket when the police would be of no avail. Armories are required that these bodies of men may be drilled and taught their duties and they must be large that the evolutions may be conveniently gone through. Then if we build of necessity, build large and strong, and build not unsightly barns but armories that will be a credit to our city and not eyesores to their neighborhoods. We hope there may never be occasion to be called for more than dress parade, but if sterner duties are laid on us you will find us in those handsome armories, ready to march forth for the defense of our homes and the upholding of the law.[41]

In the end the elected officials gave the regiments the additional money. Perhaps they thought it made more sense to pay $1.4 million for three finished armories than $900,000 for three unfinished ones. And for a while the opposition to armories subsided. But it surfaced again in 1898, shortly before the consolidation of New York and Brooklyn, when Troop C, a Brooklyn cavalry unit, asked the city for a site for a new armory. Although the state was willing to pay for the building, the *Eagle* objected. Rejecting "the assumption that the state treasury was the legitimate prey of any locality that can get its arms in it," the paper wrote that "the question arises as to when a halt is to be called to these armory raids on the legislature." Pointing out that when it came to armories no county had been treated as well as Kings, it stressed that every time a new armory had gone up the public had been assured that "the appetite of the militia was at last satiated . . . But it never has been and apparently it never will be." Commenting on the Troop's proposals for a gymnasium, bowling alleys, swimming pools, and a drill hall that could be used for social functions, the *Eagle* said: "If the county and the state are going into the business of creating social clubs and supplying them with the luxuries of existence, they manifestly ought to do so on no mean basis, and instead of supplying ordinary swimming baths should see that they are flavored with cologne."[42]

The other group that was sorely troubled by the erection of so many armories consisted largely of socialists, Populists, and labor leaders. They objected to armories not on fiscal but on ideological grounds. Although they opposed spending what the Knights of Labor called "the people's money" on armories, especially when it could otherwise have been used in more salutary ways, these Americans were not greatly concerned by the cost of the buildings. Nor did it make much difference to them whether the armories were erected with private or public funds. What troubled them was rather the purposes of the armories and the guardsmen who occupied them. As they saw it, the armories were a manifestation of class warfare in America, a war of the plutocracy against the people, capitalists against workers and farmers—a war in which the national guard served as the army of the giant corporations. What the Topeka *Advocate* called "these city bastiles" were an indication that the United States was on the road to "military despotism." Once simple halls, the armories had been transformed into "strong fortresses," contended the Socialist Labor Party. With their "formidable towers and battlements," they were designed "to overwhelm organized labor and the proletarian masses in case they should ever succeed in gaining political ascendancy or making laws by which the 'interests' of the capitalistic class might be jeopardized."[43]

Few Americans expressed their antipathy to armories more vigorously than B. O. Flower, the editor of the *Arena*, a leading reform periodical whose office was in Boston, a few blocks from the new First Corps of Cadets Armory. Flower, who sympathized with Populism and organized labor, was deeply troubled by the power of corporate capital and the possibility of class warfare. In an article entitled "Plutocracy's Bastiles," which appeared in 1894, he called attention to the rapid increase of armories in big cities. Branding them "great storehouses of death" and "rendezvouses of probable man-slayers," Flower argued that the United States was turning into "a mighty armed camp," into a nation that seemed to be preparing for "a wholesale family massacre." Claiming that the "multiplication" of armories "is perilous for a republic," he stressed that "it is indeed difficult to consider anything more contrary to the spirit of republican institutions than permitting the rich men of great centres of wealth to lavish their money upon armories."

> Who is so blind that he cannot see that the men who furnished the million dollars for the Seventh Regiment [Armory], and those who are paying for the three or four hundred thousand dollar Boston armory [the First Corps of Cadets Armory], would expect the regiments thus beholden to them to see as they saw, in case starving industry should be pitted against idle wealth, or in case the industrial millions overthrow the money changers in the temples of legislation with their ballots and plutocracy beholds the intelligence of a great republic prepared to assert the cause of justice for all the people?[44]

On one occasion the opposition to armories—and to the national guard and the social classes it defended—was expressed in poetry. Outraged by the erection of the First Corps of Cadets' new armory, T. W. Curtis wrote "The Boston Bastile" in 1896.

See rise in the heart of the city, that pile of granite stone,
With port-hole, turret, and dragon with teeth and claws full shown.
O'er-topping warehouse and dwelling, and vieing with steeple and
    dome,
And facing the grand old Common where Liberty once made its
    home! . . .

Tis the rendezvous they say of the Corps of volunteers,
The scions of the wealthy, a brood of these latter years;
A clubhouse and a fortress for drill and song and jest,
With stacks of arms and cards and wines, a moral leper's nest!

Curtis then wrote of the Corps's commander, "a multimillionaire,/
Who rides his steed with portly grace on our broad thoroughfare,"
and its rank and file, "crack marksmen who only shoot to kill,/
Parading betimes these streets to instil a wholesome awe,/Into the
baseborn rabble for the supremacy of law!" And after a few nasty
words about the Corps's chaplain, who believes "That Christ if he
were living would do as he does now,/Hobnob with the plutocrat,
and to war's insignia, bow!" Curtis concluded:

Ah! better take yon bastion down, slowly stone by stone,
And thus unseat the beast you've raised on to a human throne!
And for spasmodic virtue show an eternal vigilence,
Lest Freedom die, or lest it wear, the blood-red robes of France![45]

No group was more outspoken in its opposition to armories than
the Socialist Labor Party. To the party, the growth of the guard and
the spread of its armories reflected changes in the relationship between capital and labor in the United States. When the labor movement was in its infancy, the SLP held, the militia was a social
organization and its armories were ordinary halls. But after a long
period in which capital degraded and demoralized labor, the people
awakened. And with the railroad strike of 1877, the labor movement
came of age. Capital answered by turning the militia into a repressive force and weeding out unreliable units. In case labor rose up
to claim what rightfully belonged to it, capital also built fortresses
for the guardsmen. By the 1880s the machinery of repression was
in place throughout the nation. Nowhere was it more elaborate than
in New York City, declared the SLP's newspaper, *The People*, in
1891:

No one who beholds the half score moated and battlemented armories which dot the streets of New York and cover every strategic vantage point; no one who knows how those have been weeded out of her militia who could not be relied upon to shoot down their neighbors mercilessly when ordered, until that militia has become merely an organized portion of the ruling class; no one who knows of the vast sums spent annually for enginery of repression, but refused for education; no such person can do aught but tremble for the future of New York and his country.[46]

The Socialist Labor Party's opposition to armories was highlighted by its response to two events that took place at the end of the century. In 1899 the London, Ontario, City Council adopted a proposal to build an armory at a cost of $50,000. The local section of the SLP issued a vigorous protest. "Armories," it declared, "are representative of war, are an incentives [sic] to war, are reactionary, in tendency, and subversive of the true interests of our citizens." They are symptomatic of the "damnable and destructive military spirit that has ruined the old world, and is now being imported to our country." Armories also waste money that could be used to pave streets, repair buildings, care for the old and infirm, and provide concerts, lectures, and musicals, which "elevate, comfort and cheer and make happier" the working people. Above all, the SLP objected to armories on the grounds that they oppressed the working classes. As the protest put it:

The purpose served by armories erected at other places has served to pit one portion of the citizens trained to arms against the other part trained to labor; as at Brooklyn, Chicago, Pittsburgh, and other places. [D]uring these labor strikes against the unjust conditions in which wage workers found themselves, the military were called out of the Armories, identical with that now proposed to be erected here[,] to put down with the rifle and bayonet these efforts of labor, to free itself from wage slavery.[47]

The other event took place in Haverhill, Massachusetts. It began in 1898, when James F. Carey, a recently elected Socialist city councillor, voted in favor of a proposal to renovate the Haverhill Armory. Long annoyed by Carey's refusal to toe the party line, the SLP expelled him. For a long time, during which Carey was a prominent member of the SLP's rival, the Social Democratic Party, the SLP continued to hound him. At a meeting in 1901 a member of the SLP named W. S. Dalton charged that Carey's vote to renovate the Haverhill Armory had given "aid and comfort" to an organization whose only purpose was to oppress workers and shoot strikers. Carey answered that the sanitary conditions in the armory had been terrible. To which Dalton replied, "Mr. Carey, you have just proclaimed yourself a dirty traitor to my class." Dalton attacked Carey again at a meeting a week later. Carey, he said, "voted money to fix up and make more comfortable and sanitary an armory in which the militia—whose only reason for existence is that they may shoot unarmed strikers—drills and practices for future massacres." The SLP never forgave Carey. And it took obvious pleasure in reporting in 1903 that "Armory Builder Carey" had been defeated in his bid for reelection to the Massachusetts legislature.[48]

Despite this opposition, hundreds of armories were built between 1880 and 1910. And though many were erected in the 1910s and 1920s and even more in the 1930s, it was plain by 1910 that the great wave of armory construction was slowing down. This was partly because so many armories had already been built and partly because the fears of class warfare were on the wane. Of the hundreds of armories that were built by 1910, very few were located in the South or the Far West. The South was preoccupied not by fears of class warfare, but by fears of racial equality; and southerners devised other ways to maintain segregation than building armories. A few southern armories went up before 1910, including the Savannah Volunteer Guards Armory and the Portsmouth, Virginia, Market and Armory, but they were no more formidable than Baltimore's old Richmond Market Armory. Although the scene of industrial strife that often bordered on class warfare, the Far West was dominated by rural interests who believed that armories were mainly for the benefit of big cities and saw no reason to pay for them. At the turn of the century three militia companies in Butte, Montana, used the basement of the public library as an armory; and a decade later much of the Far West's national guard still rented rooms or buildings for meetings and drills.[49]

Some states in other regions also lacked adequate armories. Indiana was one, its adjutant-general charged in 1914. The "armories are usually on the second or third floor of an old business building, with dark halls, easily broken into by thieves, poorly lighted and poorly ventilated and in many cases not heated at all or poorly heated by stoves." Among the worst was the Bloomington armory, an old and dilapidated church. Things were much the same in South Dakota, General C. M. Englesby pointed out in 1908. In the absence of state support for armory construction, most of the national guard units "have been compelled to rely on society hall rooms, town halls, and vacant store rooms." In other states there were units that lacked suitable quarters. A good example is Baltimore's Fourth Regiment, which was housed in a high school that had been converted into an armory. Inspired by the success of the Fifth Regiment, which had secured a new armory in 1903, the Fourth launched a campaign for a new home in 1910. Six years later it was still waiting for the legislature to provide the funds. Slightly better off was Pittsburgh's Eighteenth Regiment, which had been trying to raise the money for a new armory since the 1890s. With the aid of the Pennsylvania Armory Board, the Eighteenth obtained a new administration building in 1911 and the promise of a large drill shed in the future.[50]

Particularly demoralizing to national guard leaders was the situation in Washington, D.C., where local guardsmen had been unable to prevail upon Congress to build a new armory. As late as 1912 the armories in Washington were more appropriate for a southern town than for the nation's capital. The District guardsmen rented space in eight rundown buildings, only one of which had a drill shed. That one, an assistant secretary of war testified, smelled "of bad odors from the market below and gases from an ice plant in the building." These armories were crowded, uncomfortable, and unsafe. As Brigadier-General Robert K. Evans observed: "It is not extravagant to say that a combination of evil-disposed people could destroy the equipment and armament of the militia very easily in an hour or two by just going around to these wretched hovels [where the materiel is stored], some of which are really inflammable and not much better than chicken coops." It was very hard, Evans stressed, for the federal government to press the states to put up armories, when in "our own Capital, the only place Congress has a militia directly under its wing, we find a condition worse, probably, than anywhere else."[51]

But if there were no adequate armories in the capital, there were plenty of them elsewhere in the nation, especially in the vast, heavily populated, urbanized, and industrialized part of the nation that extended from Boston west to Minneapolis, south to St. Louis, and east to Baltimore. There were hundreds of armories, small one- or two-company armories, huge regimental armories, plain small-town armories, luxurious big-city armories, and armories that housed infantry, cavalry, and artillery units. By 1910 New York (by then consolidated with Brooklyn) had roughly twenty armories. Philadelphia had half a dozen. Boston, Buffalo, Cleveland, and other big cities had two or more. Among the states, Pennsylvania probably had the most armories (though, as a group, they were much less imposing than the New York armories). Not far behind Pennsylvania was New York. Massachusetts, New Jersey, and Ohio also had a good many armories. These armories pleased most Americans, especially the guardsmen, who boasted that their armories had no equal anywhere in the world. And they impressed some foreigners. After making a trip to the United States expressly to see its national guard armories, an Englishman named A. W. A. Pollock regretfully concluded that to build even "the least pretentious" of these armories "is in our case absolutely out of the question.[52]

As it stood in 1910, thirty years after New York's Seventh Regiment moved into its new quarters, the American armory was more than the home of the citizen-soldiers—the place where they stored weapons, held meetings, drilled, socialized, and assembled in the event of a riot or other uprising. In the minds of many Americans, it was also an integral part of the state military system that had developed after the railroad strike of 1877. Indeed, declared Charles Sidney Clark, a longtime guardsman who attempted to explain the guard to a British audience in 1908, "the armory is the very cornerstone of the system." Along with New York State Adjutant-General Josiah Porter, who argued in 1888 that "there must be an armory or there will be no soldiers," Clark and others believed that it was through spacious and handsome armories, more than anything else, that the guard attracted members and retained them. Whereas some units have a great deal of difficulty in recruiting, Clark contended, the ones with fine armories have no empty places, long waiting lists, and high morale.[53] Although Clark may have overstated the point, the armory was as integral a part of the national guard that emerged after 1877 as its military discipline, street maneuvers, and summer encampments.

The armory was also a schoolhouse—"a Military Schoolhouse," wrote Colonel Edmands of Boston's First Corps, "wherein citizen soldiers prepare themselves to defend the lives and property of their fellow citizens." It was in the armory that the guardsmen took part in regular drills, took turns on the rifle range, and presented themselves for periodic inspections. It was there, said Colonel S. V. S. Muzzey, commanding officer of New Jersey's Second Regiment, that the citizen-soldiers learned "the science of warfare." In the eyes of many Americans, the armory was more than just a military schoolhouse. Within its walls the guardsmen were also taught patriotism, nationalism, obedience, discipline, self-control, respect for authority, and other middle-class values. There they learned to be better citizens as well as better soldiers. Judge George H. Williams summed up these sentiments at the laying of the cornerstone of the new Portland armory in 1887. In return for their financial support, the people of Portland expect the guardsmen to better themselves, Williams claimed:

> To learn the manual of arms and perfect themselves in military practices follow as a matter of course, but the beneficiaries and graduates of this institution ought to be gentlemen as well as soldiers. There will be an opportunity and every reasonable inducement for the young man who comes here to drill, to acquire the habit of correct deportment, to cultivate self-respect and a sensitiveness to his honor[,] to learn civility to his superiors and politeness to his equals, and to become what is known to the military code as a soldier and gentleman.[54]

Morality, Williams concluded, should be as sacred to an armory as religion is to a church.

The armory was a club house too—"a sort of club house," wrote one journalist about the Seventh Regiment's new home, "where the members may find means of enjoying themselves in leisure hours, and where the surroundings are as well calculated to create social habits as to encourage military ardor." In addition to a regimental drill hall and several company rooms, a well-equipped armory contained a saloon and dining room, a reception room, a library or reading room, a gymnasium and swimming pool, and a wide range of other "conveniences and accommodations," wrote one journalist in 1892, "not deemed necessary in armories erected 25 years ago." There the guardsmen ate, drank, and talked, held dinners, dances, receptions, and an occasional ball, wined and dined visiting regiments, read military histories and popular magazines, listened to the regimental band, played billiards and even lawn tennis, and participated in what Colonel Emmons Clark referred to as "manly sports and exercises." The American armory's social, athletic, and recreational facilities greatly impressed A. W. A. Pollock. "The officer or man who belongs to an organization possessed of a good armoury," he wrote in 1909, "has an exceedingly pleasant club at his disposal during his service, and in the hereafter he will further enjoy as a veteran, if discharged with credit, many of its advantages as long as he lives."[55]

The armory was a fortress as well—"an impregnable fortress," said a journalist of Chicago's new First Regiment Armory. It was "a refuge and sanctuary . . . in times of public commotion," declared Judge Henry Clay White at the laying of the cornerstone of the Cleveland Grays Armory in 1893. It was "a centre of safety in the hour of danger," remarked the Reverend Newland Maynard at the cornerstone ceremonies of New York City's Ninth Regiment Armory four years later. The armories were not, however, just defensive structures. As Colonel Edmands pointed out, they served "not only as places of refuge but as depots and bases of supplies and strategic points of vantage from which the militia may sally." In the event of an uprising, the guardsmen would be summoned to their armory— before the Civil War by bells tolling at regular intervals and flags hoisted at company headquarters, afterwards by telegraph, telephone, messengers, and announcements in churches, theaters, and other public places.[56] At the armory they would put on their uniforms, pick up their weapons, pack their gear, and, except for the few who would remain behind to defend the building, wait for the order to move out. In other words, the armory was a fortress in which the guardsmen would assemble if summoned, from which they would sally if ordered, and to which they could retreat if required.

The armory was not only a building, it was also a symbol. Speaking at the formal opening of the Seventh Regiment's new home in 1879, George W. Curtis said that the armory was a symbol of the community's gratitude to the militia. Several other citizens made the same point. At the laying of the cornerstone of the Seventh Regiment Armory, which took place a few months after the railroad strike of 1877, Secretary of War William M. Evarts declared that the building was a way of repaying "in some small degree the immense debt that the community owes to this regiment." At the cornerstone ceremonies of New Jersey's Fifth Regiment Armory, which were held during the railroad strike of 1894, Governor George T. Werts remarked that by erecting the armory "we may in a measure discharge a debt and obligation that we owe to our citizen soldiers." The armory symbolized the grandeur of the city as well. Speaking of the new home of Philadelphia's First Regiment, Colonel William McMichael pointed out in 1882 that it was a sign of "the liberality, the order and the prosperity of this great city which it will adorn."[57]

The armory was also a symbol of the lofty quality of American society. "It is," said Bishop Samuel Fallows about Chicago's formidable First Regiment Armory, "a visible expression of the indomitable sentiment of patriotism which God has planted in every human breast." City Council President Randolph Guggenheimer called New York's many new armories "silent, outward signs" of the people's loyalty to the flag and the Constitution. "They show that, under the surface of New York's commercial and professional activities, there are those depths of patriotism and self sacrifice which are ready to be outpoured at any moment when danger menaces our beloved nation." In a nation where change seemed relentless, where everything seemed transient and cities were transformed in a generation, the armory was a symbol of permanence as well. To many Americans, it seemed that these massive structures would last forever. Referring to the cornerstone of Portland's new armory, Judge Williams remarked in 1887: "Many generations will come and go; a great city will grow up here with its rush and rattle and noise; dumb forgetfulness will make our memories its prey, while this stone remains unchanged and unmoved."[58]

Above all, the armory was a symbol of authority, of a commitment to maintain order and, if need be, a determination to use force. Of New York's new Twelfth Regiment Armory, "a massive and handsome fortress" on the Upper West Side, the real estate *Record and Guide* wrote in 1886 that it was "a tower of strength to lovers of civic order and peace who remember the possibilities, remote ones it is to be hoped, of riot and disturbance." At the cornerstone ceremonies of New Jersey's Fifth Regiment Armory, Colonel Muzzey told the crowd that the building was "a menace to that spirit of lawlessness and unrest which if not checked culminates in open violence and insurrection." Much like the soldiers for whom it was erected, the armory was supposed to have a "moral force," in the words of New York State Adjutant-General John F. Rathbone, that would deter the dangerous classes from joining in riots and other uprisings. "Its plain, massive walls," one observer wrote of the new Seventh Regiment Armory, were meant to remind the disorderly of "the utility and dignity and firmness and strength of the National Guard." These symbols of what the orator Curtis called the "resistless power" of the state allowed the city to sleep "in peace" and the citizen to go quietly "to his work."[59]

Perhaps no one depicted the symbolism of the armory more vividly than the Reverend T. De Witt Talmadge, who spoke out so strongly against the Cincinnati Courthouse Riots of 1884. Talmadge was minister of the Tabernacle, a large Presbyterian church in Brooklyn, and probably the city's best known preacher since Henry Ward Beecher. His sermons attracted huge audiences and appeared in thirty-five hundred newspapers. A prolific author and popular lecturer, he was also chaplain of Brooklyn's Thirteenth Regiment, one of the city's two leading military units, and a logical choice as speaker at the cornerstone ceremonies of its new armory in 1891. Before a large and cheerful crowd, Talmadge paid tribute to the officials who had funded the armory and the workers who would build it. Then, referring to the impressive armory that would soon rise on Sumner and Putnam avenues, Talmadge said: "Let the building go up in all its grandeur and stand long after the smallest child that from any window has to-day witnessed these ceremonies shall have died of old age. An armory saying to all the people as they pass by: 'Be good citizens! Honor the law! Keep the peace! and if you don't keep it, I will make you keep it!'"[60]

chapter three

The Location of the Armories

Late in 1888, less than a decade after the Seventh Regiment moved into its new home on Park Avenue and Sixty-sixth Street, the New York *Times* ran a scathing editorial on the location of the city's armories. Deferring to the wishes of the regiments, which wanted quarters in "the most fashionable neighborhoods possible," the municipal officials were allowing the sites of the new armories to be determined "not so much by military as by social considerations." They were building all the new armories in mid-Manhattan, north of Fifty-ninth Street, within one or two blocks of Central Park—a solid upper-middle- and upper-class residential community that "is as little exposed to riot" as any part of New York. As a result, the city did not have "a single defensible armory" in Lower Manhattan, south of Fourteenth Street. Yet as the locus of the great banks and stores as well as the home of the "dangerous classes," Lower Manhattan was "precisely the quarter which is at once most vulnerable in case of disorder and most exposed to disorder." "With all the armories above Fifty-ninth street, and all the dangerous parts of the city below that line," the *Times* concluded, "we should not be better off than we were before the armories were built."[1]

Strictly speaking, New York had several armories south of Fifty-ninth Street. The Tompkins Market Armory, which had been built for the Seventh Regiment and now housed the Sixty-ninth, stood below Fourteenth Street. So did the Essex Market Armory, which had once housed the Sixty-ninth Regiment and later served as home for the recently disbanded Eleventh. The Ninth Regiment rented quarters on West Twenty-sixth Street, and the Seventy-first leased space on Broadway at Thirty-fifth Street. But most of these buildings were armories in name only; none was a "defensible armory." Moreover, all the new armories were located north of Fifty-ninth Street. The Seventh Regiment moved from Tompkins Square to the Upper East Side in 1880. A few years later the New York City Armory Board acquired sites for the Eighth, Twelfth, and Twenty-second Regiments, all of which were located uptown. For the Twelfth and Twenty-second, both of which wanted an armory on the West Side, the board bought one site on Columbus (then known as Ninth) Avenue between Sixty-first and Sixty-second streets and another between Broadway and Columbus and Sixty-seventh and Sixty-eighth. For the Eighth Regiment, which favored an East Side location, preferably further uptown than the Seventh Regiment Armory, the board purchased the block bounded by Park and Madison avenues and Ninety-fourth and Ninety-fifth streets.[2]

During the next decade and a half the Armory Board acquired armory sites for the other regiments too. But despite the *Times*'s criticism, none of them was located south of Fourteenth Street, much less on the Lower East Side or in other neighborhoods further downtown. By military criteria, which were based upon the assumption that the primary purpose of the national guard was to preserve order and protect life and property, the location of New York's armories left much to be desired. According to guard officials, the armories should have been "judiciously distributed," spread all over the city in such a way as to minimize the time lost in moving the troops from their quarters to the trouble spots.[3] But the armories were located largely in the solid upper-middle- and upper-class residential neighborhoods of mid-Manhattan—even though it was widely held that Lower Manhattan was the home of both the groups most likely to resort to violence and the institutions most likely to be their targets. And from mid-Manhattan to Lower Manhattan was a long trip, especially before the construction of the subway. Moreover, many of the armories were clustered in a way that defied military logic. The Twelfth Regiment, Twenty-second Regiment, and First Battery were all housed in the West Sixties, within a short walk of one another (and not too far from the Seventh Regiment

Armory on the other side of Central Park). The Seventy-first Regiment Armory was less than half a mile from the Sixty-ninth Regiment Armory, which was a little over half a mile from the Ninth Regiment Armory.

The armories were located in much the same sorts of places in other cities too. Brooklyn's Thirteenth, Fourteenth, Twenty-third, and Forty-seventh regiments were all housed in solid middle- and upper-middle-class communities in the western portion of the city. Boston's First Corps of Cadets Armory stood at the edge of fashionable Back Bay, within a half mile of the city's two other large armories. The Minneapolis First Regiment Armory was located at the foot of Lowry Hill, one of the best residential neighborhoods in the city, and across the street from a very attractive park. In light of the purpose of the national guard, some of the armory sites were especially incongruous. Buffalo's Sixty-fifth Regiment Armory was located on the site of an old abandoned cemetery, which the Buffalo *Express,* said was "thickly shaded by large trees" and endowed with a view "exceedingly broad and interesting in every direction." Baltimore's Fifth Regiment Armory was built on what the Baltimore *Sun* called "one of the most beautiful" spots in the city, "a veritable *rus in urbe,* a lovely bit of country lingering in the lap of town and pleasing the eye by its contrast with the unpicturesqueness of city surroundings."[4]

Hence the location of the armories is a puzzle. Although they were supposed to help preserve order and protect life and property, most armories were in neighborhoods where the likelihood of rioting was very low. Although they were supposed to symbolize the might of the state, most armories were in communities that were seldom visited by the "dangerous classes." In short, most armories were not built where they should have been. Contemporaries tried to account for this paradox. The New York *Times* attributed it to the authorities' inclination to accommodate the regiments, most of which wanted sites in "the most fashionable neighborhoods possible." Brigadier-General Albert Ordway, a member of the Washington, D.C., National Guard and an authority on riot control, held that armories were "generally located by the accident of convenience or value of ground" (by which he meant real estate values).[5] But these were only some of the reasons. To uncover the others, it is worth taking a look at the situation in New York City. Such a look reveals why

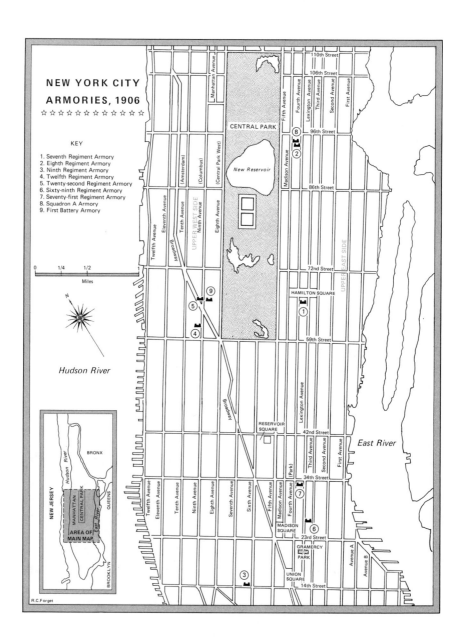

NEW YORK CITY

ARMORIES, 1906

☆ ☆ ☆ ☆ ☆ ☆ ☆ ☆ ☆ ☆ ☆

KEY

1. Seventh Regiment Armory
2. Eighth Regiment Armory
3. Ninth Regiment Armory
4. Twelfth Regiment Armory
5. Twenty-second Regiment Armory
6. Sixty-ninth Regiment Armory
7. Seventy-first Regiment Armory
8. Squadron A Armory
9. First Battery Armory

0   1/4   1/2

Miles

Hudson River

BRONX

NEW JERSEY   QUEENS

AREA OF
MAIN MAP

BROOKLYN

R.C.Forget

CENTRAL PARK

New Reservoir

UPPER WEST SIDE

UPPER EAST SIDE

110th Street
106th Street
96th Street
86th Street
72nd Street
HAMILTON SQUARE
59th Street

East River

RESERVOIR
SQUARE
42nd Street

34th Street

MADISON
SQUARE
23rd Street
GRAMERCY
PARK
UNION
SQUARE
14th Street

the new armories were all built north of Fourteenth Street (and, with a few exceptions, north of Fifty-ninth Street). It indicates what considerations other than military ones influenced the selection of armory sites. Not least of all, it tells a good deal about armories, the national guard, and urban America in the late nineteenth century.

Perhaps the best place to start is in the early 1870s, a decade and a half before the great surge of armory construction. At the time New York's armories (or, at any rate, the buildings that served as armories) were scattered throughout the built-up part of the city, with the bulk of them located in Lower Manhattan. The Seventh Regiment was housed in the Tompkins Market Armory at Third Avenue and Sixth Street. Also below Fourteenth Street were the Fifth Regiment, which rented a room on the second floor of a saloon on Hester Street; the Eighth, which had quarters in the Centre Market; the Seventy-ninth, which had space on the fifth floor of a dilapidated building at Greene and Houston streets; and, among others, the Ninety-sixth, which was housed in Germania Hall on the Bowery. Located on Fourteenth Street were the Sixth and Twenty-second regiments, the Sixth on the East Side, on the top floor of Tammany Hall, and the Twenty-second on the West Side, in an armory of its own. Above Fourteenth Street were the First Regiment, which was housed over a stable on West Thirty-second Street; the Ninth, which was quartered above another stable on West Twenty-sixth Street; the Twelfth, which rented rooms at the corner of Broadway and Thirty-fourth Street; and the Seventy-first, which leased space at the corner of Broadway and Thirty-fifth Street.[6]

The location of these armories was the outcome of a process by which the Tweed Ring, the Democratic organization headed by William M. Tweed, turned the housing of the national guard into what the *Times* called "a source of pecuniary profit." The process worked as follows. James A. Ingersoll, Tweed's business partner and political associate, rented empty lofts and other spaces for very little. The city's Board of Supervisors, which was under Tweed's control, then leased the properties as armories—even though, said the *Times,* they had been chosen "without any regard to their adaptability for armory purposes, or any reference to the conve-

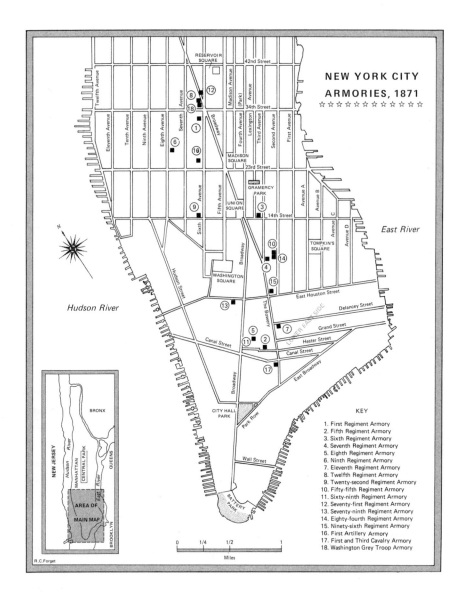

NEW YORK CITY
ARMORIES, 1871
☆ ☆ ☆ ☆ ☆ ☆ ☆ ☆ ☆ ☆ ☆ ☆

East River

Hudson River

KEY

1. First Regiment Armory
2. Fifth Regiment Armory
3. Sixth Regiment Armory
4. Seventh Regiment Armory
5. Eighth Regiment Armory
6. Ninth Regiment Armory
7. Eleventh Regiment Armory
8. Twelfth Regiment Armory
9. Twenty-second Regiment Armory
10. Fifty-fifth Regiment Armory
11. Sixty-ninth Regiment Armory
12. Seventy-first Regiment Armory
13. Seventy-ninth Regiment Armory
14. Eighty-fourth Regiment Armory
15. Ninety-sixth Regiment Armory
16. First Artillery Armory
17. First and Third Cavalry Armory
18. Washington Grey Troop Armory

0   1/4   1/2   1

Miles

R.C.Forget

nience of the troops that were intended to occupy them." Moreover, the board leased the properties for much more than Ingersoll rented them, leaving a handsome profit for Tweed and his associates. The city paid $10,000 per year for the Fifth Regiment's room on Hester Street, a room that could not otherwise have been rented for more than $1,000. It spent $16,500 for the First Regiment's loft on West

Twenty-sixth Street, which would not otherwise have brought in more than $2,000. According to the *Times*, the board paid $196,000 for space worth $46,000 to house the regiments—and another $85,000 for space that none of the regiments occupied.[7]

Although skullduggery may explain why the armories were located in some buildings as opposed to others, it does not explain why they were located throughout the built-up part of the city. The reasons are twofold. One is that through the late 1870s most regiments did not insist on buildings of their own. The Seventh Regiment, the city's most prestigious, shared the Tompkins Market Armory with the shopkeepers on the first floor. The Eighth and Sixty-ninth were housed above the Centre Market. Most of the others were quartered in buildings which were also used as stables, saloons, and other business enterprises. Of all the regiments, only the Twenty-second had a building of its own.[8] The other reason is that until the late 1870s most of the regiments did not need much space. Some of them had so few members that they were regiments in name only. For them one or two rooms was enough. For the larger regiments several rooms were necessary, but not much more. Of all the regiments, only the Seventh had a large drill hall, but even it was barely large enough for the entire regiment. As long as most regiments did not insist on buildings of their own and did not need much space, they could be housed virtually anywhere in the city.

During the 1870s and 1880s, however, several developments occurred which made it very hard to locate armories in Lower Manhattan. In the wake of the railroad strike of 1877, many national guard leaders began to fear not only that class warfare would soon break out, but that when it did the armories would be one of the mob's prime targets. Perhaps no guardsman was more troubled by this prospect than General E. L. Molineux, a New Yorker who headed the state's Second Division and would emerge as one of the nation's leading authorities on riot control. "What is to be most dreaded [in a riot]," he wrote in 1878, "is the seizure of the armory, with the arms and ammunition contained therein, as the first step by rioters." Six years later he warned that "the practically exposed and defenceless condition of the majority of the National Guard armories offers a tempting field of operations to the lawlessly disposed."[9] This concern prompted many national guardsmen (and some civilian officials) to wonder whether the existing armories were defensible in the event of a serious uprising. And it forced them to take a close look at the traditional practice of housing the guardsmen in buildings which were also used for nonmilitary purposes.

What they found was extremely disturbing. For the most part the buildings were completely unprotected, especially vulnerable to attack from the basement and ground floor. Even worse, some of the buildings were veritable fire traps, full of hay, straw, oil, turpentine, and other flammable material. In many of them the soldiers were quartered on the upper floors, with one or two narrow stairways as the only exits. If a few "evil-disposed persons" set fire to the stables beneath New York's Ninth Regiment, Colonel William Seward warned, the troops would have a hard time getting out safely. General Louis Fitzgerald, commander of the First Brigade and member of the Armory Board, considered these buildings so vulnerable that in 1886 he spoke out against a proposal to use the Gansevoort Market as an armory. He was "decidedly opposed to putting an armory over a market, or any kind of stores." Major Winthrop Alexander, Inspector-General of the Washington, D.C., National Guard, summed up the new conventional wisdom when he wrote in 1896, "The practice of locating armories over markets or in buildings not exclusively used for military purposes is to be avoided."[10]

Some national guard leaders went further, arguing not only that the guardsmen should have their own buildings, but also that these buildings should stand apart from other buildings—preferably detached "on all sides," wrote Colonal Thomas F. Edmands of Boston's First Corps. Underlying this position was the fear that in the event of a serious uprising the rioters would occupy the nearby buildings, many of which were taller than the buildings in which the guardsmen were quartered. From there they could drop bombs on the roofs, fire into the windows, and turn the troops' quarters into death traps. The West Twenty-seventh Street Armory is a good example. Located in the loft of a building that served as a stable and depot for a street railway company, it was first occupied by the Eighth Regiment and later assigned to the Seventy-first, which did not want it. A *Times* reporter revealed one of the reasons.

> Directly in front [of the building] is a large white house, with a parapet, having a direct command not only of the entrance to the

armory but of the windows opening on the avenue, and the roof of the building. A hand-grenade, a bottle of Disney's fluid, or any other incendiary compound, could be easily thrown into the building from this house. [Nearby] is a large tenement house, towering three or four stories above the surrounding buildings. It, too, has a parapet which commands all the buildings around; the west wall, if crenellated for musketry, would effectually sweep the north and east faces of the armory building and completely "bottle up" whatever force might be so unfortunate as to be caged in such a position.[11]

In the aftermath of the railroad strike, many national guard leaders also began to believe that the company was no longer an effective military force. With at most one hundred men, it was much too small to deal with a turbulent mob. In the event of a serious uprising, a company would be hard pressed to defend itself and guard its weapons, much less to restore order. For this a much larger force was required, the guardsmen reasoned. That force was the regiment, which consisted of six to ten companies and, at full strength, six hundred to a thousand men. The authorities adopted this position in many places, including New York City, which in 1870 had about twenty regiments, many of which were regiments in name only.[12] They consolidated or disbanded so many of them that by the late 1880s the city's national guard had just seven infantry regiments (and a few cavalry and artillery units), all of which were strong military forces. Although few in number, these outfits needed much more space than the paper regiments of the early 1870s, much more space, say, than the top floor of Tammany Hall. As many of them were at or close to full strength, the regiments required a minimum of six to ten company rooms, one room for the commander, another room for the officers, a rifle range, and a drill hall (large enough for regimental maneuvers and preferably on the ground floor).

At about the same time many national guard leaders came to realize that, in Colonel Sewards' words, "a regiment nowadays, to be a success, must be a military club." And if the regiment had to be a success, the armory had to be a clubhouse and not just a place to store weapons, hold meetings, and drill. If the armory was to be a clubhouse—if it was to be, as Colonel Edmands wrote, "so attractive that after drills and meetings are concluded, the members will be glad to linger and enjoy themselves"—it would have to contain a gracious saloon and dining room, a pleasant reading room or library, and a room for the band.[13] Also essential were a room for the veterans, who were so helpful in raising funds, a room for the ladies, who would join the guardsmen at dinners, dances, and other festive occasions, and, what with the growing enthusiasm for athletics and physical fitness, a gymnasium, a swimming pool, and perhaps even a bowling alley. These facilities, many of which would have been unheard of a generation before, took up a good deal of space.

The guardsmen also wanted more space because of what might be called regimental rivalry, a rivalry that permeated the guard. The regiments strove to outdo one another in the accuracy of their shooting, the precision of their marching, and, not least of all, the size of their armories. As a rule, each regiment took the position that it was entitled to at least as large and imposing an armory as any other regiment—and, if possible, an even larger and more imposing one. Buffalo's Sixty-fifth Regiment, for example, was adamant that the state should build it a new armory at least equal to the huge armory recently erected for the Seventy-fourth Regiment.[14] This rivalry was extremely intense in New York, in part because it had more regiments than other cities and in part because the regiments had been competing with one another for decades. The city's guardsmen were convinced that an impressive armory would enhance their regiment's standing and give it a great advantage in the competition for recruits.

These developments redefined the meaning of an adequate armory. It was no longer a couple of floors above a public market or a few rooms in a private building. Instead it was now a building that was used exclusively for military purposes and that stood apart from other buildings. It was a structure with an administration building large enough to house an entire regiment (and a fully equipped club) and with a drill shed large enough to hold regimental maneuvers. Such an armory required a piece of land, the size of which would have been inconceivable a generation earlier. Hence many of the big-city armories built after 1877 stood on a full acre, twice as large as the site of the Tompkins Market Armory. Some were erected on even larger parcels. Boston's East Newton Street Armory occupied nearly two acres, Brooklyn's Thirteenth Regiment Armory almost three acres, and Buffalo's Sixty-fifth Regiment Armory roughly ten acres. Things were much the same in New York

City. The Seventh Regiment Armory stood on nearly two acres; its drill hall alone was about three times the size of the old armory in Tompkins Square. The Ninth Regiment Armory, which had a smaller site, covered one acre, and the Eighth, Twelfth, Twenty-second, and Seventy-first regiment armories one and a half acres. The Kingsbridge Armory, the city's largest, stood on a little more than four acres.[15]

It was, however, very hard to find an acre or an acre and a half for sale below Fourteenth Street (and, for that matter, even below Fifty-ninth Street). That was the most heavily developed part of the city, full of stores, offices, warehouses, lofts, and tenements. It was more congested than any part of any other American city. Indeed, one or two of its wards were as congested as parts of Bombay and Calcutta. A real estate dealer named Leopold Friedman described the problem to a legislative committee in the mid-1880s. He had recently been approached by Colonel Schuyler V. R. Cruger of the Twelfth Regiment, who said, "'I would like to have a plot of ground [for a new armory] of twenty lots [or about an acre and a half] on the west side, not above Fifth-ninth street.' I told Colonel Cruger, 'It is very difficult to find a plot of ground below Fifty-ninth street, because everything has been pretty nearly built up.'"[16] The city could have attempted to put together fifteen or twenty lots in Lower Manhattan, but it would probably have had to negotiate with several different owners, a difficult and costly procedure. The city could also have resorted to condemnation, as it did in order to acquire part of the site for the Ninth Regiment Armory, but condemnation was a long drawn out process that often produced a lot of ill will.

Even if an acre or an acre and a half had been for sale below Fourteenth Street, it would have been extremely expensive. Property values there were very high not only in the prime commercial districts, but also in the worst residential neighborhoods, where the tremendous demand for housing pushed the rents way up. In 1888, for example, a parcel of close to six interior lots located on the Lower East Side sold for $96,000, more than $16,000 a lot. Although property values varied widely, with corner lots bringing more than inside lots and avenue lots more than street lots, they were generally lower north of Fourteenth Street and especially north of Fifty-ninth Street. As late as the mid-1880s it was not hard to find lots for less than $10,000 apiece on the Upper West Side, for under $6,000 each above Ninety-sixth Street, and for several hundred dollars apiece in Upper Manhattan and the Bronx. General George W. Wingate, a member of the Twenty-second Regiment, noted that some New Yorkers objected to locating the new armories uptown "on the ground that it would leave the lower part of the city comparatively undefended." "But," he wrote, "the enormous value of land down-town rendered it impossible to procure the area needed at a price which would be within any reasonable appropriation." An uptown site therefore "became a necessity."[17]

There was one parcel in Lower Manhattan that was more than large enough for an armory and was already owned by the city. It was Washington Square, a plot of slightly more than nine acres located at the southern end of Fifth Avenue, about a third of a mile south of Fourteenth Street. The parcel had been used as a potter's field until the mid-1820s, when it was set aside for military purposes. Later the adjacent property owners deeded the bulk of the plot to the city on the condition that it be maintained as a park and parade ground. Still later the city planted trees and laid out promenades, along which the militia drilled, held inspections, and sometimes assembled in an emergency.[18] It was perhaps only a matter of time before the militia leaders, who were determined to obtain adequate quarters for their troops, realized that Washington Square would make a splendid site for a new armory. The time came shortly after the railroad strike of 1877, when the local officials held that the militia deserved a new armory but felt that the city could not afford to purchase a site for it. Had the militia leaders obtained Washington Square—and despite a good deal of opposition, they came very close—at least one of New York City's new armories would have been built below Fourteenth Street.

The issue arose at a meeting of what was known as the Armory Conference Committee in early February 1878, when the fears of class warfare were just emerging in the United States. The committee consisted of Mayor Smith Ely, Controller John Kelly, a few aldermen, General Alexander Shaler, commander of the First Division, and other national guard officials—all of whom agreed, said Shaler, "that it was absolutely necessary that something should be done in order to furnish quarters for the regiments." Shaler's first choice was Reservoir Square, a large parcel between Fifth and Sixth avenues and Fortieth and Forty-second streets that was owned by the city. Kelly disagreed. Well aware of the Seventh Regiment's abortive effort to obtain Reservoir Square as the site for its new armory a few years earlier, an effort that will be discussed later, he felt that the scheme would run into opposition from nearby property owners. Kelly recommended instead Washington Square, which was Shaler's second choice and was also owned by the city. Mayor Ely concurred. He too preferred Reservoir Square; but he believed that "if that property could not be had, then Washington-Square was the next best place." Confident that this proposal would generate little controversy, the committee adopted a resolution that an armory be erected in Washington Square and that the mayor and the controller join forces with national guard officials to secure the necessary authorization from the state legislature.[19]

The committee's confidence was misplaced, to say the least. The proposal to build an armory in Washington Square infuriated many nearby property owners. They objected not to the building of an armory—indeed one of them, Robert Lenox Kennedy, had contributed $500 to the Seventh Regiment's campaign for a new armory and served as one of the three trustees of the new armory fund—only to its location. The property owners spelled out their objections in a petition that was submitted to the committee one week later. They stressed that Washington Square was one of the city's most beautiful parks, a park vital to the health and well-being of the neighborhood. The erection of an armory would destroy the square and do irreparable damage to the adjacent property. Other sites were more appropriate for an armory, among them the Manhattan Market, a large building on Eleventh Avenue and Thirty-fourth Street that stood on four acres and was easily reached by streetcar. The property owners were backed by the New York *Times*, which argued that the city had far too few "breathing-spaces" to permit the destruction of Washington Square (or, for that matter, any of its parks). Also on the side of the property owners were 150 physicians, whose endorsement of the petition strengthened the case that the preservation of Washington Square was essential to the health of the neighborhood.[20]

Saying that he was "astonished at the course the matter had

taken," General Shaler responded to the property owners' objections. The national guard did not intend to cover the square with an eyesore that would destroy the park and lower the value of the adjacent property. To the contrary, it intended to take only a small part of the square, leaving the bulk of it as a park, and to erect a building "to which the residents would look with pride." "The time had come," he said, "when the question of providing accommodations for the National Guard should be considered, and when no obstacles to the movement should be presented." (One of the other national guard officers went even further than Shaler. He argued that the proper course "was to put up an armory in each of our public parks," a remark that did little to ease the fears of the opposition, and added that it was too bad that the issue had not come up at the time of the railroad strike.) Controller Kelly agreed with Shaler. He declared that the presence of an armory would make Washington Square more attractive to youngsters and, if anything, would increase property values in the neighborhood. The city, he said, should ask the legislature for permission to build an armory in the square. Despite the mounting opposition, the committee adopted the controller's proposal.[21]

Outraged by the committee's action, the property owners intensified their opposition. In the process they received help from the Public Parks Protective Association (PPPA), an association of upper-middle- and upper-class New Yorkers formed to prevent the national guard's takeover of Washington Square and to protect the city's other parks against similar encroachments. Not only was the PPPA afraid that the proposed armory would destroy the beauty and utility of Washington Square; it was also convinced that buildings did not belong in parks. Parks, the PPPA believed, could do much to enhance urban life (and even to maintain public order), but only if they were preserved as open spaces. The New York *Times,* which viewed the national guard's proposal as another in a series of misguided efforts to use city parks for inappropriate purposes, supported the association. To Shaler's statement that the guard wanted only part of the square, the *Times* replied that "a park which has been partly frittered away for building purposes ceases to be a park." To his claim that the armory would be a credit to the neighborhood, it responded, "No wall, however highly ornamented, can be accepted in lieu of an open and breezy space."[22]

An anonymous New Yorker, who called himself "Protest," wrote a letter to the *Times* on February 17 that nicely expressed the concerns of the PPPA.

> Have the gentlemen who are contemplating this change ever chanced to pass through the square on a Summer's afternoon? Have they seen the crowds standing close around the fountain drinking its freshness, or sitting on the benches provided for them? . . . Do these gentlemen realize what the park is in Summer to the vast population between the City Hall Park and Madison Square? Do they know that from sunrise till long after sunset this place is thronged with invalids who have crawled out, with sick children and tired men and women? Do they know that this spot is air, light and health—the one bright spot in the discomfort and often the misery of those to whom the heats of an American Summer bring no country, no green fields, no release from the slums and alleys where they are forced to live?

The issue does not concern only the poor (or, for that matter, only New Yorkers who live near Washington Square), he added. It concerns all New Yorkers, even the wealthy.

> Should this thing really come to pass, should one of the few parks of this great city, full of fine trees, surrounded by noble residences, consecrated by gift to the purpose, hedged about with all the safeguards of law—should I say this place be condemned for private ends, what can we, who live in this city, hope for the future? Who or what is safe? Can the millionaires on Madison Square save it in the future from the greed of a board of Aldermen? Who will assure them that a hospital or barracks will not soon drive them from their homes?

And what about Central Park, he asked, the centerpiece of the city's park system. "Who can say that at some approaching election it may not be in danger."[23]

The Armory Conference Committee was unmoved. On February 25 it approved a petition asking the state legislature to pass a bill that would allow Washington Square to be used as the site for an armory. The bill provided that the proposed armory would house at least two regiments of infantry and four of cavalry and artillery (as well as the headquarters of the First Division and its two brigades). Although the armory would cover 80,000 square feet, or about as much space as the site of the new Seventh Regiment Armory, General Shaler stressed that it would take up only one-seventh of the square, an estimate that was off by about 50 percent. The PPPA, which was rapidly assuming leadership of the opposition, appealed to the Board of Aldermen. On February 26 it presented a petition, signed by 5,000 New Yorkers, protesting the location of an armory in Washington Square. It also prevailed on Alderman John J. Morris to move that the board request the legislature to reject the bill that would allow Washington Square to be used as an armory site. Both the petition and the motion were referred to committee. The PPPA spent the next few days drumming up support for its position; and by March 4, the day before the board's next meeting, it had 7,500 signatories, including 200 doctors and many members of the Union, Lotus, and other clubs.[24]

The PPPA found strong allies in the medical and scientific communities, both of which subscribed to the theory that disease was the product of miasma, the noxious vapors that polluted the atmosphere of big cities. According to this theory, which would be discredited by the end of the century, parks were vital to the health of cities because their open spaces, grass, and trees helped to purify the air and reduce the miasma. As Dr. A. C. Castle, a resident of Washington Square for more than thirty years, wrote, the park is "a heart-lung" of the city, "a reservoir of 'ozone,'" which was extremely beneficial to ailing children and other invalids. Doctors widely agreed, wrote one New Yorker, that the most effective way to prevent (and, if need be, to cure) childhood illnesses was to take the youngsters into a park and leave them under the trees. Pointing to the extreme congestion of Lower Manhattan and its high mortality rates, Dr. Willard Parker spoke out against the takeover of Washington Square or any scheme that would diminish the city's "open spaces" or "breathing-places." Citing medical evidence, E. Randolph Robinson, counsel to the Washington Square property owners, contended that "to take away the parks of the city would destroy more lives than the militia have saved in a score of years."[25]

The opposition got a big boost on March 4, when the New York Academy of Sciences, the city's leading scientific organization, issued a report that attacked the proposal to put an armory in Washington Square. "Like every populous city," the report pointed out, "New-York contained numerous sources of impurity," chief among which were its vast population, countless animals, many fireplaces, crowded tenements, and defective drainage. They generate "carbonic acid gas" and other dangerous vapors, which take a great toll on the residents, and especially on the children. "Medical skill is powerless here; pure air is the only remedy," the Academy claimed. The only protection against miasma "is to be found in the free circulation of air, and the decarbonizing of the air or its restoration to its original purity. The first can only be gained from parks, the second from vegetation." For the children, the poor, and the sick who live on the Lower West Side, Central Park is much too far away. Washington Square is their only hope. "For these reasons," the report concluded, "the Academy regards it as essential for the interests of the beauty of the city, the education of its children, and, more than all, their health and life, that a protest be made against the short-sighted policy of reducing the area of the city parks."[26]

The issue came to a head at the Board of Aldermen's meeting on March 5. The Committee on County Affairs, to which the PPPA's petition and Alderman Morris' motion had been referred, reported in favor of erecting the proposed armory in Washington Square. It argued that the national guard badly needed a new armory and that, despite the PPPA's objections, "the [Washington Square] site was the most desirable one that could be obtained." In defense of its recommendation, the committee made three points. One was that in view of the widespread opposition to increasing the city's debt the municipal authorities could not afford to buy a site for an armory. Another was that it would be hard to find a site for an armory (or indeed any public building) without arousing opposition from nearby residents. Yet another was that as the armory would occupy only two of the square's nine acres it would not "destroy the park or interfere in any measurable degree with its uses by the public." The report sparked a spirited debate. When it became clear that the board was closely divided, the matter was put off for a week. When the aldermen met again on March 12, the militia prevailed. By a vote of twelve to ten, the board favored building an armory in Washington Square and requesting the necessary permission from the legislature.[27]

The opposition now focused its efforts on the state legislature. The PPPA, which had vowed that "no armory or public building shall be erected in any park or square in New-York City as long as we have breath and strength to oppose it," sent a protest. So did the Academy of Sciences. At the urging of these organizations, the Public Health Association approved a resolution saying that the maintenance of Washington Square as a park was "of great importance to the health and welfare of the City of New-York, and especially to that part of the closely-inhabited City, to which it is thus the only breathing space." The New York Academy of Medicine also joined the fight, taking the position that a scheme "which proposes, on the score of economy, to poison the atmosphere . . . is most wasteful and destructive extravagance." Whether the Republican-dominated legislature was swayed by the force of the opponents' arguments or by the strength of their political connections is impossible to tell. But in any event it brought the controversy to an end in June by passing a law that expressly prohibited the use of Washington Square in any way other than as a park.[28]

The law did more than block the erection of an armory in Washington Square. It also killed what turned out to be the last opportunity to build an armory in Lower Manhattan. After this debacle, the local authorities made one more unsuccessful effort to locate an armory south of Fourteenth Street, which will be discussed later. They also made two more attempts to put an armory in a park, both of which failed. In 1887 a committee of the Armory Board recommended that the city erect two new armories, one for the Ninth Regiment and another for the Seventy-first, in Bryant Park (formerly Reservoir Square). The scheme had the backing of the president of the Tax Department, who saw it as a way to acquire an armory site at no cost to the city, and the New York *Tribune,* which regarded the abandoned reservoir on the site as "an eyesore." But the board, perhaps afraid of a run-in with the park lobby, shelved the proposal. Twenty-two years later the state legislature passed a bill which, if approved by the city, would have set apart six acres of the Bronx's Crotona Park as the site for a new Eighth Regiment Armory. The nearby residents, the park lobby, and the *Times* strongly urged the city to withhold approval. After a heated debate, in which the guardsmen and their opponents repeated many of the same arguments they had made in the fight over Washington Square, Mayor George McClellan vetoed the bill, putting an end to the project.[29]

Unable to find armory sites downtown, the local officials looked uptown. The situation there was much more favorable. Although New York was pretty well built-up between Fourteenth and Fifty-ninth streets, plenty of land was available north of Fifty-ninth Street. Much of it was one- and two-acre parcels, with some larger pieces. Much of it was also owned by one party and clear of buildings, making it fairly simple to acquire and prepare the site. Most important of all, much of the property was on the market. Shortly after the Armory Board was organized in 1884, its historian wrote, "owners of real estate awoke to its importance, and for a time its Secretary was busily employed in tabulating offers from all parts of New York of plots that, in the opinion of the owners at least, were peculiarly adapted for armory sites." General Shaler, the most influential member of the board, remarked that it received more than forty offers in the first year alone. The owners and their agents tried hard to sell these parcels. Some pointed out that they were well located and partly graded. A few pledged to purchase armory bonds if the city bought their property. One real estate agent even offered Shaler a bribe, as a result of which the general was arrested, indicted, tried, and eventually forced to step down as commander of the First Division.[30]

Not only was property available north of Fifty-ninth Street, but much of it was available at what by New York standards were low prices. For example, H. F. Dimock offered the Armory Board twenty-eight lots on Amsterdam (then known as Tenth) Avenue between Seventy-ninth and Eightieth streets for $265,000 (just under $9,500 apiece). He stressed that the elevated railway stopped at Columbus Avenue and Eighty-first Street, the horsecars ran along Amsterdam Avenue, and the lots "have no rocks on them, not even below grade, and could be built upon with the smallest possible expense." Jos. H. Goodwin offered to sell the board twenty-two and a half lots between Broadway and Columbus Avenue and Sixty-seventh and Sixty-eighth streets for $265,000 (just under $12,000 each). To sweeten the deal, he pledged to purchase $125,000 worth of armory bonds. F. Yoran asked the board to consider the block bounded by Park and Madison avenues and Ninety-fourth and Ninety-fifth streets (or thirty-four lots) for $350,000 (just over $10,000 apiece). To make the sale, he would buy $100,000 worth of armory bonds. Upon learning that the board was considering Yoran's proposal, H. B. Gardner called its attention to the block bounded by Park and Lexington avenues and 100th and 101st streets, which had thirty-four lots too. "Now here is a block (or more) in the same vicinity that can be had for $6,000 per lot [or] $204,000, which is considerable of a saving," he wrote the board. "Would you entertain it?"[31]

There were two strong inducements to locate the new armories north of Fifty-ninth Street other than available land at reasonable prices. One was that an uptown site was highly unlikely to run into opposition from neighbors, if only because so few New Yorkers lived north of Fifty-ninth Street. And neighborhood opposition could be an obstacle to the construction of an armory even when the proposed site was not part of a city park. An even stronger inducement was that the guardsmen favored an uptown location. It was in deference to their wishes, said the *Times,* that "the new armories have been disposed without much reference to what ought to be the controlling question, the question of efficiency." The guardsmen preferred an uptown location in part because of what the *Times* called "a desire to be in the most fashionable neighborhoods possible."[32] And as the histories of the Seventh and Ninth regiment armories reveal, these preferences played a crucial role in the location of the city's new armories.

The Seventh Regiment started its campaign for a new armory in 1868, less than a decade after it moved into the Tompkins Market Armory—and nearly a decade before the fears of class warfare erupted in the United States. Although the Tompkins Market Armory was the country's most impressive armory, the Seventh felt that it was no longer convenient for its members. Like other affluent New Yorkers, most of them had moved uptown to escape the influx of immigrants into Lower Manhattan and the growth of commerce and industry there. Located at Third Avenue and Sixth Street, Tompkins Square now seemed too far away. It was a serious problem, Colonel Emmons Clark pointed out a few years later:

> A large majority of the officers and members of this Regiment now reside above 30th Street, and the centre of the population which it represents is constantly moving Northward. It has already become onerous to its members to attend the weekly drills and other military duties at a place so distant from their residences as Tompkins Market. For the same reason it has become difficult to obtain new recruits to fill the places of those who are discharged at end of their legal terms of service. And thus not only the prosperity and efficiency, but the very existence of this Regiment is endangered.[33]

As the site for the new armory, the Seventh proposed Reservoir Square. Situated two miles north of Tompkins Square and about half way between the East and Hudson rivers, it was a very convenient spot. As it was already owned by the city, it could be obtained at little or no cost.

The Seventh Regiment then made the first of what turned out to be several attempts to persuade the state legislature to authorize the city to lease part of Reservoir Square as the site for the new armory. It got nowhere. A second effort, which took place in 1869, succeeded in the senate but, as a result of opposition from nearby property owners, failed in the assembly. In the early 1870s, according to Colonel Clark, the Tweed Ring offered to give the regiment a site in Reservoir Square and to build a large armory on it. But afraid that its reputation would be tarnished by any association with the Ring, the Seventh turned down the offer. In the meantime, the Tompkins Market Armory was having severe problems. The roof leaked, requiring constant repair, and as a result of doubts about the safety of the building, the regiment was forced to suspend battalion drills in the third-floor drill hall. Thus in 1873 the Seventh made its third attempt to obtain Reservoir Square. It prevailed on 20,000 of the city's leading businessmen and taxpayers to sign a petition in favor of using Reservoir Square as the site for the new armory. It also warned New Yorkers that its members lived so far from Tompkins Square that in the event of an emergency a good deal of time would be lost in assembling them.[34] Above all it lobbied hard in Albany.

The Seventh Regiment's third attempt provoked a strong protest, a protest that foreshadowed the great furor over the national guard's proposal to erect an armory in Washington Square five years later. The protest was led by nearby property owners who feared that the armory would lower the value of their holdings and spoil the square as a park. Reservoir Square, they claimed, "is now in use as a park for all citizens, and especially for large schools and children in the vicinity, who have no other place for recreation, and is so indispensable as a sanitary feature that it should never be disturbed, even if the City had the power to do so." And that, they insisted, it did not have, at least not without the consent of the adjacent property owners. The property owners also contended that the city was in such poor financial condition that it could not afford to give away a parcel of land worth more than $1 million, much less to build an armory that might cost even more. These objections were incorporated into a resolution that was sent to Albany; with it went a protest containing the signatures of five hundred property owners. Joining the opposition were other New Yorkers who thought that the city had too few "breathing-places" and worried that the erection of an armory in Reservoir Square might set a precedent that would jeopardize Madison Square and even Central Park.[35]

Colonel Clark did his best to defend the regiment. In a letter to the *Times,* he pointed out that his troops badly needed a new armory in Reservoir Square. An armory there "would be accessible to a large majority of the regiment during the next half century." "There is no other property belonging to the City which is properly located or available as a site for an armory for this regiment." Turning to the objections of the property owners, he contended that "Reservoir-Square is not large enough to be of any great service as a public park, and is not necessary for that purpose on account of its proximity to Central Park"—which was about one mile north. The erection of an armory on a small portion of the square would not deprive the city of a "breathing-place," he added. Nor would the proposed building have an adverse effect on property values in the neighborhood. Clark managed to persuade the assembly, but not the senate. And in the end the regiment had to accept a compromise, the heart of which was that the city council was authorized to provide the regiment with a centrally located site north of Twenty-third Street, though not necessarily Reservoir Square. If the council did not act within three months, the Board of Supervisors was directed to lease or purchase a suitable site for the armory.[36]

The city council took no action, however. Neither did the Board of Supervisors. In an effort to resolve the impasse, a group of New York City legislators asked the regiment to consider the block bounded by Park and Lexington avenues and Sixty-sixth and Sixty-seventh streets, a part of which was formerly Hamilton Square. A two-acre plot that was owned by the city, the Hamilton Square site was well suited for an imposing armory. At first the regiment was unenthusiastic. Many of its leaders thought that Hamilton Square was too far north. During the summer, however, the regiment made a map showing the location of the homes of its members. It revealed that for a large majority of the regiment Hamilton Square was at least as convenient as Tompkins Market (and perhaps even more so). Realizing that Reservoir Square was probably out of the question, the Seventh opted for Hamilton Square. "With each succeeding year," it claimed, "an Armory at this locality will be more and more convenient to the young men of the city." When rapid transit comes, as it is bound to, the site will be accessible to residents "in even the most distant parts of the city." Once located in a new armory in Hamilton Square, the regiment will be able to move swiftly to the rest of the city "when called into service by the civil authorities."[37]

A bill was introduced at the next session of the legislature instructing the city to lease the Hamilton Square site to the regiment for twenty-one years. It ran into little opposition from nearby residents, largely because there were few residents nearby, and became law in April 1874. The city leased the site to the regiment in September, a couple of months after the roof of the Tompkins Market Armory was badly damaged by a fire. Five years later the legislature instructed the city to extend the lease in perpetuity, a step designed to help the regiment's fund-raising campaign.[38] The Seventh's acquisition of the Hamilton Square site did more than just provide the regiment with a large, convenient, and extremely valuable plot for its new armory. It also ensured that the city's first great armory would be located uptown rather than downtown, at a spot that was about three miles north of Tompkins Market and by far the northernmost of the city's armory sites. Even more important, the Seventh's acquisition of the Hamilton Square site prompted the city's other regiments, many of whose members were also moving uptown, to look north of Fifty-ninth Street for armory sites of their own.

The first regiment to follow the Seventh's lead was the Eighth, which was quartered above a stable on Ninth Avenue and Twenty-seventh Street. In 1878 the Eighth prevailed on the state legislature to appropriate $100,000 for a new armory, provided that the local authorities supplied a site. Two years later the regiment asked for most of the block bounded by Park and Lexington avenues and Sixty-seventh and Sixty-eighth streets, which was owned by the city. The request went to the Sinking Fund Commission, a commission consisting of the mayor and four other city officials that had final say over the acquisition of sites for armories and the allocation of funds for construction. Comptroller Allan Campbell, one of the commissioners, objected that the site was too close to the Seventh Regiment Armory. For protection against mobs and rioters, he argued, "the armories of the National Guard should be distributed in different parts of the city and in situations where danger from such sources is most likely to be apprehended." In one of the few cases where military logic prevailed, the commission turned down the application. The regiment returned to the commission two years later, this time asking for a site between Sixty-seventh and Sixty-eighth streets east of Lexington Avenue, which was also owned by the city. If this was not acceptable, it requested a site north of Seventieth Street and east of Park Avenue.[39] Before a decision was reached, the state legislature set up the city's new Armory Board, which was authorized to review potential armory sites and make recommendations to the Sinking Fund Commission.

The Armory Board, on which the national guard was well represented, was favorably disposed to the regiments. Within a year it found large uptown armory sites for the Eighth, Twelfth, and Twenty-second regiments, all of which were approved by the commission and bought by the city. For the Eighth Regiment, which favored the Upper East Side, it picked the block bounded by Madison and Park avenues and Ninety-fourth and Ninety-fifth streets. For the Twelfth, which preferred the Upper West Side, it chose a site on Columbus Avenue between Sixty-first and Sixty-second streets. For the Twenty-second, which also preferred the Upper West Side, it selected the block bounded by Broadway and Columbus Avenue and Sixty-seventh and Sixty-eighth streets.[40] Later the board purchased a site on Park Avenue between Thirty-third and Thirty-fourth streets for the Seventy-first Regiment. For the Ninth Regiment it picked a spot on the north side of Fourteenth Street between Sixth and Seventh avenues, the location of the old Twenty-second Regiment Armory and the southernmost of the new armory sites. And for the Sixty-ninth Regiment it acquired a parcel on Lexington Avenue in the East Twenties. Still later the board assigned Troop (later Squadron) A to the same site as the Eighth Regiment, which subsequently moved to new quarters on Kingsbridge Road and Jerome Avenue in the Bronx. It gave the First Battery a site on West Sixty-sixth Street and the Second Battery a parcel on Franklin Avenue and 166th Street in the Bronx. It also bought a site on Fort Washington Avenue and 168th Street, on which it built yet another armory for the Twenty-second Regiment.[41]

Of all the regiments only the Sixty-ninth came close to ending up in Lower Manhattan. A largely Irish-American regiment, the Sixty-ninth moved into the Tompkins Market Armory in the early 1880s, not long after the Seventh Regiment moved out. By the end of the decade it felt that the armory was inadequate, especially when compared to the armories recently erected for the Eighth, Twelfth, and Twenty-second regiments, and asked the Armory Board for a new one. The board, under fire by the *Times* for locating all the new armories uptown, decided to build this armory downtown, a decision with which the Sixty-ninth seemed to be in accord. In 1890 it chose a site of just over an acre that consisted of the Tompkins Market plot and several additional lots, a site that was later enlarged to nearly an acre and a half. Over the objections of Comptroller Theodore W. Myers, who favored a nearby site on Second Avenue between Sixth and Seventh streets, the Sinking Fund Commission gave its approval two years later. It turned out, however, that the Sixty-ninth wanted an uptown site. As one of its captains told a reporter a few years later, Lower Manhattan was no longer a convenient location for the regiment.

A few years ago the bulk of the membership of the Sixty-ninth was drawn from the lower wards of the city. We had a few men above Forty-second-street, but to-day the conditions in this respect are almost entirely changed, and Harlem and its vicinity is our most available recruiting field. The fact is the Irish population is moving toward the upper wards, and the Sixty-ninth Regiment will be obliged to follow the tide if it is to prosper in the future as it has in the past.[42]

In deference to the wishes of the regiment, the Armory Board reversed itself in 1896 and proposed a site on Lexington Avenue between Twenty-second and Twenty-third streets, almost all of which was already owned by the city.

The Ninth Regiment applied to the Armory Board for a new armory in May 1884, about the same time as the Eighth, Twelfth, and Twenty-second regiments. For nearly twenty years the regiment had been housed on the third and fourth floors of a building on West Twenty-sixth Street, the bulk of which was used for stables and carriage-houses. The building, wrote Colonel William Seward, was "totally unfit for the purpose of an armory." It was not defensible. The Ninth had no control over who occupied the rest of the space and what they did in it. Moreover, the regiment's quarters were "dangerously exposed to a long row of densely populated tenement-houses immediately opposite . . . from which a small body of ambushed men would have the [guards]men completely at their mercy." Nor was the building safe. If a few rioters started a fire on the ground floor, the troops would find it hard to escape by the building's two narrow staircases. When a battalion (or even a company) held maneuvers in the fourth-floor drill hall, it set off a vibration that endangered the building and everyone in it. The building, other members of the regiment pointed out, was extremely unpleasant—especially when what one member called "the delicate aroma" from the Wells, Fargo Express Company stables worked its way up to the regiment's rooms on the floors above.[43]

The regiment was dissatisfied not just with the building, but also with the neighborhood—which, by the standards of its upper-middle-class members, left much to be desired. A working-class neighborhood, West Twenty-sixth Street and vicinity was full of tenement houses and small businesses. Even worse, several of the streets were lined with houses of prostitution. "The neighborhood," protested one member, "is one of the worst in the City: houses of the worst reputation are all around it, and a lady can not be asked to take any part in the receptions [and other social activities] which they hold there."[44] The neighborhood was a source of deep concern to Colonel Seward. He believed that the Seventh Regiment owed much of its great popularity to a splendid new armory in a very attractive neighborhood. He was also convinced that the Eighth Regiment, whose armory was also located over a stable in the West Twenties, was on the decline because of its "bad locality" as well as its "wretched building." To be a success, Seward told a reporter in 1887, a regiment must be a "military club." And a club should be located in a pleasant neighborhood. So long as the Ninth was quartered in the West Twenties, it would be hard pressed to hold its own against the city's other regiments.

The Ninth had a good case. As early as 1881 the *Times* had pointed out that the West Twenty-sixth Street building was in "very bad shape," that five years earlier the building department had condemned it as "unfit for armory purposes." The *Tribune* agreed. It remarked that the walls of the building were so shaky that the regiment had to restrict the number of men who could drill at any one time. The armory was also in a "bad neighborhood," it said. To many New Yorkers it was intolerable that a crack regiment should have such awful accommodations. The Armory Board shared these sentiments. Late in 1884 it recommended that a suitable armory be provided for the Ninth Regiment, a recommendation that was approved by the Sinking Fund Commission. The commission found the Ninth's armory "very unsuitable," as Controller S. Hastings Grant put it. It also believed that the interest on the money required to acquire a site and erect a building, which the Armory Board later estimated to be about $500,000, would probably not exceed the annual rent of the present space.[45] When the commission ordered the board to select a site and prepare the plans, the regiment had good reason to believe that if all went well it would have a new armory within a few years.

All did not go well, however. Colonel Seward first suggested a site in a very attractive neighborhood on the Upper West Side. It consisted of over twenty lots on Eighth Avenue, the western edge of Central Park, between Eighty-third and Eighty-fourth streets. The Armory Board rejected the site, apparently on the ground that the price was too high, and asked the regiment to consider another site on the Upper West Side at the intersection of Broadway and Amsterdam Avenue, a much less central and less pleasant neighborhood. The regiment refused. It believed, wrote Seward, that "to go further west than 9th Ave[nue] for the erection of an armory would be seriously detrimental to the interests of the organization, and would amount to a virtual disbandment." It affirmed its preference for the Eighth Avenue site, arguing that "the location of the armory with the Central Park on its front would add incalculably to the best interests of the Reg[imen]t, as the situation would naturally attract the class of young men to whom we shall look to fill our ranks to the maximum allowed by law." The regiment also denied that the price was too high and even offered to share the site with a battery.[46] It persuaded the Armory Board, but not the Sinking Fund Commission.

During the next few years, according to the Armory Board's historian, Colonel Seward "deluged the Board with sites for a new armory." With one exception, they were all on the Upper West Side. One consisted of thirty lots bounded by Broadway and Columbus Avenue and Sixty-fourth and Sixty-fifth streets. Another of thirty-two lots was situated between Eighth and Columbus avenues and

Eighty-sixth and Eighty-seventh streets. Further uptown was yet another, which consisted of the block bounded by Eighth and Manhattan avenues and 104th and 105th streets. None of these sites was acceptable to the board. It was not that they were too expensive—in at least two of the cases, the board could have acquired the land for less than it paid for the sites for the Eighth and Twenty-second regiments. It was rather that with the Seventh, Eighth, Twelfth, and Twenty-second regiments now located uptown the Armory Board was under pressure to put at least one armory downtown. In the meantime Seward kept pressing the board. In 1888 he reminded Mayor Abram S. Hewitt that four years after the Armory Board had voted to build the new armory the Ninth Regiment was still quartered in the worst "so called armory" in the city.[47]

By early 1889 the pressure was so strong that the board was forced to act. Saying that all the city's regiments had been taken care of except for the Ninth, Sixty-ninth, and Eleventh, which would soon be disbanded, it established a special committee to consider the location of future armories. After pointing out that the Seventh, Eighth, Twelfth, and Twenty-second regiments had been located north of Fifty-ninth Street—and that the Sinking Fund Commission had recently approved a site for the Seventy-first Regiment on Park Avenue between Thirty-third and Thirty-fourth streets—the committee recommended that the Ninth and Sixty-ninth regiments be quartered south of Forty-second Street.

It is the opinion of your Committee that too many regiments are already located above Fifty-ninth Street, and that they are too far distant from the business and populous portions of the City to be speedily useful, when needed on account of the long distance they would be obliged to march in case their [s]ervices were required in the lower or central parts of the City. It will be a long period, in all probability, before the services of any regiment will be needed above Ninety-fifth Street, and the Eighth Regiment, now permanently located at Ninety-fifth Street, will be able to respond quickly to any call from the civil authorities for military services above that street. But in the part below Forty-second Street, now fully built up, and occupied by public buildings and by financial, commercial, mercantile and manufacturing establishments as well as by a large population, there is always a possibility of the services of the National Guard being required in case civil authorities and the municipal police are unable to protect the lives and property of the people and maintain public order.[48]

For the Sixty-ninth Regiment the committee proposed the expansion of the Tompkins Market Armory, a proposal that was the beginning of the abortive effort to locate a new armory on the Tompkins Market site and several adjacent lots. For the Ninth Regiment the committee suggested a couple of sites. One was a large plot, already owned by the city, which lay between Sixth and Seventh avenues and Twenty-ninth and Thirtieth streets. The other was a small plot on Fourteenth Street near Sixth Avenue, which consisted of the former site of the old Twenty-second Regiment Armory and two adjacent lots. After the committee submitted its report, Commissioner Michael Coleman informed the other members of the Armory Board that Colonel Seward "was opposed to the purchase of the Thirtieth-street site, on the theory that the neighborhood was not attractive to citizen soldiers." Presumably Seward was troubled that the site was in the middle of the Tenderloin, New York's infamous hive of saloons, brothels, gambling dens, and dance halls. Indeed the Haymarket, perhaps the most notorious of the Tenderloin's dance halls, was located on Sixth Avenue just south of Thirtieth Street. Seward would prefer a site in Harlem, Coleman advised his colleagues. If that was not agreeable, he would be "fairly well pleased" with one at Lexington Avenue and Thirty-fourth Street. As a last resort he would accept the West Fourteenth Street site.[49]

Seward's preference for a site in Harlem reflected the widespread assumption that the old Dutch village would develop into one of New York City's most desirable middle- and upper-middle-class communities. Long independent, Harlem had been annexed by New York in 1873. Located above 110th Street, the northern border of Central Park, it lay squarely in the path of the city's expansion. As the elevated railways were extended up to 125th Street, Harlem began to attract prosperous businessmen and professionals who were looking for a quiet residential setting away from the tumult of Lower and mid-Manhattan. By 1893 *Harlem Monthly Magazine* confidently predicted that the community would eventually be made up entirely of the "mansions of the wealthy, the homes of the well-to-do, and the places of business of the tradespeople who minister [to] their wants."[50] It seemed a fine place for the Ninth Regiment's new home. (It was roughly two decades after Seward expressed his preference that Harlem started to turn into the foremost black community in the country. And it was about two decades later that the city erected an armory in Harlem, an armory located on Fifth Avenue between 142nd and 143rd streets and occupied not by the Ninth Regiment but by the Fifteenth—later the 369th—the so-called Harlem Hell Fighters, the best known black regiment in the nation.)

The Armory Board would not consider a site in Harlem, however, not after it had rejected other sites south of 110th street on the grounds that they were too far north and not after its special committee had recommended that the Ninth Regiment Armory be built south of Forty-second Street. Nor would it approve the site at Lexington Avenue and Thirty-fourth Street, which was only one block from the site of the proposed new Seventy-first Regiment Armory. And in the face of Colonel Seward's opposition, the board would not choose the West Thirtieth Street site. It therefore picked the West Fourteenth Street site, which seemed the only alternative, a choice that was promptly ratified by the Sinking Fund Commission.[51] Six years after it first applied for a new armory, the Ninth Regiment had a site. From the board's perspective, the site had much to recommend it. Although part of it had to be acquired by condemnation, it was not too expensive. It was also south of Forty-second Street and by half a mile the southernmost of all the city's armory sites. From the regiment's viewpoint, the site left much be desired. With just over one acre, it was the smallest of all the city's armory sites. And for the many members who lived uptown, it was the least convenient. But West Fourteenth Street was a more attractive neighborhood than West Twenty-sixth Street. And in the end that was crucial.

Although the regiments were attracted to the fashionable neighborhoods, the attraction was by no means mutual. Take the case of the Sixty-ninth Regiment, for which the Armory Board proposed in 1896 to erect a new armory on Lexington Avenue between Twenty-second and Twenty-third streets, only a block or two from posh Gramercy Park. The nearby property owners strongly objected. Like the Washington Square property owners, they objected not to the proposal to build a new armory, but to the proposal to build it in their backyard. Banded together as the Twenty-third Street Protective Association, they drafted a petition saying that the armory would place "a blight upon all further improvements of property in the neighborhood." At a meeting of the board in April the association's counsel, former Judge Ernest Hall, presented the petition, with more than one hundred signatures, and claimed that "if the city did not own the land, the proposition of putting an armory on it would never be considered seriously." He urged the board to look for another site. Former Mayor Abram S. Hewitt, who owned several parcels in the neighborhood, also spoke out against the scheme, saying that "if the armory is built as proposed it will place a blank wall opposite the house where I was married, where I have lived all my married life and where my children were born." Another speaker pointed out that the Twenty-third Street site was very close to both the Ninth Regiment Armory on Fourteenth Street and the Seventy-first Regiment Armory on Thirty-fourth Street and questioned "the advisability of grouping the armories so close together."[52]

The Armory Board held another meeting in January 1897, by which time it had reached a decision in favor of the Twenty-third Street site. The opposition turned out in full force. Judge Hall voiced the concerns of the property owners. Mayor Hewitt spelled out his reservations in a letter. Charles F. Wingate, a spokesman for the Social Reform Club, contended that the building on the site, the old College of the City of New York, should be used as "a meeting place for workingmen to keep them out of the saloons." Thaddeus Moriarty—an Irish-American furniture dealer who had said at the previous meeting that if anti-Irish sentiment was behind the opposition he would "cut off his right hand before appearing"—wanted to know why all the armories had to be located above Fourteenth Street. The board was not swayed, however. After the opposition had its say, a subcommittee consisting of General Fitzgerald and Commissioner of Public Works Charles H. T. Collis recommended the Twenty-third Street site, a recommendation that was adopted by the entire board. At the same time the board rescinded the resolution adopted in 1892 designating the Tompkins Market Armory plot as the site for the new Sixty-ninth Regiment Armory.[53]

It seemed that the issue was settled in July 1897, when the Sinking Fund Commission, informed by its engineer that "no better location could be selected as a site for the armory," gave its approval.

But it was not. The property owners continued their battle against the Twenty-third Street site; and though the board, in its historian's words, "stood to its guns with the pertinacity of veterans for a while, it finally gave up the fight." In September 1899 the board selected a site on Lexington Avenue between Twenty-fifth and Twenty-sixth streets. The site was very large, about one and a half acres, and, as the property was privately owned and worth about $800,000, very expensive. But it was not controversial. And the Sinking Fund Commission gave its approval shortly thereafter.[54] This time the issue was really settled. It had dragged on for about ten years, during which the Armory Board considered four different sites and made one decision, only to rescind it, and another decision, only to reverse itself again, before it finally chose the site on which the armory was eventually built. In the end the choice reflected not so much the preference of the board for a site south of Forty-second Street as the reluctance of the Sixty-ninth Regiment to stay in Lower Manhattan and the unwillingness of the East Twenty-third Street property owners to have an armory in their neighborhood.

Ultimately most of the city's regiments got what they wanted, which was a large site at a convenient location and in a pleasant neighborhood. Even the few that did not get their first choice were satisfied. Although the Seventh Regiment was unable to obtain the Reservoir Square site, it was happy with the Hamilton Square site. Although the Seventy-first Regiment had some reservations about the site on Park Avenue and Thirty-fourth Street, they did not last long. And though the Ninth Regiment would have preferred a site on the Upper West Side, it was not averse to the West Fourteenth Street site.

There were three main reasons that most of the regiments got what they wanted. One was that they wanted to be uptown, preferably north of Fifty-ninth Street, which was a part of the city where plenty of land was available in large parcels and at moderate prices. It was also a part of the city where a proposed armory site was unlikely to run into opposition from nearby residents, if only because there were few residents nearby. In other words, the municipal authorities were inclined to accommodate the regiments in part because their wishes were compatible with the nature of the city's real estate market and the attitudes of its property owners.

Another reason that most of the regiments got what they wanted was that they had a great deal of influence with the Armory Board, which chose the sites for all but one of the new armories. To begin with, the guard was well represented on the board. From 1884 to 1886, when the board consisted of the mayor, commissioner of public works, and commander of the First Division, the guardsmen held one of three seats. After 1886, when the state legislature enlarged the board by adding to it the president of the Department of Taxes and Assessments and another high-ranking military official, usually a colonel and commanding officer of a regiment, the troops had two of five seats.[55] With the seats filled by such men as Generals Alexander Shaler, commander of the First Division, and Louis Fitzgerald, commander of the First Brigade, and Colonels Emmons Clark of the Seventh Regiment and James A. Cavanagh of the Sixty-ninth, the regiments had good friends in high places. Shaler and his fellow officers were not able to ignore the pressures on the board to live within its means, pay some attention to military considerations, and maintain cordial relations with the Sinking Fund Commission. But they were able to take the lead in urging the board to give the regiments a sympathetic hearing and to accommodate them whenever possible.

And where General Shaler and the other guardsmen led, the civilian commissioners followed. As Commissioner of Public Works Hubert O. Thompson, one of the original members of the Armory Board, remarked in 1885, "Gen[eral] Shaler was the military man on the board, and the other members relied very much upon him." A year later former Mayor Franklin Edson testified that he and Thompson "left the details of the work of the board to Gen[eral] Shaler." Shaler, who served as secretary of the board and custodian of its records, made much the same point, saying that "every application for armory sites was referred to him by the board for a report, and his recommendations were always accepted."[56] The deference to the guardsmen is not surprising. The mayors, commissioners of public works, and presidents of the Department of Taxes and Assessments were all very busy, overwhelmed by a wide range of responsibilities, of which the siting of armories was not one of the most important. Few of them knew much about martial matters or had the time and inclination to learn. Even if they had, it would have done little good because of the high turnover rate. None of the civilian commissioners served even half as long as Generals Fitzgerald and McLeer, both of whom sat on the Armory Board for eleven years.

Yet another reason that most of the city's regiments got what they wanted was that the city needed the regiments more than the regiments needed the city. As Major Francis V. Greene remarked, the national guard was "a voluntary and unpaid organization of men, to whom soldiering is an incident and not the main object of their lives." They "can not be enlisted by force," observed General Louis Fitzgerald, "nor, from the very nature of the service, can they be compelled to perform their duty." If greatly displeased with a proposed armory site, the guardsmen could leave the service (if not right away, then in the near future) or threaten to do so. It was fine for the *Times* to criticize the local authorities for deferring to the regiments' wishes—and even to suggest that "probably the best thing that could have been done when the armories were first authorized would have been to establish their sites throughout the city according to purely military considerations, and perhaps even to build them before assigning them to any particular regiments."[57] But in view of the voluntary character of the national guard, it is hard to see how the authorities could have compelled a regiment to accept an armory site that its members regarded as incompatible with the well-being of their organization.

Some of the regiments were prepared to go to great lengths to prevent the authorities from sending them to an unacceptable building or an unacceptable site. In 1879, for example, the Board of Aldermen ordered the Eighth Regiment, whose armory on West Twenty-third Street had recently been destroyed by fire, to move into an armory on West Twenty-seventh Street. The board had long been trying to find a regiment for this armory, which had initially been rented by the Tweed Ring. But as it was located above a large stable in a diladipated building, the Eighth did not want to be quartered there. Its leaders drafted a strong protest, claiming that the building was "unfit and unsafe," vulnerable to fire, and prone to an "intolerable" stench. Rather than occupy the armory, they would recommend that the regiment be disbanded.[58] The Eighth eventually agreed to move into the armory, but only because it assumed that its new armory, for which the state legislature had recently appropriated funds, would soon be erected, an assumption that turned out to be extremely optimistic.

Whether New York was typical is hard to say. The process by which armories were located varied from city to city. Some sites were selected with little trouble. Chicago's First Regiment built its new armory on Michigan Avenue and Sixteenth Street largely because Marshall Field virtually gave it the site. But most sites were chosen only after a long and hard struggle involving the national guard and other groups. A look at these struggles suggests that the constraints and pressures which existed in New York were present in other cities as well and that they were the primary reasons that most armories were located in places where the likelihood of rioting was very low. Guardsmen and others claimed that military considerations should play the main role in the siting of armories. Speaking of the new Connecticut State Arsenal and Armory, the chair of the Senate Committee on Military Affairs asked a member of the state Armory Committee whether the site should be chosen on military grounds "regardless of pleasing the people of Hartford." "Unquesionably that should be so," he replied. But it rarely was—not even in Hartford, where the state legislature rejected a site for a new armory that was admirable from a military viewpoint and approved another whose chief virtue was that it fit nicely into the city's plans for a civic center.[59]

chapter four

The Design of the Armories

Early in 1861 New York's Seventh Regiment opened the new Tompkins Market Armory (figure 1), an armory that the New York *Times* described as "undoubtedly the finest" in the world. Located on Third Avenue between Sixth and Seventh streets, it covered 18,000 square feet and stood three stories high. On the first floor was a public market, on the second eleven company rooms and two company drill halls, and on the third a regimental drill hall, the largest drill hall in the nation. The armory was a "handsome" building, wrote the *Times,* "elegantly ornate, and yet not bewilderingly complex." A rectangular and highly symmetrical structure, it was designed in an Italianate style. Perhaps its most striking feature was the long rows of fluted columns, a combination of Corinthian and Ionic orders that was then referred to as "composite architecture." Although it housed a military unit, the armory looked much like many of the city's prominent commercial and civic structures. "If the fluted columns which decorate its front were removed," the *Times* wrote, "it would resemble the TIMES building." At first glance, the New York *World* said, "the country visitor inevitably mistakes [it] for the Astor Library."[1] With the possible exception of the vaulted roof, which covered the regimental drill hall, nothing about the Tompkins Market Armory indicated that it was the home of a military organization.

Much the same could be said about the handful of other armories

Figure 1. New York City's Tompkins Market Armory.

that were built in the 1850s and 1860s. New York's Twenty-second Regiment Armory (figure 2), erected in 1863, was a two-story French Empire building that was dominated by a medieval French tower. Notwithstanding its machicoulis gallery, reminiscent of the machicolations of medieval castles and fortresses, the armory could easily have been taken for a public market. Even less martial was Brooklyn's Henry Street Armory (figure 3), the cornerstone of which was laid in 1858. A solid, rectangular building, four stories high, it was designed in early Romanesque Revival style. With rows of round-headed arched windows and a simple cornice, it resembled many of the city's mid-century office buildings. Philadelphia's National Guards Hall (figure 4), erected in 1857 and regarded by some as "one of the finest military edifices in our Union," was an imposing three-story building that was designed along the lines of an Italian Renaissance villa. It featured an elaborate cornice, overhanging

Figure 2. New York City's Twenty-second Regiment Armory.

Figure 3. Brooklyn's Henry Street Armory.

balcony, and projecting pilasters. Far less imposing was Philadelphia's First Troop Armory (figure 5), which was put up in 1864 by the city's elite cavalry unit. It was a nondescript building, two stories high, with a one-story riding ring attached. With its small gate, low fence, and front lawn, it looked a lot like a country schoolhouse.[2]

To put it another way, these armories lacked a distinctive architectural form that would have made it clear what kind of buildings they were (and what kinds they were not). They did not look much like the homes of a military organization, much less like the forts which dotted the eastern seaboard of the United States or the fortresses which covered much of Western Europe.[3] Nor did they look much like one another. The elegant Tompkins Market Armory had little in common with the eclectic Twenty-second Regiment Armory, though it bore a strong resemblance to Boston's Faneuil Hall, the attic of which had once been the home of the First Corps of Cadets. Neither of them looked much like Brooklyn's austere Henry Street Armory. The Philadelphia armories did not have much

Figure 4.
Philadelphia's National
Guards Hall.

in common with one another, let alone with the New York and
Brooklyn armories. The ornate National Guards Hall differed in
many ways from the plain First Troop Armory, though it closely
resembled New York's Tammany Hall, the home of the city's Democratic machine, the top floor of which later housed the Sixth Regiment. In the absence of a distinctive architectural form that would
have distinguished armories from retail stores, office buildings, and
other commercial and civic structures, it is no surprise that the
nation's most prominent armory was often mistaken for a library.

A few more armories were erected in the early and mid-1870s,
but in terms of design none had much in common with the others.
Brooklyn's Twenty-third Regiment Armory (figure 6), whose cornerstone was laid in 1872, was a three-story Gothic building whose
facade was broken by long rows of narrow pointed-arched windows.
Under the cornice ran a machicoulis gallery; above it stood several
medieval French towers. Until New York's Seventh Regiment com-

Figure 5. Philadelphia's First Troop Armory.

pleted its new armory in 1879, the Twenty-third's home was the largest and most impressive armory in the nation. Brooklyn's Thirteenth Regiment Armory, on which construction began in 1874, looked nothing like the Twenty-third Regiment Armory. It was a deep three-story building designed, said the New York *Times,* in a "romanesque" style and dominated by a large central gable flanked by two corner towers. Baltimore's Richmond Market Armory (figure 7), built for the Fifth Regiment in 1873, bore no resemblance to the Twenty-third or Thirteenth regiment armories. It was a sober rectangular structure with four floors, the lowest of which was used as a public market. With the administration building in front, the drill shed in back, and a large cupola on top, the armory looked if anything like a railroad station.[4]

Of the few armories erected before 1877, by far the most intriguing was the new Philadelphia First Troop Armory (figure 8). Built in 1874 to commemorate the troop's centennial, it replaced the old armory that had been built only a decade earlier. The armory was designed by Furness and Hewitt, a local architectural firm, one of

Figure 6. Brooklyn's Twenty-third Regiment Armory.

whose principals was Frank Furness, a student of Richard Morris Hunt who would soon achieve national renown for his plans for Philadelphia's Guarantee Trust and Safe Deposit Company, the Pennsylvania Academy of the Fine Arts, and Philadelphia's Provident Life and Trust Company Bank. Located at Twenty-first and Barker streets, on a quarter of an acre adjacent to the troop's old riding ring, the new armory was a far cry from the nondescript building it replaced. A squat three-story structure, which had a drill hall on the first floor and meeting and storage rooms on the second and third, it looked like "an ancient fortress," wrote the Philadelphia *Evening Bulletin*. It stood on a massive rusticated base of battered stone about twenty feet high. Above it rose thick walls of pressed red brick. In most of its features—and, above all, in the sturdy corner tower that was pierced by a few very narrow and heavily

Figure 7. Baltimore's Richmond Market Armory.

guarded windows and crowned by a fully crenellated battlement—
the First Troop Armory followed closely the conventions of medieval military architecture.[5]

The First Troop Armory was a striking building, but there was
no reason to think it was a harbinger of things to come. Although
architects had designed other buildings in a castellated style before
the Civil War—among them the Eastern Penitentiary in Philadelphia, the Smithsonian Institution in Washington, D.C., and state
arsenals in New York, Albany, and Buffalo—they showed little
inclination to apply this style to armories. And though the First
Troop Armory was highly praised by some critics, one of whom said
that it was designed "with great spirit and signal success," so were
other armories, including the recently erected homes of the Fifth,
Thirteenth, and Twenty-third regiments, each of which drew inspiration from a different architectural tradition. A fairly small structure, one of Furness's less imposing buildings, the First Troop Armory was also unlikely to be very influential. (It would be eclipsed
by Philadelphia's new First Regiment Armory a decade later. And

Figure 8.   Philadelphia's First Troop Armory.

two decades later Montgomery Schuyler, the country's foremost architectural critic, would be unable to remember the name of the armory and whether it was still standing—which it was.)[6] In other words, as late as the mid-1870s there was little evidence that the armory was on the verge of acquiring a distinctive architectural form, much less that this form would be based on the design of medieval castles and fortresses.

But on the verge it was—especially after New York's Seventh Regiment built its new armory on the Upper East Side in the late 1870s. Apparently the Seventh did not set out to erect anything out of the ordinary. Drawings from the early 1870s, when the regiment was still trying to obtain the Reservoir Square site, show an eclectic structure, with round-headed arched windows, a mansard roof, and corner towers topped by triangular pediments. Its most distinctive feature was a separate drill shed, which was attached to the rear of the administration building. This arrangement, which reflected the regiment's view that the drill shed should be on the ground floor, may have been inspired by the nation's new railroad stations, which were divided into a head house and an adjoining train shed. If the proposed building looked little like the Tompkins Market Armory, it looked even less like the First Troop Armory. During the mid-1870s, however, Colonel Emmons Clark and his fellow officers decided that they wanted a much larger and more imposing building and asked Charles W. Clinton to design it. A young New York architect and former member of the Seventh Regiment, Clinton was the first in a long line of guardsmen who drew plans for armories after 1877. Although Clinton retained a mansard roof and a separate drill shed, he incorporated into the design a few features of medieval military architecture. And by the time construction began, he revised the plans in a number of ways which made the new armory look even more like a medieval castle.[7]

Completed in 1879, the Seventh Regiment Armory (figure 9) was much more eclectic than the First Troop Armory. Unlike Furness, Clinton drew not only on the castellated tradition, but also on the Romanesque, Gothic, Italianate, and Second Empire styles. The administration building was a large three-story structure that stood on a rusticated base of battered granite. It had narrow windows, a

Figure 9. New York City's Seventh Regiment Armory.

mansard roof, and a tall central tower, topped by a Gothic steeple and flanked at each corner by a large square tower. A massive cornice (much like "the machicolated cornices of the middle ages," Colonel Clark pointed out) crowned the towers, and a bronze portcullis, bronze gate, and solid oak door, half a foot thick, protected the main entrance on Park Avenue. To the rear, facing Lexington Avenue, stood the huge drill shed (figure 10), one of the largest unobstructed spaces in the city. The shed had three entrances, all of which were defended by strong wooden doors, reinforced by heavy iron gates. Its walls were pierced by narrow windows, most of them shielded by iron bars or iron shutters, and strategically placed loopholes, "enfilading all approaches," said the New York *Evening Express,* through which the Seventh's marksmen could

Figure 10. Seventh Regiment Armory Drill Shed.

"pick off advancing crowds." As the regiment said in one of its appeals for funds, the armory was designed with due regard for both "architectural effect" and "easy defense." It "could at any time be defended by fifty men," wrote the New York *Times*.[8]

Although far less original than the First Troop Armory, the Seventh Regiment Armory was much more influential. One reason was that the Seventh was the foremost regiment in the nation's foremost city. Although not the oldest, it was the most prestigious military organization in the country. It was probably the only one that could have prevailed upon both the president and the secretary of war to attend the opening of its new armory. Another reason was that the Seventh Regiment Armory was by far the largest, costliest, and finest armory in the nation. It was more than twice as large and roughly four times as expensive as Brooklyn's Twenty-third Regiment Armory. It contained a wide range of facilities and amenities that other regiments could only dream about. And in its ten company rooms, its colonel's room, its Board of Officers' room, its reception room, its library, and above all its veterans' room, the armory

Figure 11. Seventh Regiment Armory Company K Room.

possessed a degree of elegance found only in the country's most luxurious homes and exclusive clubs (figures 11 and 12). For these reasons newspapers from Boston to San Francisco reported at length about the building and design of the Seventh Regiment's new home. And plans and illustrations of the building were published in military journals and popular magazines (figure 13). From the late 1870s to the mid-1880s, when the great surge of armory construction got under way in New York, the Seventh Regiment Armory was, as the historian of the city's Armory Board later wrote, "the last word in armories."[9]

The castellated style took hold in New York a few years later, when the Armory Board built new homes for the Eighth, Ninth, Twelfth, Twenty-second, and Seventy-first regiments. First came the Twelfth Regiment Armory (figure 14), completed in 1886. Located on the Upper West Side, it was designed by James E. Ware, a New York architect (and a former member of the Seventh Regi-

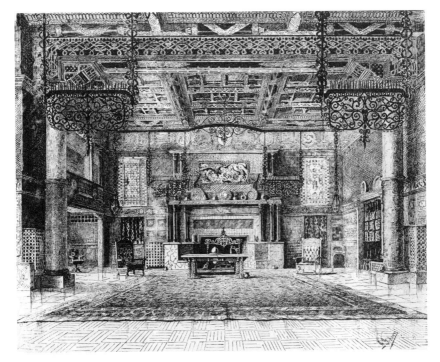

Figure 12. Seventh Regiment Armory Veterans' Room.

ment) who won a competition held by the Armory Board. Following Clinton's lead, he designed an imposing administration building and a separate drill shed. He also adhered closely, much more closely than Clinton, to the traditions of medieval military architecture. As Moses King's guide to New York described it:

> The building is a castellated structure in the Norman style of architecture, and has a solid fortress-like character, with its mediaeval bastions, machicolations and narrow slits in corbelled galleries, and grillework at the windows. At each street corner are flanking towers, with loop-holes and arrangements for howitzers, or Gatling guns, on the top. Around the entire roof is a paved promenade, protected by a parapet with many loop-holes, constituting a valuable defensive position.

With a huge battlemented tower in the center, the Twelfth Regiment Armory was reminiscent of "the military architecture of the Middle Ages," wrote one critic, who said it was, "architecturally

Figure 13. An Evening at the Seventh Regiment Armory.

Figure 14. New York City's Twelfth Regiment Armory.

speaking, much the best [armory] yet built." Calling it "a massive and handsome fortress," another observer said that the armory was "a tower of strength to lovers of civic order and peace who remember the possibilities, remote ones, it is to be hoped[,] of riot and disturbance."[10]

Even more formidable than the Twelfth Regiment Armory was the Eighth Regiment Armory (figure 15), which was completed in 1889. Located on the Upper East Side, it was designed by John R. Thomas, an architect who started out in Rochester, where he became known for his work on the Elmira Reformatory, and then moved to New York City, where he built up a successful practice. Thomas' armory was the epitome of medieval military architecture. The administration building, whose style, said the *Times*, "is somewhat imperfectly described as 'Scottish Baronial,'" featured a wide gable, recessed behind two enormous flanking towers, 50 feet in diameter and 125 feet high. Both towers were fully crenellated and machicolated and pierced by narrow windows enfiladed for muskets. With its huge towers and thick walls, its corner turrets, which protected the drill shed, its small bartizans, which projected from the great towers, and its arched entrance, through which a traditional sally-port had been constructed, the Eighth Regiment Armory was one of the most thoroughly castellated structures in the United

Figure 15. New York City's Eighth Regiment Armory.

States. The armory is the "most impressive piece of military architecture possessed by the city or State of New-York," the *Times* wrote. It "is destined to become one of the prominent 'sights' of the city" and "will stand for many years to come as a model of the ideal social and military home of the National Guard."[11]

New York's other armories were cut from the same mold. The Twenty-second Regiment Armory, which was completed in the early 1890s, was "a granite-trimmed brick fortress, in the general style of the fifteenth century," noted King's guide to New York. "It is, to an exceptional degree, a defensive structure, with re-entering angles, loop-holes for cannon and musketry, a bastion for heavy guns on the northwest corner, a machicolated parapet, and a sally-port and portcullis." Located on the Upper East Side, it was designed by Captain John P. Leo, a member of the regiment who took on the job after the Armory Board rejected a plan by George B. Post, one of the nation's leading architects, on the grounds that it could not be carried out with the funds available. Also completed in the early 1890s was the Seventy-first Regiment Armory (figure 16). Located on East Thirty-third Street, the armory was hailed by the *Times* as "one of the finest structures of its kind in the State." A building whose general outlines followed, in the regiment's words, "the style of the old Scottish baronial structures," the armory was designed by John R. Thomas, the architect of both the Eighth Regiment Armory and the Squadron A Armory—an armory that was built adjacent to the Eighth Regiment Armory, designed in the same style, and completed in the mid-1890s.[12]

Also completed in the mid-1890s was the Ninth Regiment Armory (figure 17), the last armory erected in New York before 1900. Located on West Fourteenth Street, it was designed by W. A. Cable, a former member of the Seventh Regiment and Squadron A and later an officer in the Second Battery, and E. A. Sargent, whose plan won over eighteen others in a competition held by the Armory Board. Designed, said the architects, "to be simple, strong, defensible, and distinctly military in character," the Ninth Regiment Armory was a highly picturesque and fully crenellated structure. With its rough-face granite walls, its three sally-ports, its heavy iron gates, and its many turrets pierced by narrow windows, the armory was reminiscent of "some of the most famous castles of Europe," observed the New York *Herald*. The armory "is not a fortress in

Figure 16. New York City's Seventy-first Regiment Armory.

looks only," the New York *Tribune* pointed out. "The tower, which is 27 feet in diameter and 118 feet high, and other parts of the building are pierced by loopholes for musketry fire, and the whole building is arranged so that its approaches could be fully covered in case of attack."[13] A formidable building that was defensible without and elegant within, the Ninth Regiment Armory was one of the outstanding examples of castellated architecture in New York City.

At the same time that it took hold in New York, the castellated style spread to other cities, many of which modeled their armories on New York's. In nearby Brooklyn the style first appeared in the mid-1880s, when the Forty-seventh Regiment Armory and the Dean Street Armory, which housed the Third Battery, were erected. It reached a high point there a decade later, when huge new armories were built for the Thirteenth, Fourteenth, and Twenty-third regiments. The Fourteenth Regiment Armory was designed by Wil-

Figure 17. New York City's Ninth Regiment Armory.

liam Mundell, a local architect best known for Brooklyn's Hall of Records and Raymond Street Jail. Mundell followed what was by then the standard practice of designing an imposing administration building and separate drill shed. Of the administration building, the Brooklyn *Eagle* wrote, "It is built in the style of the old Norman castles, with arched openings, high parapet walls pierced by firing holes, and has heavy overhanging battlemented towers and turrets." Even more imposing was the Twenty-third Regiment Armory (figure 18), which was designed jointly by Isaac G. Perry, de facto state architect of New York, and Fowler & Hough, a New York architectural firm, both of whose principals were members of the regiment. It was, wrote one journalist, "a castellated structure in the mediaeval style of Norman architecture," a structure dominated by a very tall, fully battlemented circular tower. "As to its utility and impregnability there can be no doubt."[14]

By far the most formidable of Brooklyn's armories was the new

Figure 18. Brooklyn's Twenty-third Regiment Armory.

home of the Thirteenth Regiment (figure 19), which was designed by Rudolph L. Daus. A local architect who had studied at the French Ecole des Beaux-Arts, the most influential school of art and architecture in the nineteenth century, Daus was only thirty years old, ordinarily too young to be given such a large commission. But he was a protégé of the Brooklyn political boss Hugh McLaughlin, who got him the job in spite of the opposition of Mayor Alfred C. Chapin and Colonel David E. Austen, commander of the regiment. The armory, wrote the New York *Times,* was "a huge castellated structure, designed after the style of the old Norman keep." It featured two large fully battlemented towers, above one of which rose an

Figure 19. Brooklyn's Thirteenth Regiment Armory.

octagonal turret that served as a signal tower. Between the towers was a deep arched entrance protected by a fortified sally-port. At the corners stood octagonal turrets, each crowned by a battlement, all "offering excellent bases of defense in case of attack," noted James de Mandeville, the regiment's historian. The *Times* saw in the armory many features of the Castle of Chapultepec in Mexico, where Daus had spent part of his life. *Harper's Weekly* noted the influence "of the French feudal castles of the eleventh and twelfth centuries." And de Mandeville held that Daus drew his inspiration from thirteenth-century Norman architecture. But all agreed that the Thirteenth Regiment's new home was, as the *Times* put it, "one of the most imposing structures of its kind in the United States."[15]

In upstate New York most of the armories were designed by state architect Perry. A well-established architect, highly regarded for his work on the state capitol and executive mansion, Perry drew the plans for armories in Albany, Binghamton, and roughly forty other cities in the 1880s and 1890s. Most were castellated structures, a few of which were modeled on Brooklyn's Twenty-third Regiment Armory, which Perry designed with Fowler & Hough. Probably the most impressive was Buffalo's Seventy-fourth Regiment Armory, which was completed in the late 1890s. A formidable building whose interior was very elegant, it was dominated by a huge square central tower and two large circular corner towers, all crowned by battlemented parapets. In New Jersey most of the armories were designed by Charles A. Gifford, the architect of the New Jersey State Building at the Chicago World's Fair of 1893. Hired by the New Jersey Military Board, Gifford drafted the plans for the First (Newark), Second (Trenton), Third (Camden), Fourth (Jersey City), and Fifth (Paterson) regiment armories, of which all but the Second were completed in the mid- and late 1890s. Guided by the board's views that the armories would probably have to be defended against a mob some day, Gifford designed them to look like "forts," wrote the New York *Times*.[16]

Of the many armories which went up in the mid-Atlantic states after 1877, one of the most noteworthy was the new home of Philadelphia's First Regiment (figure 20). Completed in the mid-1880s, after New York's Seventh Regiment Armory but before the Eighth and Twelfth, it was one of the earliest castellated armories in the country. The designer was James H. Windrim, a well-known Phil-

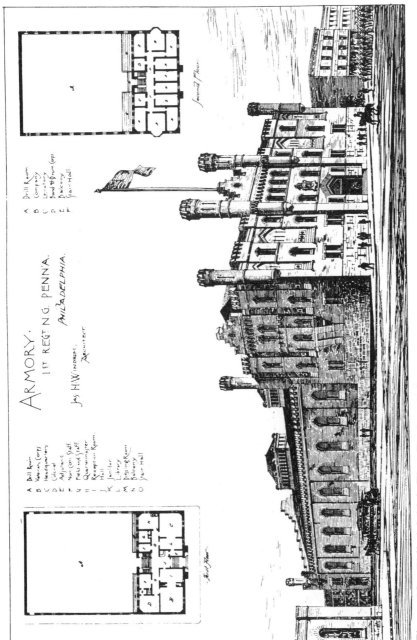

Figure 20. Philadelphia's First Regiment Armory.

adelphia architect who had recently been named a fellow of the American Institute of Architects. For the regiment Windrim designed what the Philadelphia *Public Ledger* described as "an ornamental brick building upon a stone base . . . in the castellated gothic style of architecture." Three stories high, it featured two tall central towers and six shorter corner towers, all of which were fully battlemented and pierced by slit windows. The proposed structure, wrote the Philadelphia *Press,* was designed according to "strict military principles and will be so disposed as to be readily capable of defence by a corporal's guard."[17] For reasons which are unclear, Windrim was forced to modify his plans. Besides eliminating the third floor, he got rid of much of the crenellated cornice and toned down a few of the other castellated features. But he retained the rusticated base, the recessed entrance, and most of the battlemented towers. Although not as highly castellated as Windrim's original version, the First Regiment Armory was one of Philadelphia's most striking examples of medieval military architecture.

The castellated style took hold in New England as well, especially in Massachusetts and Rhode Island. The Massachusetts armories, the clerk of the state Armory Commission remarked, were modeled on "the magnificent armories of [New York's] Seventh, Eighth and Twelfth Regiments . . . particularly the noble building of the Seventh Regiment." Shortly after it was set up, the commission and the supervising architect of Boston's Irvington Street Armory, Olin W. Cutter, went to New York to look at its new armories. These armories provided inspiration not only for the Irvington Street Armory, which was finished in 1890, but also for the Worcester and Lowell armories (figures 21 and 22), both of which were completed in the 1890s. Rhode Island built castellated armories in Pawtucket, Bristol, and Newport in the mid-1890s. And in 1897 it approved the plans for Providence's Cranston Street Armory, one of the country's most picturesque and castellated armories. Like most of Rhode Island's armories, the Cranston Street Armory was designed by William R. Walker & Son, a Providence architectural firm founded in 1881. Walker owed his success as much to his service in the national guard, which he left as a major general, as to his studies at MIT and the Ecole des Beaux-Arts. Associated with him was his son, William H. Walker, who served in the guard for twenty years before retiring as quartermaster general.[18]

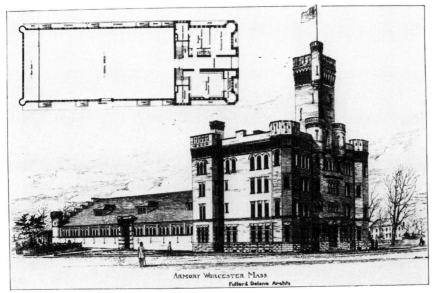

Figure 21. Worcester Armory.

By far the most imposing armory in New England was the new home of Boston's First Corps of Cadets (figure 23), which was designed in the late 1880s and finished nearly a decade later. The architect was William G. Preston. The son of one of Boston's most accomplished architects, Preston studied at Harvard and the Ecole des Beaux-Arts, worked in his father's office, and later designed several of the city's notable buildings. He was also a former member of the Corps and active member of its Veteran Association. For the Corps Preston designed a highly castellated structure, very much in the Romanesque style popularized by H. H. Richardson, the most influential American architect of the late nineteenth century. In the front was the formidable administration building, which stood on a rusticated base, rose four stories to a crenellated cornice, and was topped by a hexagonal tower, two stories high, pierced by narrow windows and crowned by a battlemented parapet. In the rear was a spacious drill shed, whose entrances were protected by triple-plate iron doors, loop-holed for muskets, and, in one case, by a portcullis, drawbridge, and moat and whose windows were guarded by musket-proof, loop-holed iron shutters. The building, wrote Col-

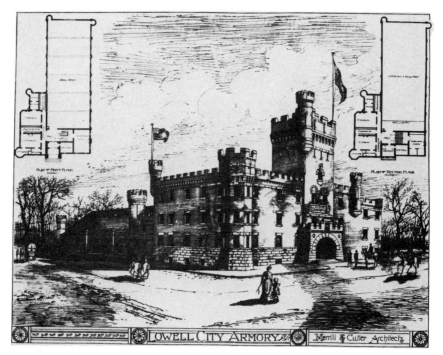

Figure 22. Lowell Armory.

onel Thomas F. Edmands, was "substantial—not ornate, but as tasteful as is required and as may be in keeping with due regard for means of defence."[19] Although Edmands did not say so, the building was extremely elegant, if not quite as elegant as New York's Seventh Regiment Armory.

The castellated style also spread to the Midwest. Cleveland's Central Armory (figure 24), designed by Lehman and Schmitt and completed in the mid-1890s, was a large castellated structure dominated by two battlemented towers, one circular and the other octagonal (and, as one scholar has noted, "reminiscent of a Florentine or Sienese thirteenth century municipal fortress tower"). Less highly castellated, but more thoroughly Romanesque, was the Cleveland Grays Armory, also completed in the mid-1890s and designed by Fenimore C. Bate. Hailed by Judge Henry Clay White as "a citadel of social strength," the armory had a rusticated base, Romanesque entrance, and five-story circular tower. Another castellated structure was the Detroit Light Guard Armory (figure 25), which was erected

Figure 23.   Boston's First Corps of Cadets Armory.

Figure 24. Cleveland's Central Armory.

in the late 1890s, after the Guard had sent a committee of three to visit the leading armories of New York and Brooklyn. Dominated by a huge circular tower, fully crenellated and machicolated, the building was probably modeled on the Eighth and Twenty-third regiment armories.[20]

By far the most formidable armory in the Midwest was Chicago's First Regiment Armory (figure 26). Built in the early 1890s, it was designed by Burnham & Root, one of the region's leading architectural firms, whose principals were John Wellborn Root, a gifted designer who died before the building was completed, and Daniel H. Burnham, a superb manager who soon went on to win national renown as supervising architect of the Chicago World's Fair. Describing the armory as "perhaps the most massive piece of masonry in the city," one observer wrote that it "impresses the beholder as if it were an impregnable fortress." The first story, he said, was a forbidding thirty-five foot high wall of large blocks of rock-faced brownstone, broken only by a sally-port, forty feet wide and ten feet deep and defended by a portcullis and steel doors. "The two

Figure 25.   Detroit Light Guard Armory.

upper stories, on top of the massive masonry of the first floor, are crowned at the angles by great bastions, from which an enfilade fire may be directed against any side of the walls. In the walls are many small windows protected by basket grating, and the top of the building is supported by a mediaeval parapet projecting over the top of the wall and penetrated with rifle slits." Speaking of the armory, Captain Charles G. Fuller claimed that "for use as the home and fortress of a regiment it leaves nothing to be desired. And no visitor to the World's Fair will ever need ask the character of the towering, frowning, massively magnificent structure which is so rapidly growing into being."[21]

A few armories were not designed in the castellated style. Among them were Philadelphia's Third Regiment Armory and the J. J. Bagley Memorial Armory, which was built for the Detroit Light Infantry. These armories were the exceptions, however. After 1877 the vast majority of the armories, and especially of the most impressive armories, were designed in the castellated style. Whether inspired by Norman, French, or Scottish Baronial styles (or by the

Figure 26. Chicago's First Regiment Armory.

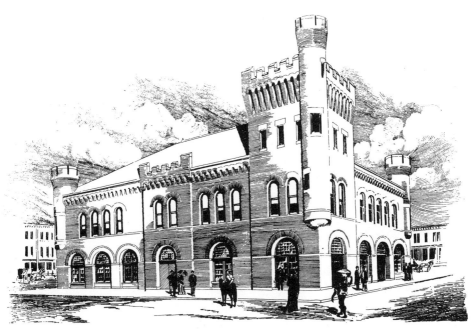

Figure 27. Portsmouth, Virginia, Market and Armory.

architecture of the eleventh, twelfth, or thirteenth century), they all exhibited what the Providence *Journal* called a distinctive "'armory' style of architecture," whose cardinal features "are reminders of the feudal strongholds of the Middle Ages."[22] This style was a national style. It was found everywhere in the country where armories were built, in big cities and small ones, in the Northeast, Midwest, and Far West. It was even found here and there in the South, the home of the Portsmouth, Virginia, Market and Armory (figure 27), a small, far from formidable castle that was designed by Carpenter & Peebles.

The consensus that the castellated style—or what *Architectural Record* referred to in 1911 as "military Gothic" architecture—was "the appropriate style and manner for an armory" emerged not long after the railroad strike of 1877 and remained intact through the rest of the century.[23] Subscribed to by virtually all architects (as well as virtually all national guardsmen and public officials), this consensus was so strong that nearly all the armories were designed in the castellated style. It did not make much difference whether the architects had their own practices, as most of them did, or were on the public payroll, as Isaac Perry was; whether they were employed by the regiments, which relied on private contributions, or by public agencies, which depended on legislative appropriations. Nor did it make much difference whether the architects obtained their commissions by virtue of their professional reputation, their affiliation with the national guard, or, as in the case of Rudolph Daus, their political connections. Finally, the castellated style was followed by well-known architects who had established offices and as much business as they could handle as well as by little-known architects who had just joined the profession and for whom a commission to design an armory was a great opportunity.

Two architectural competitions, one for New York's Ninth Regiment Armory and the other for Providence's Cranston Street Armory, revealed just how strong the consensus was. The competition for the Ninth Regiment Armory was held by the New York City Armory Board in 1897. It drew nineteen entries, of which eight have survived. Besides Cable and Sargent, the winners, the architects included James E. Ware, who had designed the Twelfth Regiment Armory, Walter A. Dickson, who had supervised the erection of the U.S. Immigration Bureau buildings on Ellis Island, and Harding & Gooch, a New York firm that had designed several Manhattan office buildings. Each closely followed the conventions of medieval military architecture; and the result was eight castellated buildings that differed only in details. The same was true of the competition for the Cranston Street Armory, which was held, also in 1897, by the Providence Armory Commission. It drew forty-two entries, of which four have survived. They came from W. T. Smith and R. D. McPherson, Walter Atherton and Herbert D. Hale, Howard & Cauldwell, and William R. Walker & Son, the winner. Following the Armory Commission's stipulation that "the whole building must be adapted for purposes of defence," they all designed huge castellated structures. The designs were so similar that it is hard to avoid the conclusion that Walker probably won because of (and his son's) standing in the guard.[24]

To begin to grasp why the architects who designed armories opted for the castellated style, it is helpful to bear in mind that the armory was one of the many new building types which appeared on the

American landscape in the second half of the nineteenth century. Among the others, wrote the prominent architect and architectural critic Henry Van Brunt, were

> railway buildings of all sorts; churches with parlors, kitchens, and society rooms; hotels on a scale never before dreamt of; public libraries, the service of which is fundamentally different from any of their predecessors; office and mercantile structures, such as no pre-existing conditions of professional and commercial life have ever required; school-houses and college buildings, whose necessary equipment removes them far from the venerable examples of Oxford and Cambridge.[25]

Like most new building types, the armory did not have a form of its own, a form that could have served as a model for the architects. Thus the architects had to do for the armory what they had already done for the railway station and the state capitol. They had to find for it a distinctive form, one appropriate for a building that served not only as the home of the guardsmen, a place for them to get together, hold meetings, and store weapons, but as a schoolhouse, clubhouse, fortress, and symbol as well.

In the search for such a form, the architects labored under a few powerful constraints. One was that the armories (or, at any rate, the big-city armories) had to be very large in order to house the wide range of facilities and amenities demanded by the guardsmen. Among them were an officers' room, several company rooms, a veterans' room, and a room for ladies; a library (or reading room), band room, trophy room, dining room, and saloon; a gymnasium, swimming pool, rifle range, and maybe a bowling alley; and, above all, a regimental drill shed. The armories also had to be very impressive, not only because the guardsmen insisted on it, but also because the buildings were symbols of the community's generosity and integral features of the city's landscape. As Bishop Samuel Fallows said at the cornerstone ceremonies of Chicago's First Regiment Armory in 1890, "We do not want the headquarters of our soldiers to be inferior to any other monuments of our city's architecture."[26] Given these constraints, the architects could not model the new armories on the country's existing military structures. The eastern forts, which stood at strategic points along the coast, were starkly utilitarian buildings, most of which would have been out of place in the ornate landscape of late nineteenth-century urban

America. And the western forts, which dotted the frontier, were small wooden structures.

Another constraint was that the guardsmen felt very strongly that the drill shed should be on the ground floor, preferably attached to, yet separate from, the administration building. As the guardsmen saw it, the common practice of putting the drill shed on the upper floors of the armory was extremely inefficient and dangerous. Even if the drill shed was big enough to hold a regiment, the maneuvers would place a heavy strain on the structure.[27] And a regiment which was restricted to company drills could not develop proper military discipline. Even worse, if a mob attacked the armory and set it afire, the troops would have a hard time getting out alive if they were caught drilling on the upper floors. To the volunteers, it was as reckless to put the drill shed on top of the administration building as it was to put an armory on top of a public market. Given this constraint, the architects could not design the new armories along the lines of the Tompkins Market Armory, National Guards Hall, and other antebellum armories which had a drill shed on the upper floors.

Despite these constraints, the architects had a good deal of leeway. They did not have to worry about whether their designs might be too advanced for the existing technology. For by the late 1870s the armory posed no technological problems. To build a huge drill shed was far from simple. But it was much less difficult than it was before the engineers figured out how to use iron trusses to create huge unobstructed spaces for the country's new railroad stations. Nor did the architects need to worry about whether their designs might be incompatible with the prevailing national style. For no such style existed. The country lacks an architectural style "of its own," a well-known firm declared in 1871, and its architects can therefore "choose among all styles and all ages." The same point was made by Edward A. Freeman, a prolific English historian with a strong interest in architecture. "The architect of our age," he wrote in 1892, "finds himself in a position which no architect of any other age ever found himself. He has to choose his style." At other times in history the architect might have had two styles to choose between. "But the architect of the nineteenth century can choose among all the styles that have been in use since men began to build."[28]

How did the architects who designed the armories choose from what *American Architect and Building News* called "an unlimited supply of architectural forms?" The answer lies in the growing influence of functionalism. According to this theory, which should not be confused with twentieth-century functionalism, a building should be designed in a way that clearly expresses its purpose. Functionalism had been very much out of fashion in the United States in the early nineteenth century. At that time most architects believed that beauty in no way reflected the harmony of form and function. This view was well summed up by William Hosking, professor of architecture at King's College, London, who declared in the eighth edition of the *Encyclopedia Britannica:*

> The merit or demerit of a composition is not at all affected by the use to which the edifice is applied; neither would its front be more tolerable, nor its cupola less beautiful if St. Peter's in Rome were by the course of events to become a democratic forum instead of a Papal basilica; nor is the Monument of London a more or less elegant object, whether it be understood to record a triumph or a defeat, the burning of the city or its re-edification.

A good sign of the strength of this belief was the Greek Revival architecture of the early nineteenth century—which one scholar has called "the great unifying American style of its time." Convinced that this style was appropriate for all kinds of buildings whatever their purpose, the architects filled the land with Greek temples. As the mid-century architect Leopold Eidlitz wrote, "We had Greek temples for churches, school-houses, libraries, courts of justice, custom-houses, exchanges, post-offices, colleges, theaters, and beer-shops, all Greek temples alike."[29]

By the middle of the century, however, functionalism found a few advocates in America. They were inspired by the ideas of European architects and architectural theorists, in particular the Englishman A. W. N. Pugin, who held that "a building should look like the type of building it is," and the Frenchman E. E. Viollet-le-Duc, who believed that "a thing has style when it has the expression appropriate to its uses." They were also inspired by their antipathy to the Greek Revival style, which they thought had been applied to many building types for which it was inappropriate. The most forceful of the functionalists was Horatio Greenough. A sculptor and critic, Greenough objected to the practice "of forcing the functions of every sort of building into one general form" and ridiculed the phenomenon of "the Greek temple jammed between the brick shops of Wall Street or Cornhill, covered with lettered signs, and occupied by groups of money-changers and applewomen." He urged the architects to design buildings so that henceforth "the bank would have the physiognomy of a bank, the church would be recognized as such, nor would the billiard room and the chapel wear the same uniform of columns and pediments."[30] Although few architects were prepared to go that far, some were persuaded that a single style was no longer suitable for civic, ecclesiastical, and domestic structures alike.

After the Civil War, moreover, functionalism attracted even more supporters. Writing in 1876, A. F. Oakley, a New York architect who later moved to San Francisco, pointed out that "a building, or any part of one, should suggest its uses as far as possible." It would be absurd "to be unable to decide, even at the distance of half a mile, which of three buildings is a church, a prison, or a dwelling-house." Another architect held that at first sight a church should look like "a place of worship." Following the same logic, still another said that a Protestant church should not look like a Gothic cathedral, which has as little in common with modern Protestantism as "a Hindoo temple, a Turkish mosque, or a Roman basilica." The cruciform, vaulted roof, stained glass, and other features of the Gothic cathedral "are as foreign to Protestant worship as the barefooted friars, the sackcloth and penance, the processions, the incense, the relics, and the confessional." American architecture, wrote Barr Ferree, an architect who earned his living as an author, editor, and lecturer, should follow the lead of Roman architecture—which was based "not on some mistaken idea of the beautiful, but on the single thought that if the building answered its purpose it was satisfactory and accomplished all that was to be expected of it." Since buildings express different ideas and perform different functions, Ferree argued, the architect makes a great mistake when he tries to force them all into the same mold.[31]

By the late nineteenth century functionalism was the conventional wisdom of most architects. In their eyes—as a French writer whose remarks were published in *Public Opinion* in 1891 put it—the task of architecture was "to express[,] by its appearance, the use for which a building is destined."

A church that resembles a barracks, a hall that is like a church, a private house built on the model of a fort, are the absurdities that disgrace an architect. A single look at an edifice should show to what use it is to be put, and whether it is to be the dwelling place of gods or of men; whether the gods are amiable or terrible; whether the men are resting or working, amusing themselves or . . . defending themselves; whether they are citizens or monks, kings or peasants.

Among the many architects who espoused functionalism were John Wellborn Root, designer of Chicago's First Regiment Armory, and John R. Thomas, designer of New York's Eighth and Seventy-first regiment armories. "As far as material conditions permit it to be possible," Root declared in 1888, "a building designated for a particular purpose should express that purpose in every part." Thomas made the same point a few years later. Speaking about the prison, he remarked that "its purpose should dictate its expression. The requirements call for massive walls. The expression of such a wall must be severe. An 'elegant' prison, an 'ornate' prison is as inconsistent with artistic architecture as it is with common-sense."[32]

From a functionalist perspective, an armory was supposed to look like an armory—not like a school, court, library, hospital, marketplace, or city hall, let alone like a house or church. It was supposed to look like what it was, namely a building that housed a military organization and served as a schoolhouse, a clubhouse, and, in the event of siege, a fortress. An armory was also supposed to stand as a symbol of authority, of the overwhelming power of the state, of its determination to maintain order and, if need be, its readiness to use force. In their efforts to design an armory along these lines, the architects had a wide range of historical styles to choose from, one of which was the castellated. An offshoot of the Gothic Revival, which originated in England in the late eighteenth century, the castellated style arrived in America in the early nineteenth. It was used in a good many churches, penitentiaries, college buildings, and suburban homes in the antebellum years.[33] And though the style dwindled in popularity afterwards, it remained part of the standard repertoire of most architects.

To the architects of the armories, the castellated style was extremely appealing. Based on the medieval castle and fortress, it was one of the few styles that readily identified a building as the home of a military organization. It was a style that could serve as a model for a very imposing structure, at once formidable on the outside and elegant on the inside. A castellated armory could also serve as an attractive clubhouse for the citizen-soldiers because, unlike the coastal fort and frontier stockade, it fit into the landscape of late nineteenth-century urban America. Its rusticated walls and battlemented towers were very much in style at a time when the Romanesque and other medieval styles were in favor. According to a poll of the members of the American Institute of Architects that was taken in 1885, nine of the ten best buildings in the United States were inspired by medieval models and five were designed by the Romanesque master H. H. Richardson.[34] Boston's First Corps of Cadets Armory blended nicely into a landscape graced by Richardson's Trinity Church. Chicago's First Regiment Armory went well with the Marshall Field Wholesale Store, also a Richardson building. And Detroit's Light Guard Armory had more than a little in common with the city's Museum of Art, which bore more than a slight resemblance to the Cleveland Grays Armory.

The architects found the castellated style appealing for at least two other reasons. One was that most of them believed that it would help keep the "dangerous classes" under control. Underlying this belief was the assumption that architectural forms, through their emotional, intellectual, and historical associations, had a strong impact on ordinary people. As one writer put it in 1886:

> In our more elaborate public buildings—the school, church, library, court-house—if the building is architecturally adapted to its intended use, it will awaken ambition, reverence, love of knowledge, respect "for the powers that be," as the case may be. A gaol or prison, whose forbidding aspect, barred windows, and massive walls bespeak its intended use, will have a more wholesome influence on a community of young rascals than a dozen sermons preached from the text, "thou shalt not steal."[35]

Designed along the lines of a medieval castle or fortress, an armory would have a "wholesome influence" too. As most architects saw it, the thick walls and narrow windows, the towers, turrets, and bartizans, and the crenellations and machicolations had an aura of might and force. They inspired awe and fear and fostered respect and obedience.

The other reason was that most architects believed that the United States was going through a period very much like the Middle

Ages. Like other Americans who were appalled by the railroad strike of 1877, the Haymarket Affair, and the Homestead strike, they feared that the country was, in the words of E. L. Godkin, the editor of the *Nation,* "on the road to mediaeval anarchy." Wherever they looked, they saw the collapse of authority, the breakdown of the rule of law, and the growing tendency to resort to violence—all problems commonly associated with the Middle Ages. The analogy between modern America and medieval Europe was farfetched. But in light of the widespread enthusiasm for the Middle Ages in the late nineteenth century, it was understandable. An expression of longing for a more vivid and intense time, this enthusiasm was reflected in the popularity of medieval romances, the passion for medieval forms of punishment, and the proliferation of Protestant youth groups inspired by medieval chivalry.[36] To the enthusiasm for the Middle Ages, the architects were as susceptible as other Americans.

Convinced that the armories were castles and fortresses in looks only, formidable but not defensible structures, some observers held that the architects chose the castellated style for purely symbolic purposes. One well-known exponent of this position was Montgomery Schuyler, dean of American architectural critics in the late nineteenth and early twentieth centuries. Schuyler spelled out his views in 1906 in an essay on New York's new Seventy-first Regiment Armory, an armory designed by Clinton & Russell and built to replace the old Seventy-first Regiment Armory designed by John R. Thomas and destroyed by fire in 1902. The armory, he wrote, was designed in the castellated style, full of "the conventions of mediaeval warfare to which distance lends romantic enchantment, contrariwise to the actual and prosaic art of murder." But these conventions are anachronistic. "The parapets are crenellated, though nobody is expected to shoot between the crenelles. The cornices are machicolated, though nobody expects to pour hot lead from the machicoulis." These architectural devices call to mind the warfare "of the bow and arrow period, or at most of the ballista and catapult period," Schuyler added. They are no longer relevant to the "art of war." Despite their concessions to "past modes of warfare," the armories are designed in a way that acknowledges their impotence "to cope with actual modes of warfare."[37]

Schuyler, who was right about most things, was wrong about the armories (or, at any rate, about the armories built in the 1880s and 1890s). The guardsmen, the architects' clients, wanted genuine fortresses, not just symbolic ones. Afraid that the armories would some day be attacked by the mob, they insisted on defensible as well as formidable structures. One guardsman who took this position was Colonel Thomas F. Edmands, commander of Boston's First Corps of Cadets and leader of the Corps's campaign for a new armory. An armory, Edmands believed, should be a fort—a fort, he wrote in 1884, that should be "impregnable to mobs." When the Corps built its new armory a few years later, it adhered closely to Edmands' position. In its instructions to architect William G. Preston, the Board of Officers said that the armory should "be placed apart from other buildings on all sides." The walls should be "so pierced as to afford means of securing flanking fire to sweep the several facades [of the armory], as well as for direct fire from windows upon the several streets or passages around the building." The windows should be "so placed as to be inaccessible directly from street level" and, in some cases, should be protected by "stout sliding shutters of iron, rifle bullet-proof."[38]

The architects shared the guardsmen's fears. "Sooner or later," warned the editor of *American Architect and Building News* in 1894, "the great city armories will be the objects of attack, probably by mobs, bent on getting possession of the arms that they contain; and they ought to be designed expressly to resist such attacks." One architectural firm that did just that was Burnham & Root, designer of Chicago's formidable First Regiment Armory. As Burnham & Root saw it:

[The armory should] be the perfect embodiment of the spirit of regimental life in peace or in war; which practically means accommodations of every sort for occupation by the organization, for maintaining them in health, for sustaining life in case of siege, and, so far as construction is concerned, that perfect defence without should be possible against all weapons but heavy artillery. The result is a building which should be held against any mob, unless it rise to the dignity of a revolutionary force, and be possessed of heavy ordnance. The conditions are practically identical with those which caused the building of mediaeval castles, and the design[,] being thus caused by analogous conditions, is strongly suggestive of a fortress.

With massive walls, a huge sally-port, heavy iron grills, and other defensive features, "the design is to the last degree business-like in a military sense, and [the armory] cannot fail to impress a passer-by with the full extent of its purpose, and its ability to carry it out."[39]

These remarks make it clear why Schuyler missed the point. The armory was not supposed "to cope with actual modes of warfare." It was not supposed to stand up to heavy artillery and other weaponry which would be employed in a war between states. No building, no matter how well designed, could hold up against such force. Rather the armory was supposed to be able to hold off a mob of ordinary citizens, armed, if at all, with rocks, bricks, handguns, and possibly muskets and rifles. It was, after all, the fear of indigenous mobs, not foreign armies, that had spurred the building of the armories in the first place. Of the armory's ability to stand up to the mob, few observers had much doubt. Speaking of New York's Seventy-first Regiment Armory, *Harper's Weekly* pointed out that "while it has not the defensive strength of a fort to resist modern artillery, it is strong enough to withstand the attack of any ordinary unorganized street mob." *Harper's* made the same point about Brooklyn's Thirteenth Regiment Armory, stressing that while it was vulnerable to dynamite and heavy artillery, "a handful of men properly posted could defend it against a very large mob." Referring to Portland's First Regiment Armory, the *Oregonian* wrote that "troops stationed in [its] bastions could easily defend the four walls of the armory from successful attacks by a mob."[40]

A close look at the armories confirms the point that they were designed to withstand an ordinary mob. Consider the walls. Most armories had rusticated and tapered walls, the bases of which were usually made of huge blocks of stone or granite. Reminiscent of medieval castles and fortresses, these walls conveyed a sense of impregnability; they also symbolized the strength of the building and, by implication, of the troops quartered in them. But the walls not only seemed massive; they were massive. In many armories they were more than two feet thick (and, in some cases, reinforced by heavy buttresses). The walls were close to three feet thick in Brooklyn's Thirteenth Regiment Armory and nearly four feet thick in parts of Boston's First Corps of Cadets Armory (or more than half as thick as the walls of Chicago's sixteen-story Monadnock

Building, the last of the Windy City's tall masonry structures). Since most armories were only three or four stories high, the walls were more often than not at least twice as thick as necessary. And according to one description of New York's Twelfth Regiment Armory, the walls were designed to be extra thick for the express purpose of "enhancing the defensive nature of the building."[41]

As revealing as the walls were the entrances. For defensive purposes, most armories had very few entrances. The First Corps of Cadets Armory had three, one for the administration building and two for the drill shed. Chicago's First Regiment Armory had two, a main entrance, at ground level, and a basement entrance. Philadelphia's First Regiment Armory had only one—an arrangement, wrote one newspaper, that ensured that the armory would be "readily capable of defence by a corporal's guard." The guardsmen's preference for few entrances was clearly revealed in the early 1900s by General McCoskry Butt's response to the original plans for New York's Sixty-ninth Regiment Armory. Drawn by Horgan & Slattery, Tammany Hall's favorite architect and designer of the recently completed First Battery Armory, the plans called for four entrances. Butt, commander of the First Brigade and member of the Armory Board, objected that with so many entrances the armory would be "absolutely indefensible in case of a riot." Horgan responded that the armory would also be used for social activities and that without several exits it would be unsafe in the event of fire. Butt answered that "armories were not built for dance halls and crowds, but at a large expense to the City for protection, and that was the first and last consideration in my mind."[42] Horgan & Slattery revised the plan, but when the reformers ousted Tammany Hall, the board gave the job to another firm.

The entrances, as a rule, were strongly defended. The main entrance to Chicago's First Regiment Armory, a large sally-port forty feet wide and ten feet deep, was protected by a portcullis of chains and steel bars and by firing slots in the heavy reveals on both sides. The basement entrance, wrote *Inland Architect and News Record*, was "so amply provided with gates, bolts and locks that any attempt to force an entrance would be practically an impossibility." Solid oak doors, half a foot thick and shielded by a heavy bronze gate, guarded the main entrance to New York's Seventh Regiment Armory. Triple-plate iron doors, pierced by loopholes for rifle fire, defended the entrances to the First Corps of Cadets Armory. The entrances to New York's Twelfth Regiment Armory were protected not only by well-fortified doors but also by overhanging bays, "in the floor of which are apertures through which grenades or bombs can be dropped upon a mob assailing the doors." Indicative of the architects' fears of the mob were William G. Preston's remarks about the entrance to the First Corps of Cadets Armory. Speaking of the "massive gateway" that was designed to defend the entrance to the drill shed, he advised Colonel Edmands that the gates "should open outward and *not inward*." In that way "the pressure of a crowd against them [would] not tend to break them loose, but to close them tighter against the entrance."[43]

The windows had much in common with the entrances. Following the conventions of medieval military architecture, most armories had very few windows, about as many as a commercial warehouse and far fewer than other public buildings of similar size. More often than not, the windows were extremely narrow, in many cases nothing more than long slits which barely broke the plane of the massive walls. A powerful symbol of invulnerability, they were also a strong defensive feature. The windows of New York's Seventh Regiment Armory were protected by rolling steel shutters, the windows of the nearby Twelfth Regiment Armory by immense iron grills on the outside and bullet-proof steel shutters on the inside. In Brooklyn's Twenty-third Regiment Armory, the windows were covered by heavy wrought iron guards; in Chicago's First Regiment Armory, they were shielded by heavy basket gratings, iron grills, and steel plates. In an effort to make the First Corps of Cadets Armory defensible, and still allow air and light to enter, William G. Preston designed sliding iron shutters which were placed in recessed pockets and set into the walls on each side of the windows. Like other architects, Preston pierced the shutters with loopholes for rifle fire.[44]

The windows were designed not only to prevent the mob from trying to force its way into the armory, but also to keep the mob from laying siege to it in the first place. With this objective in mind, the architects placed the windows at strategic points from which the guardsmen could direct rifle fire along the approaching and surrounding streets. Speaking of New York's Seventh Regiment Armory, the *National Guardsman* observed that "at every angle there are loop-holes for riflemen, enfilading all approaches, and twenty sharpshooters would keep all enemies at a respectful distance." The same was true of Newark's First Regiment Armory, whose towers had narrow windows, reported the *Daily Advertiser,* "from which an enfilade fire could be poured upon an attacking party no matter from what point it might come." The architects also designed the windows in ways which enhanced the effectiveness of the guardsmen without increasing their risk. Speaking of Chicago's First Regiment Armory, Burnham & Root wrote that beneath each window was a narrow porthole for rifle fire, "which is splayed on the outer and inner jamb to give greater range." A similar device was used in Brooklyn's Twenty-third Regiment Armory. The jambs of its windows, remarked the architect Isaac G. Perry, "are beveled so that the soldiers can command the entire length of the building."[45]

Even more striking than the deep sally-ports and narrow windows were the huge towers and projecting turrets. Some stood in the center of the armories, others hugged the corners, and still others flanked the entrances. Although they came in all shapes, some square, some circular, and even some hexagonal and octagonal, they were all reminiscent of medieval castles and fortresses. For all their symbolic value, the towers and turrets served several defensive purposes. Most of them were pierced by loopholes and portholes, and not only for rifles but, in a few cases, for howitzers and Gatling guns as well. Moreover, they were placed at such points that, as Burnham & Root said of Chicago's First Regiment Armory, "an enfilading fire can be maintained along the outer face of all main walls." At the top of many of the towers and turrets were parapets, from which, said New York's Twelfth Regiment, sentries "may observe all that is going on in the streets below and at the same time command the roofs and houses in the immediate vicinity." And this they could do without exposing themselves, the New York *Times* pointed out. A few of these towers and turrets were designed to serve as signal towers. The uppermost turret of Brooklyn's Thirteenth Regiment Armory was one. Another was the imposing tower of Boston's First Corps of Cadets Armory, which commanded a clear view of the State House, from which orders could be sent to the troops by flag.[46]

Most of the towers and turrets were crowned by formidable battlements, which were pierced by narrow machicolations and topped by heavy crenellations. These battlements were evocative of the Middle Ages, when soldiers defended their castles and fortresses against attack by firing arrows, pouring melted lead, and throwing large rocks. In some armories the crenellations and machicolations were meant to be purely symbolic. In several others, however, they were supposed to be practical as well. Speaking of New York's Twelfth Regiment Armory, one architectural critic pointed out that above the round arch over the entrance to the drill shed was "a machicolated gallery with slits in front and at the sides and with real apertures in the machicolations, from which the entrance could be defended in the mediaeval manner with boiling oil and melted lead, or even in the modern manner with musketry fire." Much the same was true of the First Corps of Cadets Armory, whose central tower, flanking turrets, and impressive cornice were crenellated, machicolated, and, in spots, pierced by loopholes and portholes. "The building is so contrived that all parts of the walls may be swept by flanking fire and musketry, and by water, boiling, if need be," *American Architect and Building News* wrote. "This should render the building invulnerable to mob-attack at close quarters."[47]

Some architects went to extraordinary lengths to make the armories defensible. Besides designing a drawbridge (and a dry moat) for the First Corps of Cadets Armory, William G. Preston provided it with an independent water system, which had had no symbolic value whatever. It worked as follows. When rain fell on the armory's immense roof, water was carried into a cistern in the basement, from which it was pumped into a tank at the top of the central tower. Besides supplying soft water for the boilers and showers, the system served two valuable defensive purposes. One was that in the event of a serious uprising, it was impossible, wrote the Corps, "for a mob to jeopardize the building by cutting the city water mains." The other was that by means of steam pumps, "for which provision is made," the troops could shoot water under enormous pressure, an effective "element of defence," said the Corps, "against a troublesome crowd at close quarters."[48] Few architects went as far as Preston, but as late as 1908 Lieutenant-Colonel J. Hollis Wells, a member of Clinton & Russell, designer of New York's new Seventy-first Regiment Armory, recommended that if possible an armory should be equipped with its own heating, lighting, and power plants "so as to be absolutely independent of all outside connections which might be destroyed in time of riot and insurrection."

The armories were designed to be defensible as well as formidable because most Americans assumed that sooner or later the armories would be attacked by the mob. This assumption was a corollary of the fears of class warfare which led to the building of the armories in the first place. Among the many Americans who harbored these fears were the guardsmen and architects, the two groups that had the most to say about the design of the armories. The fears of class warfare were extremely strong among the guardsmen, most of whose leaders came from the upper-middle and upper classes and shared their views about American society. Pointing to the growth of Communism in the United States, the influx of refugees from the Paris Commune, the inflammatory statements of the radicals, and the arming and drilling of their followers, the *National Guardsman* warned in 1878 that "the gravity of the impending danger can hardly be overestimated." A decade and a half later a prominent guardsman declared, "We are in the midst of the greatest conflict ever known between capital and labor," and then, referring to the riots of 1877, predicted that we "shall witness like scenes again, so soon as hard times prevail once more in these United States."[49] The fears of class warfare were expressed not only in what the guardsmen said, but in what they did—in the exclusion of union members, the adoption of military discipline, and the staging of riot drills and mock battles.

To the guardsmen, it was clear who was responsible for the impending class warfare. At the top of the list were the socialists, communists, and anarchists, most of them foreigners, declared Major-General Arthur D. Ducat of the Illinois National Guard, who "have drifted to our shores, invited, perhaps, by the liberty so freely offered and which they are disposed to abuse." Also high on the list were the "dangerous classes," most of whose members were poor immigrants who congregated in big cities, many of them "idlers and miscreants," charged Lieutenant-Colonel David B. Williamson of the New York State National Guard, who were loath to engage in "honest toil," but "ever ready to disturb the peace." This position was summed up by Albert Ordway, a brigadier-general in the Washington, D.C., National Guard and an authority on riot control, who predicted in 1891 that rioting would be "more frequent and more formidable" in the future than in the past. Things have changed for the worse since 1877, he insisted:

> Since that time our country has been overrun by hundreds of thousands of the most criminal and ignorant classes of Europe, who can neither assimilate with our people nor appreciate or understand the meaning of our institutions or the force of our laws—men who know no law but force and can appreciate no punishment less than death. Following in the wake of this horde of immigrants have come the professional agitators, who may be called the pimps of the professional leaders, who have come to live on the tolls they levy on these ignorant people while they organize and train them for their own diabolical purposes.[50]

The guardsmen claimed that they were strictly neutral, that they were the servants not of capital or labor, but of law and order. They protected owners and workers alike. They were committed to preserving order, no matter who threatened it or what the issue. "Our duty," Ordway told the District of Columbia guardsmen, "is both simple and clear—to maintain and enforce law without consideration of the class of people that may be resisting it, and without regard to our personal views of the injustice of the law or the justice of the grievances that may arise under it." Despite the guardsmen's claims, there was no doubt that they sided with management. Most guardsmen subscribed to the notion of "freedom of contract," which held that every man had the right to sell his labor, or, if dissatisfied with the wages or terms of employment, not to, but that no man had a right to force another to withhold his labor. Most guardsmen also felt a deep animosity towards radicals and union leaders, an animosity that was revealed in Ordway's remark that if the troops had to deal with the mob, "let us hope that the anarchists will constitute the front ranks, if not the entire body of it. What otherwise might be a duty will then become a pleasure."[51]

The fears of class warfare were extremely strong among the architects as well. Members of a profession that worked mainly for the upper-middle and upper classes, they harbored a deep animosity towards labor unions—and especially towards the building trades, which they regarded as the bane of the construction industry. Their fears emerged in the wake of the railroad strike of 1877, which led many Americans to conclude that the country was polarized between capital and labor. "The antagonism of the two classes adds to the embarrassment of class-interests the perils of class-warfare," *American Architect and Building News* declared. In the labor unrest and radical agitation the journal saw reminders of "how slight[,] on the whole, the barriers are that defend modern society from anarchy." Speaking of the radicals, it conceded that their leaders "disclaim at present any intention of violence," but cautioned that "so much arming and drilling is not undertaken for nothing." The fears of class warfare reached a peak in the early 1890s, not long after the Buffalo switchmen's strike and other industrial disputes. Full of "wanton bloodshed and destruction," which triggered the mobilization of thousands of guardsmen, these disputes were among the worst in U.S. history, wrote *American Architect and Building News*. A few years later came the Brooklyn streetcar strike, a bitter struggle that *Architecture and Building* called "the first step in the inauguration of riot and internal warfare."[52]

To the architects, the heart of the problem was the thousands of uneducated workers, many of whom were recent immigrants. For them, said *American Architect and Building News* a week after the Haymarket Affair, happiness is "to give up thinking for themselves, to obey passively and implicitly, [and] to eat, drink and sleep at some rascal's signal." Accustomed to being led, craving "a yoke of some kind," they are "at the mercy of whoever is most willing to flatter them." Ever ready to exploit the workers were the socialists, who "make cat's paws of the trades-unions everywhere," wrote *American Architect*. Worse still were the "walking delegates," the union representatives who manipulate the workers for their own aggrandizement. Crafty and unscrupulous, they use not only flattery, but also intimidation and terror. Spokesmen for the architects left no doubt where they stood. Advocates of "freedom of contract" and defenders of property rights, they praised the Carnegie corporation for employing the Pinkertons at Homestead, lauded the Pullman company for evicting workers who fell behind in their rent, and hailed Attorney-General Richard Olney for his decision to break the railroad strike of 1894. They also favored using soldiers to prevent strikers from tying up the railroads, called for the death penalty for anyone who tried to stop nonstrikers from doing their job, and proposed that the striking Buffalo switchmen be executed—and their bodies "hung in chains . . . from telegraph poles" along the railroad lines.[53]

One reader took issue with *American Architect and Building News,* charging that it treated "the great mass of citizens as stupid, ignorant, blind followers of mercenary, selfish leaders." Far from daunted by the attack, the editors responded, "Let us say frankly that he is not very far from right." And in a statement at once condescending and indignant, they summed up the profession's position on the labor problem.

> We think the majority of our fellow-citizens to be trusting, inexperienced, and faithful to a degree which exposes them to all sorts of fraud and terrorism, and it is their very simplicity and unselfishness which should commend them to the protection of those better acquainted with the ways of the world. We are not at all ashamed to say that for examples of the most perfect purity, honesty, and faithfulness that the world can show, we must look . . . to the class of our fellow-creatures who live upon their daily wages. But in the continual movements and demonstrations which we have lately been compelled to witness we cannot help seeing myriads of happy little families plunged into destitution, the lives of thousands of women made miserable with privation and terror, and the characters of men degraded by tyranny and despair. If any good has ever come out of the colossal strikes, of which agitators are so fond, sufficient to pay for the misery which they cause, we have not yet heard of it, and until we do hear of some such great advantage, we shall be likely to hold to our unfavorable opinion of the practice of blowing up street-cars with dynamite, or fracturing the skulls of their drivers with bricks, or of placing hand-grenades under the seats of ferry-boats, or carpet-bags full of lighted bombs in the cabins of steamboats, or the other similar devices by which men with families dependent upon them are kept in the state of subjection, which appears to be necessary to the management of labor organizations.[54]

In the end, the United States was not racked by class warfare. Nor were the armories attacked by the mob. A good many riots took place after 1877, but in none of them did the rioters lay siege to the armories.[55] They did not attempt to break into the buildings, set them afire, toss dynamite into the basements, or hurl rocks through the windows. Nor did they try to kill the guardsmen. The guardsmen, for their part, did not have to fire bullets through the loopholes and portholes, sweep the surrounding streets with rifle fire, drop hand-grenades from the parapets, or pour boiling water through the machicolations. Nor did they have to fire howitzers and Gatling guns. It is possible that the armories were not attacked because they were defensible, just as it is possible that the United States was not racked by class warfare because the national guard was on hand. But it is more likely that if the mob had been bent on attacking the armories, it would not have been deterred by their massive walls, narrow windows, and battlemented towers.

To us, the fears that the armories would be attacked by the mob may seem farfetched. But they did not seem farfetched to the guardsmen and architects who had lived through the Draft Riots of 1863 and the railroad strike of 1877. In both uprisings the armories (and arsenals) were prime targets of the mob. Not long after the Draft Riots erupted in New York City, a mob armed with iron bars and staves marched on the state arsenal on West Thirty-fifth Street. Aware that the mob had broken into armories and made off with weapons in the past, the authorities posted guards around the arsenal. They also sent troops to protect the state's downtown and uptown arsenals and the city's Seventh, Eighth, and Ninth regiment armories. The mob spared these buildings, but it attacked an armory on East Twenty-first Street, a rifle factory whose upper floor was used as a drill hall by the militia. At first the rioters threw stones at the armory. Later they tried to storm the entrance and set the building afire. The New York City police fired at the rioters, killing a few and driving off others. But the mob regrouped, and the police, afraid that it would make another attempt to burn down the building, fled. The mob then broke into the armory, took the weapons, and set fire to the place. By the time the battle of East Twenty-first Street was over, the armory had been destroyed and a dozen people had been killed.[56]

New York was not the only city in which the mob attacked (or was rumored to attack) the armories. In Boston a mob formed shortly after the draft was started and, after a run-in with the police, assembled at the North End's Cooper Street Armory. Home of the city's Light Artillery, the armory was then occupied by the state's First Battery, commanded by Captain E. J. Jones, and two companies of federal troops. The mob threw bricks and stones at the building and then, using brickbats and other weapons, broke the windows and attempted to batter down the door. When it was clear that the police could not control the crowd, the troops fired a round of blank cartridges at the rioters and charged them with bayonets. The mob retreated, but, when the troops returned to the armory, it launched another attack, making a sizable hole in the door. At that point Captain Jones ordered his troops to fire a round of canister from a six-pound cannon that stood near the door, a round that killed and wounded several rioters and drove off the mob. The Draft Riots made a lasting impression on many Americans. When the editors of *American Architect and Building News* warned in 1894, fully thirty years later, that the armories would be attacked by the mob sooner or later, they reminded readers of the Draft Riots and, in particular, the attack on the Cooper Street Armory.[57]

The mob also attacked (or threatened to attack) the armories during the railroad strike. In Harrisburg, Pennsylvania, the rioters broke into a gun shop (though when the police arrived they gave back most of the stolen weapons). Afraid that the mob would go after the armories next, the state authorities ordered the troops to move their weapons to a state arsenal outside the city. Similar fears led the authorities to take the arms out of the Allegheny City Armory and to post guards at the Allentown and Norristown armories. A tense situation developed at the U.S. Allegheny Arsenal, when a mob from Pittsburgh demanded arms to do battle with the Philadelphia guardsmen who had been brought in to help restore order. Major A. F. Buffington, commanding officer of the arsenal, refused. Although the arsenal was full of weapons and, in Buffington's words, "utterly defenseless" in places, the mob eventually disbanded without attempting to force its way in. Elsewhere the mob was more determined. In Pittsburgh, Captain John J. McFarland of the Washington Infantry told a legistative committee, the rioters threatened to break into the armories and gun stores. It was not an idle threat. Shortly thereafter the mob ransacked a few gun shops and, before McFarland could do anything to stop it, broke into his armory, which was located over a city marketplace, and made off with the weapons.[58]

The mob behaved in much the same way in other cities in 1877.

It tried to force its way into the Fulton Market Armory in Troy, New York, only to be driven off by the local police. And according to Major-General Thomas S. Dakin, commanding officer of New York State's Second Division, the mob was planning to attack the Brooklyn armories and carry off the arms and ammunition stored there. Much more serious was the assault on Maryland's Sixth Regiment and its armory. Shortly after the rioting erupted in Baltimore, the Sixth was ordered to assemble in its armory, which was located on the second and third floors of a warehouse in a neighborhood whose residents were in sympathy with the strikers. As the troops made their way to the armory, they were harassed by a mob, which had surrounded the building. When the troops moved out, the mob renewed its attack, driving some of the guardsmen to seek refuge in a railroad station and forcing others to return to the armory. The mob then attacked the building, throwing stones and rocks at the door and smashing in the windows. The railroad strike left an indelible impression on many Americans. One of them was Senator Weldon B. Heyburn of Idaho, who recalled in 1912, thirty-five years later, that during the rioting in Pittsburgh he had led a militia company that was forced to retreat to one of the armories. For him and his men, he said, the armory "became the fortress."[59]

The guardsmen and architects had good reason to think that the pre-1877 armories could not withstand a serious attack by a strong mob. For one thing, most of the armories were located on the upper floors of public markets and other commercial buildings, the lower floors of which were sometimes filled with flammable materials. Often overlooked by adjacent buildings, they stood in an extremely "exposed and defenceless condition," wrote General E. L. Molineux. Pittsburgh's Washington Infantry Armory, which was broken into by the mob in 1877, "could not have been defended at all," Captain McFarland testified. It was so vulnerable that during the riots McFarland ordered his men to assemble at the mayor's office instead. For another thing, many of the mobs were more than a match for the guardsmen, who were the principal force that stood between the rioters and the armories. The assault on Maryland's Sixth Regiment was only one of several instances in which a mob overpowered the troops, forcing them to retreat and, in one case, capturing and disarming them. The Pittsburgh mob was so dangerous, Captain McFarland testified, that it was foolhardy for a guardsman to appear in the streets in uniform.[60] Certain that the old armories would be attacked by the mob and uncertain that they could withstand it, the guardsmen and architects came to the conclusion that the new armories had better be designed in a way that was defensible as well as formidable.

chapter five

The Demise of the Castellated Style

Early in 1899 a heavy snowfall severely damaged Philadelphia's First Troop Armory, the little castle that had been designed by Frank Furness twenty-five years earlier. A report showed that it would cost more to repair the old armory than to build a new one. The Troop therefore launched another campaign, which brought in roughly $100,000, enough to buy half an acre at Twenty-third and Ranstead streets and to erect a three-story administration building and behind it a one-story riding hall. To design the new armory the Troop hired Newman, Woodman & Harris, a firm that had recently been formed by three young Philadelphia architects. Newman, Woodman & Harris followed closely in Furness' footsteps, designing, if anything, an even more highly castellated building. Of the armory (figure 28), the Troop's historian wrote:

> The principal facade is patterned along the lines of a mediaeval castle. A heavily rusticated base of coursed ashlar extends to the sill of the closely barred ground floor windows. Above this the walls rise unbroken for two stories, pierced only by narrow openings. At the third floor level the surface of the wall is broken by projecting turrets at the corners, while heavy stone corbels support a wide projecting bay in the centre and the embattlemented cornices.[1]

Figure 28.   Philadelphia's First Troop Armory.

Finished in 1901, the First Troop's armory was a sign that even after the turn of the century some of America's new armories would be designed along the lines of medieval castles and fortresses.

And some of them were. To give a few examples, Horgan &

Slattery, Tammany Hall's favorite architect, designed a small castle for New York City's First Battery in 1900. Later in the decade a large castellated armory was put up in Rochester, the work of State Architect George L. Heins, an eminent church architect and designer, with Christopher LaFarge, of New York City's Cathedral of St. John the Divine. A similar but smaller armory was built in White Plains according to a plan by Franklin B. Ware, Heins' successor as State Architect and brother of James E. Ware, the architect of New York City's Twelfth Regiment Armory. During the early 1900s Hartwell, Richardson & Driver, a well-known Boston firm, designed an imposing, if not especially forbidding, castle in Cambridge, and George A. Moore produced a picturesque little fortress in nearby Somerville. A few years later Captain Ernest W. Langdon and George E. Turner designed a new armory in Minneapolis, a large building with a rusticated base, circular battlemented towers that flanked a recessed entrance, and square battlemented towers that guarded the corners. In Seattle Kerr & Rogers won the competition for the new state armory (figure 29) with a huge rectangular structure that featured an arched portal, iron portcullis, crenellated cornice, and strategically placed and fully battlemented bartizans.[2]

Of the many armories which were designed in the castellated style in the early twentieth century, two stood out—New York City's new Seventy-first Regiment Armory (figure 30) and Buffalo's Sixty-fifth Regiment Armory (figure 31). Built by the city's Armory Board at a cost of $750,000, the new Seventy-first Regiment Armory was located on the site of the old Seventy-first Regiment Armory, which had been erected in 1892 and destroyed by fire ten years later. The architect was Clinton & Russell, a prominent New York firm, one of whose principals had designed the Seventh Regiment Armory. The designer was Lieutenant-Colonel J. Hollis Wells, a member of the regiment and an authority on armories. For the Seventy-first Wells designed a large "baronial" building, much like the city's other armories, "only more elaborate." In it, Montgomery Schuyler observed, "one finds[,] in full force, all the conventions of mediaeval warfare"—the thick walls, narrow windows, rusticated base, recessed entrance, flanking towers, corner bastions, and crenellations and machicolations. Standing over the structure was a battlemented tower that rose 230 feet above the ground. Completed in 1905, the Seventy-first's new home was not only one of "the finest and most

Figure 29. Seattle Armory.

commodious" armories in the city, wrote the *Times*, but also one of the most imposing buildings in mid-Manhattan.[3]

Although it was less expensive than New York's Seventy-first Regiment Armory, Buffalo's Sixty-fifth Regiment Armory was even more impressive. Erected by the State Armory Commission, the Sixty-fifth's new home was located on the site of an old abandoned cemetery. It may have been, as *Harper's Weekly* claimed, "the finest [armory] in the world." Covering a full four acres, or roughly 40 percent of the site, it was certainly the largest. Perhaps even more important to the members of the Sixty-fifth, the armory was in no way inferior to the home of their rivals, Buffalo's imposing Seventy-fourth Regiment Armory, which had been erected at the very end of the nineteenth century. The Sixty-fifth Regiment Armory was designed by Major George J. Metzger, a local architect and member of the regiment, in consultation with State Architect Heins. Inspired by what *Harper's Weekly* called "the Norman style of the eleventh century," Metzger produced a huge castle, with battlemented towers

Figure 30. New York City's Seventy-first Regiment Armory.

flanking the entrance, a crenellated cornice, and battlemented turrets guarding the corners. "The style," wrote the Buffalo *Express,*
"is middle English, adapted from the days of baronial castles and
bloody fights, as befits the purpose of the structure."[4] Finished in
1909, the Sixty-fifth's new home was the capstone of the style of

Figure 31. Buffalo's Sixty-fifth Regiment Armory.

medieval military architecture that had first been applied to America's armories more than thirty years earlier.

Even before the Sixty-fifth Regiment Armory was finished, however, there were signs that this style might be on the wane. One such sign was New York's Sixty-ninth Regiment Armory (figure 32), which was built on Lexington Avenue between Twenty-fifth and Twenty-sixth streets. Although the Armory Board originally selected Horgan & Slattery, it later changed its mind and held a competition, which was won by Hunt & Hunt, a local firm whose two principals were the sons of Richard M. Hunt, one of the foremost architects of the nineteenth century. For the Sixty-ninth the Hunts designed an imposing, but by no means castellated structure. It had very little in common with New York's other armories, wrote Montgomery Schuyler shortly after it was completed in 1905: "It seems even to be a protest and token of revolt against them. It is noteworthy by the absence of the conventions of military architecture . . . Your regular thing, the architect seems to say, is not at all founded on fact. Your crenelles and machicoulis are anomalies in 'the present state of the art.' Go to. Let us build a modern armory on modern lines." Pointing to the rusticated stone work and massive corner towers, the architects noted that the armory had "a stern, unrelenting exterior." They also added that the bastions contained portholes for use "in case of riots." But Richard H. Hunt told a reporter that "he could give no specific name to the architectural design of his exterior. He said he had tried to make the building look like an armory in a city—not a mediaeval castle demanding for completeness a moat and country setting."[5]

Schuyler doubted that Hunt & Hunt's armory would have much of an impact on other architects—or, at any rate, enough of an impact to lead them to modify or abandon the castellated style. But in many cases they did so, though not necessarily because of the influence of the Sixty-ninth's new home. Two notable examples are New York's Second Battery Armory (figure 33) and its new Twenty-second Regiment Armory. The first armory built in the Bronx, the Second Battery Armory was designed by Charles C. Haight, a prominent New York architect well known for collegiate, ecclesiastical, and public buildings. Selected by the Armory Board in 1906, Haight produced what Schuyler called an "admirably consistent, restrained, and effective" building. Although it had a few signs of

Figure 32.· New York City's Sixty-ninth Regiment Armory.

Figure 33. New York City's Second Battery Armory.

"military Gothic," the building "might have taken the same forms if the designer had never heard of a Gothic castle." Somewhat more castellated was the new Twenty-second Regiment Armory, which was erected in Upper Manhattan, six miles north of the regiment's old home on the Upper West Side. After a sharp dispute, the Armory Board gave the job to Walker & Morris. Submitted in 1909, the plans provided for a huge rectangular structure, with a clerestory, peaked roof, and semicircular arched windows as well as several towers, at the entrance and in the corners, that were only slightly reminiscent of medieval military architecture.[6]

Another significant departure from the castellated style was Brooklyn's Troop (later Squadron) C Armory (figure 34), which was designed in 1903 by Pilcher & Tachau, a young firm whose principals had studied together at the Columbia School of Architecture. According to Professor A. D. F. Hamlin, an advisor to the Armory Board, their plan was chosen because of its simplicity and conve-

ARMORY FOR TROOP C   BROOKLYN. N.Y.

Figure 34. Brooklyn's Troop C Armory.

nience as well as the admirable lighting and ventilation of the stables. Designed in a style that *American Architect* called "L'Art Nouveau," the Troop C Armory consisted of an administration building that was dwarfed by a vaulted drill shed, by far its most striking feature. Pilcher & Tachau drew liberally from the Troop C plan in 1911, when they designed the Eighth Coastal Artillery Armory. Better known as the Kingsbridge Armory, it was the second armory erected in the Bronx and the largest ever built in the United States. Here too the huge vaulted drill shed dominated a much smaller administration building. Much the same was true of Baltimore's Fifth Regiment Armory, which was erected in 1903. Designed by Wyatt & Nolting, probably the leading architectural firm in the city, the armory was a forbidding building that combined slit windows and corner bastions with several noncastellated features. By far the most important element in the design was the great drill shed, which stood in the center of the armory and loomed over the smaller administration building that surrounded it.[7]

The castellated style was modified or even abandoned in other armories as well. The Trenton Armory, designed by Charles A. Gifford and completed in 1905, bore less of a resemblance to a fortress than Gifford's Jersey City and Paterson armories. Notwithstanding its crenellated parapet, Newark's Essex Troop Armory, designed by George A. Poole and finished a few years later, looked more like a high school than a castle. In Chester, Pennsylvania, Price & McLanahan produced an armory with a few features of medieval military architecture. But in Haverhill, Massachusetts, the home of the much-abused "Armory Builder Carey," Andrews, Jacques & Rantoul, a Boston firm, designed an armory with none of these features at all. The St. Paul Armory, which was completed in 1904, was much less castellated than the Minneapolis Armory erected a few years later. And the San Francisco Armory (figure 35), designed in 1912 by State Architect John W. Woollett and his brother William L. Woollett, both third-generation architects, was much less formidable than the Seattle Armory, its only peer on the West Coast.[8]

Nothing revealed the breakdown of the consensus in favor of the castellated style as well as the architectural competition for the State Arsenal and Armory in Hartford, Connecticut, which was held in 1907. The drive for a new armory got under way in 1901, after the

Figure 35. San Francisco Armory.

state legislature refused to appropriate funds to repair the old Elm Street Armory, a dilapidated structure whose drill shed was a former skating rink that had sometimes been used for revival meetings. For several years the drive was stalled by a dispute over the site in which the legislature rejected the recommendations of two special commissions, one appointed in 1901 and another in 1903. The issue was resolved in 1905, when the legislature gave in to pressure from Hartford citizens to include the armory in a proposed civic center and picked the so-called roundhouse site, roughly twelve acres next to Bushnell Park and near the state capitol. The legislature then appointed a third commission, which consisted of Governor Henry Roberts, Adjutant-General George M. Cole, and three prominent citizens, to supervise the erection of the new armory. And though the 1903 commission had hired Davis & Brooks, a Hartford firm, and George Metzger, the architect of Buffalo's Sixty-fifth Regiment Armory, to design the building, the new commission was required to hold an architectural competition.[9]

The commission opened the competition in November 1905. Along with the announcement went a list of instructions drawn up after consultation with Connecticut's First Regiment, the principal tenant of the new facility. The instructions called for a three-story building, with a large drill shed, company, officers', and storage rooms, headquarters for the state guard, a gymnasium, a pistol range, and other amenities of a fully equipped armory. The commission stressed that the building should not cost more than $400,000, but did not specify in which style it should be designed, nor insist, as the Providence Armory Commission did ten years earlier, that the armory "must be adapted for purposes of defence." Twenty-one architects entered the competition. A varied group, they included Hunt & Hunt, the New York firm that designed the Sixty-ninth Regiment Armory; McFarland, Colby & McFarland of Boston, the architect of the Gloucester Armory; Davis & Brooks of Hartford, the choice of the prior commission; and W. L. & J. W. Woollett, an Albany firm whose principals later designed the San Francisco Armory. The commission exhibited the drawings in the state capitol in February 1906 and soon after held a public hearing at which the architects were given a chance to promote their plans.[10]

Unlike prior competitions in New York and Providence, wherein all the entries followed the castellated style, the Hartford competition produced a good deal of diversity. Most of the architects designed one building, but some proposed a group of buildings. Although many favored a high arched roof over the drill shed, some called attention to it and others attempted to conceal it. Some followed the castellated style. Chief among them was William J. Dilthey of New York, who produced an extremely picturesque building (figure 36) that featured a rusticated base, two tall, square, fully battlemented towers, crenellations and machicolations galore, and a mansard roof over the wide sally-port. Others abandoned this style. Herbert W. Colby stressed that his plan aimed for simplicity, included no projections, and did not draw inspiration from "the feudal castle." Speaking of his own plan, W. L. Woollett stated bluntly that "the idea of a modern armory is not that it should be a fortress." Impressed by the diversity of the entries, the Hartford *Times* said, "If the commission desires to provide for the new armory the exterior of a mediaeval fortress it will still have to make a selection from among several designs, while it if prefers that the big structure shall resemble a modern railway station or even a grain elevator it has the material at hand."[11]

What the commission wanted, it turned out, was not a medieval fortress (though not a grain elevator either). With the help of John Merven Carrère, a principal in the well-known New York firm Carrère & Hastings, it first narrowed the field to five and then picked Benjamin Wistar Morris. A New York architect, Morris had close ties to Hartford; he had attended Trinity College, married the daughter of a local minister, and designed the Aetna Life Insurance Company Building there. Inspired far more by classical than medieval architecture, Morris proposed a highly symmetrical building (figure 37) with no towers, no turrets, no crenellations and machicolations, plenty of windows, and a high peaked roof covering the drill shed. Of the other finalists whose drawings have survived, Pell & Corbett of New York designed a castellated structure, though not nearly as castellated as William J. Dilthey's, which was not one of the final five. And Gay & Nash of Boston produced a similar, though less picturesque, building. After the competition, moreover, Morris revised his proposal. He added a few windows to the facade, put mansard roofs at the corners, and removed the few castellated features at the side entrance.[12] Morris, whose estimate exceeded the $400,000 limit by upwards of 50 percent, may have made some

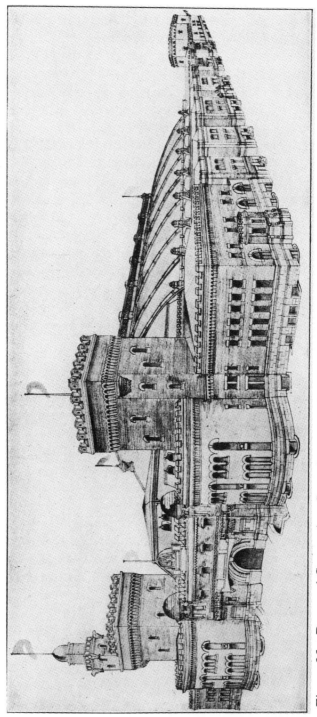

Figure 36. Proposed Connecticut State Arsenal and Armory.

The Demise of the Castellated Style

Figure 37. Connecticut State Arsenal and Armory.

of the changes to cut costs. But it is noteworthy that most of them tended to eliminate what little there was of medieval military architecture in the building.

By the time the Hartford Armory was erected, the castellated style was not only on the wane; it was also under attack. Writing in 1910 to the chairman of the District of Columbia Armory Commission, Tracy, Swartwout & Litchfield, a New York architectural firm, spoke with disdain of "the foolish battlemented and turreted type [of armory]." The firm—two of whose principals, Evarts Tracy and Egerton Swartwout, had once worked for McKim, Mead & White, the leading classical architects in the country—went on to say:

> Upon consideration it is hard to understand why the architecture of a mediaeval castle should have been thought to be appropriate for a modern armory. Surely, the confusion and irregularity of such a style is entirely out of keeping with modern military ideals. It was, perhaps, more appropriate at the period when the chief distinction of the militia was the splendor of its uniforms, but it has little that would seem to be indicative of the simple military spirit of the militia of to-day. A modern armory should recall the military regularity of the army, its simplicity and effectiveness, and it should have the dignity which would seem consonant with the army.

Many guardsmen now took much the same position. A good example is General Albert Mills, Chief of the U.S. Division of Militia Affairs. Testifying in 1916 on behalf of the District of Columbia National Guard's request for a new armory, he was asked if he thought it was "desirable to get away from the battlement[ed] type of armory to more of a public building [meaning classical] type." "I should think so," Mills replied.[13]

Criticism of the castellated style also came from Americans other than architects and guardsmen. Consider what happened in San Francisco in 1912, when the State Architect's office, which was headed by John Woollett, released the plans for the new state armory on Mission and Fourteenth streets. The plans—which called for a formidable structure, "an adaptation of the medieval Florentine style," wrote the San Francisco *Call*—generated a storm of protest. Local architects and nearby residents insisted that the building was "too severe, too austere, to serve the light and decorative purpose for which an armory is intended," a position inconceivable twenty years earlier. They thought that it looked "too much like a carbarn." Woollett, whose brother William had drawn the plans, supported the design. So did Adjutant-General E. A. Forbes, who approved of "the warlike front" of the building. But in the face of so much opposition, Woollett agreed to revise the plans. The revised version added numerous decorative features to "tone down the martial facade," to "eradicate the carbarnesque effect," and, observed the *Call* sarcastically, to "make the building appear a little more frolicsome, as befits the rigorous service of the national guard of California." The new, much less formidable design satisfied the critics and won prompt approval by the state armory commission.[14]

The repudiation of the castellated style had a profound impact on the design of armories in the 1910s and 1920s, a time when a good many were erected, if not as many as in the 1880s and 1890s and not nearly as many as guard leaders called for. With a few exceptions—the most conspicuous of which was the Kingsbridge Armory, which was authorized in 1909, designed a couple of years later, and finished in the mid-1910s—virtually none of them looked much like a medieval castle or fortress. (Interestingly, the one highly castellated armory that was designed in these years was not meant to be built. It was the work of a Columbia student, one of several architecture students who entered an academic competition sponsored by the Beaux-Arts Institute of Design in 1925, a competition for an armory for a regiment of field artillery. Following a style that was then out of fashion, he produced an imposing castle with slit windows, battlemented towers, and crenellations and machicolations. For his efforts, the jury awarded him a Second Medal. It also gave a Second Medal to two other students, each of whom designed a less castellated building, and a First Medal to another student, who followed very few of the conventions of medieval military architecture).[15]

Although virtually none of the armories built in the 1910s and 1920s looked like a medieval castle or fortress, some of them alluded to the castellated style. A good example is Boston's Armory for Mounted Troops, commonly known as the Commonwealth Avenue Armory (figure 38), to which the State Armory Commission gave its approval in 1913. The commission invited nineteen architects to

Figure 38. Boston's Commonwealth Avenue Armory.

The Demise of the Castellated Style

Figure 39. Chicago's Second Artillery Armory.

submit plans and, in a statement spelling out the specifications, made it clear that they would be well advised to design something other than a castellated building. The competition, which attracted fourteen entries, was won by James E. McLaughlin, a Boston architect who had previously designed a few small armories elsewhere in the state and whose proposal impressed the jury because of its simplicity, economy, and sensible handling of lighting and ventilation. Taking the commission at its word, McLaughlin did not produce a castellated structure. Neither the administration building nor the riding hall had crenellations or machicolations, turrets, bartizans, or slit windows. Perhaps as a concession to the castellated style, McLaughlin connected the armory to the street by a small bridge, thereby creating a metaphorical moat between them.[16]

In the same category as Boston's Commonwealth Avenue Armory was Chicago's Second Artillery (or 122nd Field Artillery) Armory (figure 39). The home of what was originally the Illinois First Cavalry, the armory was funded by the state and built in stages, first the administration building, finished in 1919, then the riding hall, completed in 1925. The architect was Holabird & Roche, a firm that had been founded in 1883 and gained national renown for the

Tacoma Building and other Chicago skyscrapers. The firm, whose principals, William Holabird and Martin Roche, were at the end of their long careers, had also designed many clubs, hotels, and public buildings in Chicago and other midwestern cities. For the Second Artillery, Holabird & Roche designed an unusual and by no means castellated structure. The base was broken by a row of unprotected windows, an arrangement unthinkable in a fortress. The towers were not battlemented; nor was the cornice crenellated. The architects employed a few medieval features, notably the large turrets that projected from the facade of the administration building. As the unit's commander wrote, they may have been inspired by St. Cecily Alby, a fortified church in Alby, France.[17] Without the turrets and the windows between them, the administration building would have borne more than a superficial resemblance to a grain elevator.

Also in this category were most of the armories designed by Lewis F. Pilcher. Pilcher had made his reputation as a principal of Pilcher & Tachau, the firm that had won the competition for Brooklyn's Troop C Armory, narrowly lost out to Walker & Morris in the competition for the new Twenty-second Regiment Armory, and more than made up for this loss when it was named architect of the huge Kingsbridge Armory. Based partly on his reputation for armories, he was appointed State Architect of New York in 1913, a post he held for ten years. As State Architect, Pilcher was responsible for the design of armories in Buffalo, Rochester, and several other cities. With the exception of the Troy Armory, none of these armories was as castellated as the Kingsbridge Armory, which was by no means a highly castellated structure. Buffalo's Troop I Armory had very few medieval features, and Albany's Troop B Armory had virtually none. As a group, Professor A. D. F. Hamlin observed, Pilcher's later armories were "simple and practical," without any "affectation of medievalism." Hamlin conceded that some might consider the fifteenth-century French towers that flanked the entrances to the Troy and Malone armories "an archaeological affectation." To such criticism, he responded, "The medieval note, if present, is certainly not paraded."[18]

The other armories built in the 1910s and 1920s rejected (or, in some cases, ignored) the castellated style. A notable example is Pittsburgh's Eighteenth Regiment Armory (commonly known as the Logan Armory, in honor of its commander, Colonel Albert J. Logan),

Figure 40. Pittsburgh's Eighteenth Regiment Armory.

the administration building of which (figure 40) was erected in 1911. When the regiment had tried to build an armory on its own in the 1890s, it had in mind a castle as imposing as any in the United States (figure 41). But it failed. By the time Allegheny County supplied the site and the Pennsylvania Armory Board the money, it had a completely different vision. For Colonel Logan and his men, wrote the Pittsburgh *Press,* "the paramount idea was to deviate from the medieval fortress-like style, which obtains in most of the armories throughout the country." The Logan Armory, by this measure, was a great success. Designed by the W. G. Wilkins Company, a local firm that had already worked on several small armories in Pennsylvania, it was a stately classical building, whose most prominent feature was a classical portico with four large three-story columns. In what the Pittsburgh *Dispatch* called a notable departure from the castellated style, the building had no military, let alone medieval military, features. It looked more like "a school than a fortress."[19] Located in the fashionable Schenley Farms district, near the University of Pittsburgh and Carnegie Institute, it could have served nicely as an office building for either of these institutions.

Figure 41. Proposed Armory for Pittsburgh's Eighteenth Regiment.

A more striking example was the Washington, D.C., Armory (figure 42), an armory that was designed but, as a result of a dispute in Congress over funding, not built. The armory posed an unusual problem for its architect, Tracy, Swartwout & Litchfield, the New York firm selected by the District of Columbia Armory Commission. The proposed site of the armory was on the Mall (first between Sixth and Seventh streets and later between Twelfth and Fourteenth); and only classical buildings were allowed there. Hence the architects had to come up with something other than a castellated structure. As E. D. Litchfield said in 1912, two years after the plan was submitted, they had "to design a building of classic type which should at the same time be recognized as an armory." They resolved the problem by creating a monumental Greek temple that resembled McKim, Mead & White's Pennsylvania Railroad Station in New York and featured a very long colonnade of Doric columns that surrounded the building on all four sides. As Litchfield explained: "We felt that without question there was something quite characteristic of the military organization in the simple, powerful, Doric order, and that in its repetition in a long colonnade it repre-

Figure 42. Proposed Washington, D.C., Armory.

sented the regularity, strength, and dignity of the military arm of the Government as no other type of architecture could."[20]

Designed along much the same lines as the Washington Armory was Pittsburgh's Hunt Armory (figure 43). Located in the East Liberty district, it was the home of Pennsylvania's 107th Field Artillery and one of the largest armories in the state. The work of the W. G. Wilkins Company, which also designed the Logan Armory, the Hunt Armory featured a seemingly endless row of columns that ran along the facade. In the same style was Philadelphia's imposing Thirty-second Street Armory. An armory that the First Regiment would move into after World War II, it looked more like a railroad station than anything else. Much less relentlessly classical was Providence's Armory of Mounted Commands, which was located on North Main Street. Athough the riding rink was the work of William R. Walker & Son—the administration building, which was erected later, was the work of William G. Richards—it was a far cry from the Cranston Street and other castellated armories designed by the firm in the late nineteenth century.[21] Like the Logan and Washington armories, these buildings were all representative of classical revival architecture, a style that swept the country in the 1900s, but began to wane in the 1920s.

The waning of classicism did not lead to the revival of the castellated style. To the contrary, the next wave of armory building, which started in the mid-1930s, revealed that this style had become, if anything, even less fashionable. The new armories were an outgrowth not of fears of class warfare, but of the Roosevelt administration's efforts to cope with the Great Depression by providing relief for the unemployed and stimulating the private sector. Shortly after the administration persuaded Congress to appropriate $4.8 billion for emergency relief, spokesmen for the national guard asked that $80 million be earmarked for the construction of new armories, one thousand of which they said were sorely needed. Although the request was turned down, the guardsmen later prevailed upon the Works Progress Administration and Public Works Administration to include armories among the types of public buildings eligible for federal grants. With the help of the WPA and PWA, the states built hundreds of new armories (and enlarged and improved hundreds more). Although a few were large regimental armories that cost more than $1 million, most were small one company armories that

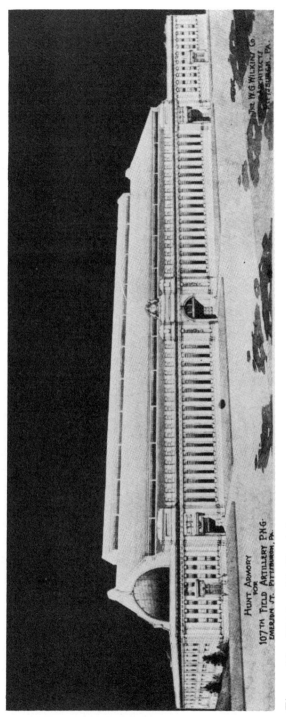

Figure 43. Pittsburgh's Hunt Armory.

cost from $20,000 to $40,000. Although many were erected in the East and Midwest, even more were built in the South and Southwest, the two regions that had lagged behind in the great wave of armory building several decades earlier.[22]

With a host of more pressing problems to deal with, neither the WPA nor the PWA was inclined to get deeply involved in the design of the armories, much less to dictate the style in which they should be built. Speaking of the "architectural treatment," the WPA's Acting Chief Engineer advised his staff that it "is purely a matter of available materials, taste and community influence and is therefore something for local determination." In the case of the WPA and PWA armories, the result of "local determination" was a good deal of diversity. Most of the small one-company armories, many of which, under WPA rules, had to cost $25,000 or less, were nondescript structures—highly utilitarian and of little architectural interest. Of the larger, more imposing armories, a few were designed in the classical style. A good example was the combined armory-office building erected, with the PWA's help, in Springfield, Illinois. Most of the others were characterized by simplicity of structure and lack of ornamentation, which reflected, among other things, the administration's determination to hold down costs and the architects' increasing use of concrete. Aside from an occasional tower, very few of the New Deal armories employed military features; and with the exception of the Durham, North Carolina, Armory, a battlemented building of sorts that was partly funded by the WPA, none of them followed the castellated style.[23] Like most of the armories built in the 1910s and 1920s, they were far less elegant inside than the Seventh Regiment and other armories built in the late nineteenth century.

Of the few noteworthy New Deal armories, most were designed in Art Deco style, a style that first appeared in Western Europe in the 1920s and quickly found its way to the United States. It was one of the early distinctly modern styles. Unlike the castellated and classical revival styles—indeed, unlike most of the architectural styles of the nineteenth century—Art Deco drew its inspiration less from historical traditions than from geometric patterns. The first attempt to apply Art Deco to armories came in the Beaux-Arts Institute of Design Competition of 1925—the same year as the Paris Exposition Internationale des Arts Decoratifs et Industriels Mod-

Figure 44. Minneapolis Armory.

ernes, which gave the style its name. A few years later Perkins, Chatten & Hammond designed Chicago's large 124th Field Artillery Armory, probably the first important Art Deco armory, and smaller but similar armories in Decatur and Cairo, Illinois. Closely modeled on the Decatur and Cairo armories were the Jersey City and Minneapolis armories (figure 44), both of which were built with the help of the PWA and looked much like municipal auditoriums.[24] A far cry from New York's Eighth Regiment Armory and Brooklyn's Thirteenth Regiment Armory (and, for that matter, from the Logan Armory and the proposed Washington, D.C., Armory), the Art Deco armories provided additional evidence that the architects had completely (and, it turned out, permanently) abandoned the castellated style.

The architects abandoned the castellated style in part because medieval architecture fell out of favor in the late nineteenth and early twentieth centuries. For decades, critics pointed out, American architects had borrowed all too freely from what Herbert Croly, editor of *Architectural Record* in the early 1900s, called "practically the whole miscellaneous mass of historical and architectural forms [of Western Europe]," much of which had emerged in the Middle

Ages. When an educated, trained, and highly gifted architect like H. H. Richardson adopted these forms, the results were often splendid. But as Henry Van Brunt, a prominent architect and architectural critic, remarked, many architects were "uneducated and untrained" and anything but gifted. Prone to excessive individualism, they were unaware that good architecture cannot be based on "undisciplined invention [and] illiterate originality." The result of their labors was a civic architecture that made the United States "the laughing-stock" of the rest of the world, wrote John Stewardson, a Philadelphia architect who had studied at Harvard and the Ecole des Beaux-Arts. It was time to call a halt to this unrestrained eclecticism, to bring order out of "the chaos of styles," declared Professor Hamlin, an architectural critic and historian who had graduated from MIT, attended the Ecole des Beaux-Arts, and later headed the Columbia School of Architecture.[25]

Medieval architecture, critics contended, was out of place in modern America. "We cannot work in the Gothic, or in any other mediaeval style, unless we return to the Gothic or mediaeval life," wrote Thomas Hastings, who had studied at Columbia and the Ecole des Beaux-Arts, worked for McKim, Mead & White, and then formed Carrère & Hastings, one of New York's most successful architectural firms. No matter how impressive, the thick walls, narrow windows, and great battlements of the Middle Ages cannot serve as models for modern America because they grew out of "a disordered social status not like our own," a time "when every man's house was indeed his castle, his fortress and stronghold." "The modern Romanesque, of which we see so much, must prove a failure, because we are not living the Romanesque life of the ninth or eleventh century . . . The revival of the Byzantine, Romanesque, Gothic, and all other mediaeval styles can be at best but an unnatural adaptation to modern thinking and living."[26] Similar sentiments were expressed by other architects, including John Wellborn Root, who argued that "no man has the right to borrow from another age an architectural idea evolved from the life of that age, unless it fits our life as normally and fully as it fitted the other." For Hastings and Root, it was incumbent upon the nation's architects to draw their inspiration from an historical period that had more in common with modern America than the Middle Ages did.

Critics of medieval architecture believed that if any period had "an intimate intellectual kinship" with modern America, if any period shared its humanism, rationalism, and faith in the future, it was the Renaissance. "This does not mean that the Middle Ages are to be entirely ignored," wrote Croly, "but it does mean that we are bound by much closer spiritual ties to the Renaissance than we are to the Age of Feudalism and Militant Catholicism." Once American architects acknowledged these ties, they would turn—as Renaissance architects did—to the classical style, the architecture of ancient Greece and Rome. The classical style would help American architects stay in touch with the source of their moral, political, and intellectual ideals. And as it required "long and fine training" to design along classical lines, a point made by Daniel Burnham, this style would force the architects to acquire a good education. Such a step would curb their extreme individualism and, in Van Brunt's words, serve as "a timely corrective to the national tendency to experiments in design." Classicism was the wave of the future, Hastings insisted. "I believe," he wrote in 1894, a year after this style was popularized by the World's Columbian Exposition, "that we shall one day rejoice in the dawn of a modern Renaissance, which, as has always been the case, will be guided by the fundamental principles of the classic."[27]

The origin of the World's Columbian Exposition went back to the mid-1880s, when a movement got under way to commemorate the four hundredth anniversary of the discovery of America. The movement gathered momentum, and in 1890 Congress authorized a world's fair and, after a lively competition, chose Chicago as its home. In charge of the fair was a corporation of Chicago's business leaders. For advice on the site, the corporation retained Frederick Law Olmsted, the country's foremost landscape architect. On his recommendation it decided to hold the fair in Jackson Park, a large undeveloped marsh on the south shore of Lake Michigan. To oversee the design, the corporation hired Daniel Burnham (and his partner John W. Root, who died not long after). Burnham invited several of the country's leading architects, including Richard M. Hunt, George B. Post, and McKim, Mead & White, to serve as consultants and share the work. The architects, all of whom, said one, opposed "the use of medieval or any other form of romantic, archaeological, or picturesque art," agreed that the buildings should be designed in classical style. With a few exceptions, they were.

Together they made up what soon became known as the "White City," a classical city of monumental buildings, sculpture, and open spaces. As well as an aesthetic theory, the White City embodied a concept of order, a concept based not so much on "the strong arm of authority" as on the moral force of rationality, coordination, beauty, and harmony.[28]

The Exposition, which was opened to the public in May 1893, had a profound impact on American architecture. It unleashed an enthusiasm for classicism that spread over the United States for a generation. Burnham had predicted as much. After telling the young Frank Lloyd Wright, to whom he had offered a job in his firm, that "the American people have seen the 'Classics' on a grand scale for the first time," Burnham went on to say, "I can see all America constructed along the lines of the Fair, in noble, dignified, Classic style." But not even Burnham expected the fair to evoke so strong and so favorable a response. Over twenty-one million people visited the White City, nearly all of whom were delighted by it. Novelist William Dean Howells praised it. So did Henry Demarest Lloyd, a muckraking reporter. Even Montgomery Schuyler, who had mixed feelings, called the fair an "architectural triumph," "the most admired group of buildings ever erected in this country." The response to the fair was nicely summed up by Elihu Root, a well-known lawyer and former secretary of war. Speaking at a dinner of the American Institute of Architects in 1905, he said, "It was reserved for the great city of the Middle West, by the example of that fair White City by the Lake, which remains with us as a dream of Ionian seas, to lead our people out of the wilderness of the commonplace to new ideas of architectural beauty and nobility." "The lesson of the Chicago Exposition has gone into every city and town and hamlet of America," he added.[29]

The Exposition had a profound impact on architectural theory too. It dealt a heavy blow to functionalism, which had emerged as the conventional wisdom a decade or two earlier. As Fiske Kimball, an architect and architectural historian later wrote, "The issue, whether function should determine form from within or whether an ideal form might be imposed from without, had been decided for a generation by a sweeping victory for the formal ideal." By the end of the century, functionalism was on the defensive. One of the strongest attacks was made by Thomas Hastings, who held that the functionalist ethos was an architectural aberration. Writing a year after the fair, he declared: "The irrational idiosyncrasy of modern times is the assumption that each kind of problem demands a particular style of architecture. Through prejudice this assumption has become so fixed that it is common to assume that if building a church, we must make it Gothic; if a theatre, we must make it Renaissance; if a bath, we must make it Moorish; and if a warehouse, we must make it Romanesque." "The time *must* come, and, I believe, in the near future," Hastings argued, "when architects of necessity will be educated in one style, and that the style of their own time," by which he meant the classical style.[30]

Formed by the growing enthusiasm for classicism and the waning influence of functionalism, what one observer called an "almost tidal wave" of classical architecture changed the landscape of urban America in the 1890s and 1900s. With McKim, Mead & White in the forefront, the architects drew their inspiration from columns, pediments, and domes rather than from towers, turrets, and steeples. They used these forms to design a wide range of building types, including clubs, hospitals, hotels, museums, and libraries, perhaps the most impressive of which was Carrère & Hastings's New York Public Library. The classical style was applied to both small banks and large railroad stations, the epitome of which was McKim, Mead & White's Pennsylvania Station in New York, whose main hall was modeled on the Roman baths at Caracalla. It was also applied to state capitols, for which it was highly appropriate, and to skyscrapers, for which it was less so. Much like the Greek Revival, the classical revival was a style that was popular everywhere in the country. Indicative of its popularity were the results of a poll conducted in 1913 by the American Federation of Arts, which asked its members to name the best works of architecture in the United States. At the top of the list were the Boston Public Library, the Capitol in Washington, D.C., the New York Public Library, New York's Pennsylvania Railroad Station, and Boston's Trinity Church, all but the last of which were designed along classical lines.[31]

The classical revival was not, however, as pervasive as the Greek Revival. It did not leave much of an imprint on domestic architecture. For every classical mansion, town house, and apartment building, the architects designed thousands of single-family homes which were inspired less by admiration for ancient Greece and Rome than by nostalgia for seventeenth- and eighteenth-century America. This vision gave rise to colonial and Georgian homes in New England, pseudo plantations in the South, and so-called Spanish and Moorish homes in Florida and California. Nor did the classical revival leave much of an imprint on church architecture. Most architects believed that the appropriate style for churches was what was known as ecclesiastical Gothic. The high priest of this style was Ralph Adams Cram, a principal of Cram, Goodhue & Ferguson, the firm that converted New York's St. John the Divine from a Romanesque church into a Gothic cathedral. But even McKim, Mead & White, a firm second to none in its devotion to classicism, designed some Gothic churches. The classical style had more of an impact on colleges and universities than on churches. Yet with a few exceptions, the most important of which were Columbia, Berkeley, and MIT, most of these institutions preferred what was known as collegiate Gothic. This style was adopted not only on Ivy League campuses like Yale and Princeton, but also at less prestigious places like the College of the City of New York.[32]

Even Cram, whose architecture was a protest against "the new paganism," his phrase for the secularization and professionalization of American life, conceded that the Gothic style was not in harmony with most American institutions. It was appropriate for high churches and elite colleges, both of which were "blazing anachronisms," but not for banks, office buildings, railroad stations, and some Protestant churches, one of which he designed as a Georgian meeting house. Cram's attitude reflected the consensus about American architecture that emerged during the heyday of the classical revival, a consensus much like the one that had prevailed just before the Civil War. At the heart of this consensus was the view that there were three kinds of architecture—domestic, religious and educational, and civic—and that each required its own style. As Professor Hamlin pointed out, the appropriate style for domestic architecture was colonial (or, in the case of apartment houses, Parisian). For religious and educational architecture, it was Gothic, Tudor, and Elizabethan. And for civic architecture, it was classical. "For great and monumental public edifices, such as State capitols, libraries, and museums," Hamlin wrote in 1905, "the dignity and stateliness, the ample scale, and the very formality of the various versions of classical architecture are now pretty generally accepted as the most appropriate form of design."[33]

As more and more architects were carried away by the wave of classicism, the style came under sharp attack. In a letter to the editor of *Architectural Record,* F. W. Fitzpatrick complained in 1908 that classicism had been overworked.

> Beautiful as classic Architecture is when well done and eminently satisfying as it should be, it has been, to use the vernacular, "run into the ground." Verily I dread looking at plans of any proposed building for I know exactly what the exterior is going to be. It will be one of three themes, one of the three variations upon which all else today is founded or is simply a variant. You get the same thing in a church or a city hall, in a forty-story office building, or a stable or a dog-kennel; columns that support nothing, entablatures as meaningless and where windows ought to be, and a dome cocked on end and there you have it.

Montgomery Schuyler made the same point a decade earlier. After saying that thanks to the Chicago Exposition and the Ecole des Beaux-Arts the classical revival was now well established, he wrote, not entirely facetiously, that it was "no longer necessary for an architect to design anything." Then tongue-in-cheek, he announced the formation of the "Classic Design and Detail Company," which would provide architects with a complete set of drawings in any classical style. All the architect had to do was to specify whether he preferred the Parthenon, the Erechtheum, or the temple of Jupiter Stator. Free from "the drudgery of the drawing board," the architects could spend their time looking for commissions.[34]

A much sharper attack came from Louis Sullivan, the remarkable Chicago architect, to whom classicism was not so much overworked as unsuitable. Just as Hastings objected to Gothic architecture on the grounds that modern America was not medieval Europe, so Sullivan objected to classical architecture on the grounds that it was not imperial Rome either. "Roman," he wrote at the turn of the century, "does not mean American, never did mean American, never can mean American." An architect who looks to Roman civilization for answers to American problems is "not a scholar, nor an architect, but a public nuisance." Along with Fitzpatrick and Schuyler, however, Sullivan was very much in a minority. The great majority of American architects agreed with John Stewardson, who forecast in 1896 that classicism would "raise the standard of our civic architecture in the beginning of the twentieth century infinitely above what we are used to to-day." And when Elihu Root said at the American Institute of Architects dinner in 1905 that "the reign of Mullet is over"—referring to Albert G. Mullet, Supervising Architect of the United States after the Civil War and designer of the highly ornate State, Army and Navy Building in Washington, D.C.—few architects mourned its passing.[35]

The rise of classicism spelled the demise of the castellated style. To a profession enamored of the simplicity, regularity, and restraint of classical architecture, medieval architecture was bad enough. The castellated style, a grandiose form of medieval architecture, was even worse. To most architects it embodied the lack of discipline and passion for experimentation that marred the age of Mullet. Now that functionalism was on the wane, the architects saw no reason why the armory should retain a distinctive style. An armory, after all, was just another public building. If classicism was the appropriate style for museums, libraries, and state capitols, it should be the appropriate style for armories. Yet another drawback of the castellated style was the prevailing view of the architectural profession that a prominent and monumental building like an armory should fit well into the urban landscape. And a medieval armory would have fit into the classical landscape of McKim, Mead & White as badly as a classical armory would have fit into the medieval landscape of H. H. Richardson.

The architects also abandoned the castellated style in part because the function of the armory changed in the first third of the twentieth century. It was still the home of the national guard. And it was still a schoolhouse. But after the guard was federalized in 1903 and turned into a more strictly military organization, about which more later, the armory was less of a clubhouse—which is one of the main reasons the armories built after 1910 were much less elegant inside than the ones built before. Even more important, the armory was no longer a fortress. Or, in any case, that was the view of most Americans, among them the editors of *American Architect*. Writing in 1911 about Tracy, Swartwout & Litchfield's design for the proposed Washington, D.C., Armory, they pointed out that it marked a striking departure from the castellated style. And about this style, the editors had serious reservations. In an illuminating passage, they explained why.

> It is not difficult to trace an analogy between the mediaeval castle and a fortress erected for defensive purposes, but this is hardly the purpose, or at least the principal purpose, of the modern armory. It is rather a building designed to accommodate the militia and afford a vast area for drills, quarters for officers, various rooms and accommodations for the transaction of the affairs of the company, and such other uses as may present themselves, not ordinarily including service as a fort.

Whether the profession should "abandon altogether the mediaeval style for armories is a question which [Tracy, Swartwout & Litchfield's] commendable type of building brings very much to the fore."[36]

The belief that the armory was no longer a fortress was also held by many guardsmen, one of whom was Colonel William E. Harvey of Washington, D.C. Testifying before the Senate Committee on Public Buildings and Grounds in 1912 about the proposed Washington, D.C., Armory, he took exception to the view that an armory should be a fortress. "That is, I believe, an exploded idea of armories. The modern idea of military operations is to take the offensive, and not to stand on the defensive if you can help it." "But here we are talking about defending the Nation's Capital," Senator Weldon B. Heyburn told him. "We are not going to protect anything by shutting ourselves up in an armory," Harvey replied. Heyburn reminded him that an uprising could take place in the District. And Harvey admitted, "That is very true; but I would not make the armory a fortress." It would suffice to make sure that the building was secure and the arms locked up. Heyburn said that during the railroad strike he had led a military company in Pittsburgh that had been forced to retreat to an armory. Harvey, who was not sure just when the strike had occurred, replied, "That is one of the historic things—I am glad to know that you took part in it."[37] But despite Heyburn's experience, he stuck to his position that an armory should not be a fortress.

At the heart of the belief that the armory was no longer a fortress was the assumption that the country was no longer on the brink of class warfare, an assumption that most Americans came to hold after

1900. If it was unlikely that the nation would be racked by insurrection or civil war, it was unlikely that the armories would be attacked by the mob. If the armories were unlikely to be attacked, said *American Architect,* they did not have to be designed like fortresses. This position was reinforced by the growing awareness that in none of the riots that took place after 1877 had the mob attacked an armory. Forgetting the Draft Riots of 1863, *Architectural Record* even suggested in 1911 that a look at New York's history would not disclose "a single attack upon an armory."[38] Moreover, it seemed even less likely that the armories would be attacked in the future. Well organized, trained, and armed, the militia was now more than a match for the mob. The rough parity between them was over. It was hard to imagine that the troops would ever again be forced to seek refuge in the armories. Henceforth the issue was not whether order would be restored, but at what cost.

The function of the armory changed in yet another way after 1900. It became a civilian as well as a military facility, a coliseum and community center as well as the home of the national guard. Before 1900 the armories had been used occasionally by nonmilitary organizations for nonmilitary purposes. To give a couple of examples, the Cleveland Grays Armory was the site of Cleveland's first auto show in 1893 and Cleveland Orchestra concerts two years later. The nearby Central Armory hosted a celebration of Cleveland's centennial in 1896, a women's six-day bicycle race in 1897, and Democratic presidential candidate William Jennings Bryan, who spoke to a crowd of over ten thousand in 1900. The armories were good sites for public gatherings because their drill sheds were among the largest unobstructed spaces in the cities. And as the soldiers seldom drilled more than once a week, the sheds were unoccupied much of the time. Before 1900, however, the armories were primarily a military facility. Thus when New York City allowed too many civilian groups to use its armories for nonmilitary purposes in the late 1880s, the adjutant-general issued an order that the armories were to be used only by the national guard (and some veterans' organizations) and for other purely military purposes which were approved by his office.[39]

After 1900 the military authorities found it much harder to say no to the many commercial, social, cultural, fraternal, and political groups which wanted to rent the armories for nonmilitary functions. In some cases the authorities were hesitant to risk offending these groups, some of which had supported the national guard in the past and, it was hoped, would support it in the future. In other cases they were reluctant to give up the income. The rentals provided a source of sorely needed revenue for units like the Detroit Light Guard, whose armory served as "Detroit's Convention Hall, Masonic Temple auditorium, Olympia and Orchestra Hall—all rolled into one," wrote one reporter. In still other cases the military authorities were hard pressed to say no because they had already gone on record in favor of the nonmilitary use of the armories. In their campaign for a new armory, Seattle guardsmen stressed the point that the building would provide the spacious auditorium needed to attract conventions to the city. Pittsburgh guardsmen emphasized that the drill shed of the Logan Armory would be the city's largest "auditorium and gathering place." And backers of the proposed Washington, D.C., Armory pointed out that it would provide a good site for the inaugural ball.[40]

As the authorities gave in to one group after another, the armory was soon turned into a coliseum—a combined convention hall, sports arena, and cultural center. Baltimore's Fifth Regiment Armory hosted the annual meetings of the Elks, Odd Fellows, and League of Municipalities in 1903, as well as the Democratic National Convention of 1912 (after which it was known as Convention Hall). Providence's Cranston Street Armory was the site of an auto and boat show in 1908 and a poultry and horticultural show in 1920. Gene Tunney, Benny Leonard, and many long forgotten boxers (and wrestlers) fought in Paterson, New Jersey's Fifth Regiment Armory, which was known as the "Madison Square Garden of Passaic County." Track meets were held in the Seattle Armory, and the National Indoor Tennis Championships were played in New York's Seventh Regiment Armory. Enrico Caruso performed in the Detroit Light Guard Armory, as did Ignace Paderewski, John McCormack, Leopold Stokowski, and Walter Damrosch. Rudolph Valentino once appeared in Newark's First Regiment Armory, and when he failed to turn up for a second show, six thousand women stormed his dressing room, forcing him to flee for safety. Probably the most memorable event that took place in an armory was the Armory Show of 1913. Held in New York's Sixty-ninth Regiment Armory, it was the first great exhibition of modern art in the United States.[41]

Once the armory was turned into a coliseum, many Americans

held that it should be turned into a community center too. If it was all right to use armories for public events on an occasional basis, they reasoned that it should be all right to use them for neighborhood activities on an everyday basis. The cities were full of children who had few places to play except the streets, which were widely regarded as incubators of crime and delinquency. To get children off the streets was a goal of many Americans. At their behest many schools were kept open in the late afternoon and early evening for social, athletic, and recreational activities. If the schools could serve as "neighborhood centers," wrote the Brooklyn *Eagle* in 1913, so could the armories. Along the same line, Gordon Battle, President of the Parks and Playgrounds Association of New York, the successor to the organization that had blocked the erection of an armory in Washington Square in 1878, argued in 1926 that armories should be used as playgrounds. "If the armories could be used for this purpose," he wrote, "it would afford the children in the crowded sections [of the city] an opportunity for play and recreation which they sorely need."[42] Having long opposed turning parks into armories, the park lobby now favored converting armories into playgrounds.

The campaign to turn the armory into a community center was highly successful. As early as the mid-1910s the Gramercy Neighborhood Association obtained the use of New York's Sixty-ninth Regiment Armory, where one thousand boys assembled to watch movies and listen to talks about citizenship. Once organized, a company to each block, the boys competed in athletic contests too. By the mid-1920s such practices were common. New York State allowed children to play in its armories. Wisconsin rented them to community groups for social and recreational activities. California turned its armories over to local recreation departments. Pennsylvania's armories also served as "community centers," Major General E. C. Shannon told a congressional committee. By the 1930s some armories were in such demand by community, civic, and commercial groups that the state authorities had to impose limits on how many days a year they could be used for nonmilitary purposes. And by the end of the decade Major General William S. Haskell, commanding officer of the New York State National Guard, was so annoyed by the commercial use of the state's armories that he lashed out against the officers in charge. Their job, he reminded them, was "not to make money but to train troops, and not to give facilities built by the city and the State to civilians and clubs and other groups for their amusement, but to make them attractive and available for the enlisted men themselves."[43]

By the time of the New Deal, the principle that the armory was as much a civilian as a military facility was well established. Calling on Congress to set aside a portion of the relief funds for new armories, national guard leaders emphasized that the armories would not only house the troops, but also serve as community centers. This position was later adopted by the WPA, which based its armory construction program on the assumption that the buildings would be used "approximately 75 per cent as a community center and 25 per cent for military purposes." Most WPA armories were built accordingly. Speaking of the fifty-one Oklahoma armories constructed with WPA funds, the Oklahoma City *Daily Oklahoman* wrote, "Not only may these armories be used to house the guard, but they also may be converted into municipal auditoriums, gymnasiums or theaters in a twinkling. And they are expected to be the center of civic functions for years to come."[44] Also noteworthy were the Sheboygan, Wisconsin, Armory, which served as a municipal auditorium, and the Stoughton, Wisconsin, Armory, which served as a school gymnasium. Half a century after Boston militiamen drilled in a university gym Wisconsin schoolchildren played in a national guard armory.

The changes in the armory's function had profound implications for its design. As a fortress, the armory was supposed to help prevent troublemakers from joining in riots and other uprisings. It had to look formidable. It had to evoke a sense of fear and awe, to symbolize the might of the state, and to convey its willingness to use force to maintain order. Walls two or three feet thick, a large, well protected sally-port, heavily guarded windows, crenellated turrets and towers which commanded the streets—all were suitable in a fortress. But as a coliseum or community center, an armory was supposed to attract people, not intimidate them, to treat them as potential visitors, not as potential rioters. It had to look hospitable, for want of a better word, not formidable. It had to arouse in passersby the feeling that they were welcome and that once inside they could enjoy themselves. As a coliseum or community center, an armory had to be accessible, not defensible. What it needed were plenty of entrances, to allow people to enter and exit quickly (especially in case of fire), and plenty of windows, to let in as much light and air as possible. Given these requirements, the castellated style was highly inappropriate.

The rebuilding of Baltimore's Fifth Regiment Armory, which was destroyed by fire in 1933, nicely illustrates the impact of the changing function of the armory. Shortly after the fire the regiment urged the state to rebuild the armory. So did the Baltimore Association of Commerce, which urged that the armory, the only structure in the city large enough to host large gatherings, be rebuilt as a convention center. Spokesmen for the state pointed out that it could not afford to build a convention center, but promised that it would do everything possible "to make the armory more suitable as a convention hall and for other community purposes." With the help of the U.S. Civil Works Administration, it did just that. Although the architects from Wyatt & Nolting, the firm that had designed the old armory, closely followed the original plans, they added a second hall, expressly for nonmilitary events, with a separate entrance, ticket office, and check room. They also provided a clerestory and other features which made the new armory less formidable than the old. To hold down costs, the architects retained the original walls. Asked if the armory could still withstand artillery fire, Adjutant-General Milton A. Reckord replied that no one expected it to. "Who would use artillery against it?" he asked. And, he added, taking the same position as Colonel Harvey, "If artillery were being used in Baltimore [why] would the troops be inside it?"[45]

Although the armory had a good deal of unobstructed space, most of which was unoccupied much of the time, it could only have been turned into a coliseum and community center if the residents wanted to use it and the guardsmen allowed them to. Neither was likely before 1900. To understand why, it is helpful to bear in mind that at that time the national guard served as the states' peacekeeping and strikebreaking force. Many Americans therefore viewed the armories as a symbol of repression and would have been loath to use them. Many guardsmen, for their part, would have been reluctant to let the lower and working classes use the armories, for fear that they might make off with the arms and ammunition stored there. After 1900, however, the national guard underwent a remarkable transformation. By the end of World War I, it was a federal as well as a state force—a force that served as the backup for the army, rather than as the "policeman of industry," a force whose mission was to defend the country against foreigners, not against other Americans. Once the guardsmen took on this new role, they stopped thinking of the lower and working classes as potential rioters, other Americans stopped looking at the armories as symbols of repression, and it became possible to turn what had long been a fortress into a coliseum and community center.

Of the many things which brought about the transformation of the national guard, probably the most important were the waning fears of class warfare and the growing fears of foreign warfare. The fears of class warfare, which reached their peak in the 1880s and 1890s, declined after 1900. And though they later surfaced from time to time, notably in the Anarchist Scare of 1908 and the Red Scare of 1919, these fears lost much of their force in the next two decades. Most Americans, guardsmen and architects included, still believed that the nation had grave problems, but they no longer thought that class warfare was imminent. They were troubled by industrial conflict, but they now perceived it as a struggle between capital and labor, not as a sign of incipient insurrection. Thus the steel strike of 1919 aroused less anxiety than the Homestead strike. The dynamiting of the Los Angeles *Times* in 1910 generated less hysteria than the Haymarket Affair. And the apocalyptic literature of these years was far less bloodthirsty than *Caesar's Column*. Most Americans now attributed social problems less to deep conflicts of interest than to misunderstanding and poor communication and assumed that these problems could be resolved by mediation and other nonviolent means. If the authorities had to employ force to maintain order, they should do so in a measured and evenhanded way—a far cry from the summary justice advocated by many Americans in the late nineteenth century.[46]

The fears of class warfare waned for several reasons, not the least of which was that both organized labor and corporate capital grew less bellicose after the turn of the century. Aside from the International Workers of the World, organized labor became less militant. Following the example of the American Federation of Labor, most labor unions embraced "pure and simple" unionism and concentrated on raising wages and improving working conditions. Committed to working within the capitalist system, they repudiated Socialism and other radical ideologies. Moreover, the socialists lost much of their power. In an attempt to enhance their electoral prospects, they abandoned their revolutionary rhetoric. But despite a good showing at the polls in the early 1910s, they were racked by internal struggles. And after opposing United States entry into World War I, they were no longer a force to be reckoned with. At the same time corporate capital became less intransigent (or, from another perspective, more sophisticated) vis-à-vis organized labor. One indicator of this was the emergence of the National Civic Federation, an association of influential businessmen (and prominent union leaders) who were willing to work with organized labor to lessen industrial strife. Another indicator was the growth of welfare capitalism, the practice by which corporations attempted to reduce conflict in the workplace by providing employees with housing, schools, pensions, and other benefits not required by industry or mandated by law.[47]

Closely related to the waning fears of class warfare were the growing fears of foreign warfare, which, it turned out, were far better grounded. Throughout the 1880s most Americans were confident that they had little to fear from other nations. Other nations had no cause to attack the United States and, even if they did, no way to do so. America was separated from Europe by one ocean and from Asia by another; it had a friendly country to the north and a weak one to the south. This confidence started to decline in the 1890s, however, as the United States became entangled in Latin American and Far Eastern affairs. Even before Congress declared war on Spain in 1898, many Americans feared that war might break out. Afterwards, as the tensions which eventually led to World War I increased in Europe, many Americans concluded that the United States was on the verge of an even more arduous struggle in the years ahead. The fears of foreign warfare were expressed in many forums, among them the ceremonies which accompanied the building of the armories. Before the turn of the century most speakers had stressed the danger of domestic disorder, of riot and insurrection; afterwards they stressed the threat of foreign conflict. For all the cries of "universal peace," Mayor William A. Magee of Pittsburgh warned at the opening of the Eighteenth Regiment Armory in 1911, it was only a matter of time before the United States was drawn into "armed strife."[48]

As fears of class warfare gave way to fears of foreign warfare, many Americans grew concerned that the nation was poorly prepared to wage war. And shortly after the Spanish-American War, which showed just how poorly prepared it was, Secretary of War Elihu Root launched a campaign to strengthen the country's military forces. Among other things, Root proposed the formation of a large reserve that would back up the regular troops. This proposal provoked a heated debate. On one side were guard leaders, who held that the guard could be turned into an effective reserve (and feared that if it were not it would eventually be dismantled). On the other were army officers, who believed that the guard was not up to the job and called for the creation of a national reserve entirely independent of the states. In 1903 Congress reached a compromise. Incorporated into the Dick Act, named after Congressman Charles Dick of Ohio, it provided that the guard would be the backup for the army, but would be accountable to the federal government as well as to the states. The act also mandated that within five years the guard had to adopt the same organization, weapons, and discipline as the army.[49] In other words, the Dick Act gave the guard a new mission, but took away much of its old autonomy. And in later years Congress passed other acts which gave the federal government even more control over the national guard.

Before the Dick Act was passed, a few Americans had warned that the national guard could not count on the support of all the citizens as long as it served largely as a strikebreaking force—a force that took for granted that labor and capital would always be "flying at each other's throat." But not until the act was passed (and the guard was turned into the backup for the army) were such warnings taken seriously. Many Americans now realized that if the guard were to be an effective reserve it had to be able to recruit from all classes, which was virtually impossible given its reputation as a strikebreaking force. To attract the lower and working classes, they argued, the guard would have to give up its role as "policeman of industry"—a proposal that struck a responsive chord at a time when few Americans were worried much about class warfare. (One critic even recommended that in order to increase recruitment among the laboring classes the guard should allow enlisted men to refuse to serve in industrial disputes, a recommendation that would have been inconceivable a generation earlier.) This proposal appealed both to federal officials, who were well aware of the advantages of a reserve that was regarded favorably by all segments of society, and to state officials, many of whom were tired of defending the guard against charges that it was a tool of corporate capital.[50]

This proposal appealed to the guardsmen as well. Even before the Dick Act was passed, many of them were more than ready to give up their role as "policeman of industry." And as spokesmen for the guard began to downplay its role as a peacekeeping force and to emphasize its place in the military system, this attitude spread through the service. By the mid-1910s most guardsmen no longer wanted to deal with industrial disputes. "There isn't a member of the Guard, there isn't an officer in the Guard," Mayor George R. Lunn of Schenectady told the annual convention of the New York State Federation of Labor in 1916, "who would not, if he had the power to-day, take the National Guard out of doing police duty." Even guardsmen who were reluctant to give up their peacekeeping role admitted that strike duty was by far "the most disagreeable feature of National Guard service." When the strike took place out of town, the guardsmen had to leave their homes and workplaces, which was bad enough. When it occurred nearby, they had to use force against their friends and neighbors, which was even worse. Strike duty was highly demoralizing as well. Many guardsmen were upset by the criticism of organized labor, which, as one Illinois officer put it, viewed the guard as "a mere servant and slave" of capital. Many of them were also weary of responding to this criticism, of stating again and again that their duty was not to serve either capital or labor, but to maintain public order.[51]

What troubled the guardsmen most about strike duty was not that it was disagreeable and demoralizing, but that it was an obstacle to recruitment. Strike duty "has stopped recruiting" in Rhode Island, reported a high-ranking guardsman. In Buffalo, the *Outlook* pointed out, strike duty severely weakened an attempt to bring the Sixty-fifth Regiment up to full strength. Asked why they were disinclined to enlist, many young men cited the obligation to police strikes. Requiring the guard to deal with industrial disputes "is probably the most effective means of depleting the ranks of the State militia which could be devised," wrote the *Outlook*. The guard, which badly needed qualified recruits if it were to serve as an effective reserve, no longer discriminated against union members. But given its reputation as a strikebreaking force, many workers were reluctant to sign up. So were many other Americans, who were not necessarily sympathetic to organized labor but were strongly repelled by the prospect of using force against their fellow Americans, particularly at a time when class warfare seemed highly unlikely.[52] So far as its leaders were concerned, the national guard would be hard pressed to attract new members unless the states relieved it of the responsibility to deal with industrial disputes.

The states were willing to relieve the guard of this responsibility, once they found another force to take it on. That force was the state police (or, as it was originally called, the state constabulary). Aside from the Texas Rangers and other frontier police forces, the first state police force was the Pennsylvania State Constabulary, which was established in 1905. A far cry from the municipal police departments, the Pennsylvania state police was a small, well-trained, highly mobile paramilitary force that was empowered to operate throughout the commonwealth. Headed by a superintendent who was accountable to the governor, it policed rural communities, patrolled state highways, and, among other things, handled industrial disputes. Based on Pennsylvania's experience, many Americans believed that the state police was a more efficient and less expensive peacekeeping force than the national guard. They urged other states to follow Pennsylvania's lead. Organized labor strongly objected to the state police. Branding the troopers "Cossacks" and "Hussars," its spokesmen declared that the state police was just as bad as the Pinkertons and corporate police and even worse than the national guard. In spite of organized labor's opposition, however, one state after another set up its own police force after World War I; and in most of them the state police took on the responsibility of handling industrial disputes.[53]

As the state police took on this responsibility, the national guard gave up its role as "policeman of industry." In Pennsylvania, where the guard had developed a well-deserved reputation as a strikebreaking force, it was not called up once for strike duty between 1905, the year the state constabulary was established, and 1930. In other states the guard was seldom used in industrial disputes after its much-criticized performance in the Colorado coal strike of

1913–14. As the guard shifted from a peacekeeping force to a military reserve, it spent less time on riot drills and more time on field maneuvers. In addition to training young Americans to defend the nation, it also sponsored athletic contests and other activities to improve their health and well-being. At the same time the guard gradually turned into an all-purpose emergency force. By the 1920s it was regularly summoned in the event of floods, forest fires, train crashes, and other disasters. The guardsmen evacuated victims, organized relief centers, and provided medical services.[54] These efforts helped the guard win the support of many groups which had long regarded it as a tool of corporate capital.

One such group was organized labor. Relations between the unions and the guard had deteriorated in the 1890s. By the early 1900s they were even worse. Expressing the view of most unions, the Illinois State Federation of Labor charged in 1902 that the national guard was nothing but "an auxiliary police force" used by corporate capital to stifle organized labor. It urged union members to refrain from joining the guard. Many other unions took the same position. One of them, the Painters' and Decorators' Union of Schenectady, expelled a member for serving in the guard—an action that was attacked by the New York *Times* as "at once wrong and absurd" and defended by many labor leaders, one of whom asked, "What business has a workingman with the National Guard?" a force that "has always been employed by the corporations to crush out the strikes." The hostility to the national guard was widespread in the AFL, where at one annual convention after another the delegates submitted resolutions instructing its affiliates "to hold absolutely aloof from all connection with the militia." Although these resolutions did not carry, it was only because some labor leaders believed that the guard would be less antagonistic to organized labor if workers served in it and felt that as bad as the guard was a standing army would be even worse.[55]

As the national guard changed its role, however, organized labor changed its mind. In 1910 the *American Federationist,* the official journal of the AFL, said that workers had the right to join the guard and that unions should not stop them from doing so. The AFL's opposition to the guard softened even more after World War I, a time when Samuel Gompers lectured annually at the Army and Navy war colleges to demonstrate organized labor's patriotism and respectability. By the early 1920s organized labor had come full circle. Writing to Adjutant-General Louis G. Lasher of Iowa in 1922, Gompers declared that a worker "has not only the right to become a citizen soldier, but that right must be unquestioned." The militia, he pointed out, is the only alternative to a standing army. And the difference between the militia and the standing army is the difference between "liberty and tyranny." Gompers's statement, Lasher declared, "is simply added proof that organized labor stands for the same brand of loyalty and patriotism as does the National Guard."[56] An outgrowth of the waning fears of class warfare and the growing fears of foreign warfare, the rapprochement between organized labor and the national guard was at the heart of the transformation of the American armory and the demise of the castellated style.

epilogue

The Fate of the Old Armories

Speaking at the cornerstone ceremonies of the Portland, Oregon, Armory in 1887, Judge George H. Williams predicted that while a great city would grow there and many generations would come and go "this stone" would remain "unchanged and unmoved." Things did not work out that way. Eighty-one years later the national guard abandoned the armory, which had long housed Oregon's First Regiment and hosted circuses and sporting events. The guard sold it to a local brewery, which knocked down part of the building and turned the rest into a parking lot. In the process workers removed the cornerstone, inside of which the state archivist found a copper box full of late nineteenth-century coins, buttons, documents, and newspapers.[1] The fate of the Portland Armory was not atypical. Few of the old armories still house the national guard. Many have been destroyed, either accidentally or deliberately. Many others have become obsolete, especially after World War II, when the federal government appropriated funds to build hundreds of modern armories, most of them in suburban and rural communities. Still others have been sold or given away and used for various nonmilitary purposes. The fate of the old armories thus gives us some insight not only into the changing role of the national guard, but also into the social and political life of urban America in the last two generations.

Of the many armories built in the late nineteenth and early twentieth centuries, some were destroyed by fire—to which, it turned out, they were extremely vulnerable. As well as arms, the guardsmen stored ammunition and other flammable material there. Many of the armories were so large that if this material caught fire it often took a long time before anyone realized it. By then it was sometimes too late to do much. What the New York *Times* described as one of the most "spectacular" fires in many years broke out in the Seventy-first Regiment Armory in 1902, less than ten years after it was built. The fire, accompanied by the explosion of cartridges and shells, destroyed the armory and spread to a nearby hotel, killing seventeen people and injuring scores of others. A fire also devastated Baltimore's Fifth Regiment Armory in 1933. The same year Detroit's Light Guard Armory narrowly escaped a serious blaze. But twelve years later, a few years before the armory's fiftieth birthday, a five-alarm fire started in the basement, spread to the roof, and in a matter of hours left nothing standing except the walls. Among the other armories destroyed by fire was New Jersey's Second Regiment Armory, which was erected by the state in the early 1900s, sold to Trenton in the late 1960s, and then used for a while as a civic center.[2]

No city was hit harder by fire than Buffalo, the home of the Sixty-fifth and Seventy-fourth regiment armories. The Sixty-fifth, an immense castle that looked as if it would last for centuries, burned down in 1931, barely two decades after it was built. The fire started in the basement, where lumber and wood shavings were being stored for an upcoming circus, and soon got out of control. One of the worst fires in Buffalo's history, it raged for several days, threatening the whole neighborhood. As over one hundred thousand spectators watched, virtually the whole Buffalo fire department battled the blaze. By the time it was over, nothing was left of the armory but a shell. The Seventy-fourth Regiment Armory, which was erected a decade before the Sixty-fifth, caught fire a half century later. The fire forced many nearby residents to leave their homes. As the ammunition exploded, a veteran of the Vietnam War said, "It was like Saigon all over again." But the Seventy-fourth suffered much less damage than the Sixty-fifth. Although much of the drill shed was gutted, most of the administration building was spared. The state therefore decided to rebuild the armory. With the help of the federal government, the Seventy-fourth Regiment Armory was completely restored a few years later.[3]

Fire also destroyed much of the Seattle Armory in 1962. The

armory, which had not been used by the national guard for years, had suffered a few other fires before, the worst of which had occurred in 1947, when it was occupied by the state's Unemployment Compensation Office. And during the 1950s several Seattle citizens had called on the authorities to demolish the building and turn the site into a waterfront park. After the fire, they renewed their efforts. Since the guard had no interest in the armory, the state was willing to sell it. But the city took no action until 1968, when it offered to buy the building, which lay within the Pike Place urban renewal area, and proposed to knock it down. Just when it seemed that the issue was resolved, several architects and preservationists launched a campaign to save the armory, claiming that it was "a remarkable example" of nineteenth-century American architecture. Since the Seattle Municipal Arts Commission had already designated the armory an historic building, it appeared for a while that the armory might be preserved. But in the end the municipal officials decided that the building stood in the way of a road that was vital to the Pike Place project and that it would cost far too much to save all or even part of it.[4] The armory (or what was left of it) was soon demolished and eventually replaced by office buildings.

Other armories were deliberately destroyed—either because the national guard no longer needed the buildings or because other groups very much wanted the sites. The destruction was especially widespread in New York City. The first to go was the old Twenty-second Regiment Armory. It was torn down in 1929 by a real estate developer to whom the city had sold the building after it decided to move the current tenant, the 104th Field Artillery, to a new armory in Queens. Starting in the late 1950s, several other armories met the same fate. The Twelfth Regiment Armory was razed in 1958 to clear the site for the Lincoln Square urban renewal project, which later became the home of Lincoln Center for the Performing Arts. The old Eighth Regiment Armory was demolished in 1966 to make way for Intermediate School 29, a school for white students from Yorkville and black and Puerto Rican students from East Harlem. Three years later the Ninth Regiment Armory was knocked down. Although some New Yorkers favored using the site for middle-income housing, the national guard built a new armory on it for the Forty-second Division. In 1971 the Seventy-first Regiment Armory was leveled. It was replaced by a nine-story high school, the money for which came from the sale of air rights for the thirty-two story skyscraper that was erected on top of it.[5]

The story was much the same in other cities. Newark's First Regiment Armory, the building from which Valentino had fled, was demolished in 1969, several years after the state had decided it was obsolete and sold it to private parties. An extended care facility for the aged ill was erected on the site. Camden's Third Regiment Armory, commonly known as Convention Hall, was torn down in 1977 to make way for a new Veterans Administration hospital. Philadelphia's First Regiment Armory, one of the oldest in the nation, is gone. It was sold to Triangle Publications, the publishing empire of Walter Annenberg, and later acquired by another company, which razed the building in the early 1980s and later turned the site into a parking lot. Also gone is Pittsburgh's Logan Armory. It was sold to the University of Pittsburgh, which knocked down the fifty-year-old structure in the mid-1960s to make room for the Michael L. Benedum Hall of Engineering. Boston's Irvington Street Armory was torn down in the early 1960s by the Massachusetts Turnpike Authority, which had taken the property in order to extend its toll road into the heart of the city. Also in the early 1960s the commonwealth turned Boston's East Newton Street Armory over to the state Department of Mental Health, which demolished it a few years later and erected the Solomon Carter Fuller Mental Health Center on the site.[6]

Several of the Midwest's old armories have been destroyed too. The Minneapolis Armory was razed in 1934, five years after it was condemned by the city's building inspector. Erected in 1907, the armory soon developed structural problems; and despite major repairs, it remained in precarious condition for much of its short life. Cleveland's Central Armory was knocked down in 1962 by the city, which had bought it a year earlier with the intention of using the site for a parking lot or public building. Shortly afterwards the federal government erected a thirty-two-story office building there. Chicago's First Regiment Armory, the most imposing of the midwestern armories, was sold after World War II to an automobile dealer, who used it to store cars. A dilapidated building in a rundown neighborhood, the armory was demolished in the 1960s. Despite its historic importance, its passing went largely unnoticed. Cincinnati's First Regiment Armory was purchased by the city in 1982, twenty-one years after it had been sold to private parties. For a while the city tried to find someone to rehabilitate it and adapt it for another purpose. When that failed, it tore down the armory and sold the site to an advertising display firm, which built a light industrial plant there.[7]

The fate of New York City's Squadron A Armory was bizarre. In 1964 New York State sold the armory, along with three others that the guard no longer needed, to the city, from which it had taken them in 1942. Some residents wanted to turn the site into a park; others favored housing; and still others pressed for a school. In the end the local authorities decided on an intermediate (and presumably integrated) school and gave the property to the Board of Education. The demolition, which got under way early in 1966, was almost finished when a few residents called on the authorities to preserve the Madison Avenue facade, with its massive walls and two tremendous towers. They won the support of the mayor's office, the Board of Education, the New York *Times,* and the Landmarks Preservation Commission, which had not hitherto seen fit to designate the armory a landmark. And the city halted the demolition. Shortly after the commission designated the facade a landmark—overriding the not unreasonable objection that it made little sense to save part of a structure that had not itself been deemed worthy of preservation (and was largely rubble). Today the armory is only a memory, but its walls and towers still loom over Madison Avenue. Behind them stands an asphalt playground and a five-story brick schoolhouse, a virtually windowless building that has the air of a fortress about it.[8]

Many other armories are still standing. But some of them have been sold or given to nonmilitary organizations. No longer the home of the national guard, they are armories in name only. Take the case of Brooklyn's Thirteenth Regiment Armory, which is now almost one hundred years old. Early in the 1970s the state decided it had no need for the armory and turned it over to the city. The city was urged to convert it into a day-care center, a senior citizen facility, or a community auditorium. For a while the city leased it to an addiction treatment center. But eventually it gave the building to the Board of Education, which turned it into the annex to Junior High School 57. The state also transferred two other Brooklyn armories to the city in the mid-1960s. Contrary to expectations, neither has been demolished. The Clermont Avenue Armory, built in the mid-1870s for the Twenty-third Regiment, is one of the very few pre-1877 armories still standing. Used for a while by the city's sanitation department, it is now vacant and in poor condition. Almost as old is the Dean Street Armory, which was erected in the mid-1880s for the Third Gatling Battery. The city tried to sell it in the mid-1970s, but the Bedford-Stuyvesant Boys' Club, which had been leasing it, brought suit to block the sale. Still owned by the city, it now houses an Afro-American cultural center.[9]

Paterson's Fifth Regiment Armory, the "Madison Square Garden of Passaic County," is another armory in name only. Closed by the state in 1982 because of budgetary pressures, it was later sold to investors and is now used to store files and records. In the same category is Philadelphia's Second Regiment Armory, which was transferred to the Pennsylvania Department of Education in the mid-1970s. The department rents it to Temple University. Another state agency, the General Services Department, leases Philadelphia's Third Regiment Armory to St. Rita's Church, which uses it as a soup kitchen, bingo hall, and community center. In the mid-1960s the state of Massachusetts sold the Cambridge Armory to MIT, which had long been using it as a drill hall for ROTC students. Just as Boston's First Corps of Cadets once drilled in the Institute's old gymnasium, so MIT students now play basketball and volleyball in the Cambridge Armory's drill shed. Nearly twenty years later the state sold the Commonwealth Avenue Armory to Boston University at what one reporter called a "bargain-basement price." The sale generated charges of corruption in the legislature and triggered a nasty conflict between the community and the university over the appropriate reuse of the armory and the ten acres on which it stands.[10]

Of the armories which have been abandoned by the troops, many have been reused in unexpected (and sometimes ingenious) ways—a fairly common fate for obsolete buildings in the recent past. Bought by ABC television in the mid-1970s, New York City's First Battery Armory has been converted into the studio in which "One Life to Live," one of the country's most popular soap operas, is produced. The White Plains Armory is now the Armory Plaza Apartments, a federally subsidized apartment house for the elderly with fifty-two studio and one-bedroom units and a senior citizens center. The Milk Street Armory, which is located in a historic district along the Portland, Maine, waterfront, was recently converted into the Old Port Regency Hotel. The Savannah Volunteer Guards Armory now houses the Savannah College of Art & Design, a private college founded in 1979. The Montgomery, Alabama, Armory is today the Montgomery Arts Center, the home of the city's Arts Council. And the San Francisco Armory, whose fate was the subject of a long controversy, was sold in the mid-1980s to Armory Studios, Inc., which intends to turn it into the largest motion picture and video studio in northern California.[11]

Also still standing, though no longer used by the guard, is Boston's First Corps of Cadets Armory. With no money to pay property taxes, much less to make overdue repairs, the Corps sold the building in 1965 to William J. Fitzgerald, a parking lot operator and one-time Boston fire commissioner. Fitzgerald leased it to the University of Massachusetts, which converted the armory into a library for its Boston campus students, using the administration building for offices and the drill shed as a reading room and book stack. When the university moved to its permanent campus at Columbia Point in 1973, the year the armory was listed on the National Register of Historic Places, Fitzgerald rented it to Boston 200, a bicentennial organization, which used the drill shed as an exhibition hall. Over Fitzgerald's objections, the armory was designated a city landmark in 1977. A few years later it was sold to Donald and Roger Saunders, the principals of Saunders & Associates, a real estate firm and owners of the nearby Park Plaza Hotel and Towers. As the armory approaches its centennial, the drill shed serves as a convention center and exhibition hall for the hotel, the site of craft shows and inaugural balls. And in the meantime Saunders & Associates has been trying to find someone to lease all or part of the administration building. Its ads read, "WANTED: A King for a Castle."[12]

Many other armories still house the national guard. Besides the Seventh Regiment Armory, there are the Fifteenth, Twenty-second, and Sixty-ninth regiment armories, all of which are in Manhattan; the Second Battery and Eighth Coastal Artillery armories in the Bronx; and the Fourteenth, Twenty-third, and Forty-seventh regiment armories, as well as the Squadron C Armory, in Brooklyn. Albany's Tenth Regiment Armory is still standing. So are Pittsburgh's huge Hunt Armory, and Philadelphia's small First Troop

Armory, one of the very few privately owned armories in the country. The Hartford Armory, which is the headquarters of the Connecticut National Guard, is in good condition. So is Baltimore's Fifth Regiment Armory, which was rebuilt after the 1933 fire and is now the headquarters of the Maryland National Guard. But Providence's Cranston Street Armory is in serious disrepair. A special task force has recommended that when the guard moves out, as it plans to do, the armory should be turned into a state archives and records center.[13]

Besides housing the national guard, most of these armories have served as coliseums, community centers, and emergency facilities. New York's Seventh Regiment Armory has a full schedule of exhibitions, including the annual Winter Antiques Show, for which its elegant interior provides a splendid setting. The Kingsbridge Armory has hosted many trade shows, among them the National Motor Boat Show. So has Boston's Commonwealth Avenue Armory, which was recently the site of a job fair that attracted hundreds of recruiters and thousands of job seekers. The Seventh Regiment Armory has leased space to a tennis club, as has New York's Twenty-second Regiment Armory. The Twenty-second has been the site of indoor track and field meets, as was Boston's East Newton Street Armory before it was given to the state Department of Mental Health. Albany's Tenth Regiment Armory is the home of the Albany Patroons, one of the teams of the Continental Basketball Association. Baltimore's Fifth Regiment Armory has been used by all sorts of social, commercial, and professional organizations. So has the Hartford Armory. As well as serving as the headquarters of the Connecticut National Guard, it has provided a site for Masonic circuses, antique shows, dog shows, tennis matches, and track and field meets for high school students.[14]

Both the Kingsbridge and Squadron C armories have served as community centers. So has the Fifteenth Regiment Armory, the home of the nation's most famous black military unit and a New York City Landmark since 1985. It was recently the setting for an "I Remember Harlem Night," a combined film festival and dinner dance. To give a few other examples, the Connecticut National Guard has allowed Gamblers Anonymous to meet in the Hartford Armory. The Cleveland Grays has shown silent movies, accompanied by organ music, in its armory and permitted local police forces to practice on its pistol range. And the Illinois National Guard has let the community use Chicago's 122d Field Artillery Armory, a building that some state officials would like to get rid of. Neighborhood youngsters have played in its gymnasium, and community groups have held dances in its ballroom. Even New York's Seventh Regiment Armory, a privately owned building full of valuable art that has long been regarded as closed to community groups, has sometimes been made available to neighboring institutions. In 1972, for example, the regiment allowed Hunter College, a branch of the City University of New York located on Park Avenue and Sixty-eighth Street, to hold its commencement exercises in the drill shed.[15]

Since World War II, when the guard took an active role in coping with floods, fires, crashes, and other disasters, the armories have also served as emergency facilities. Here New York City was in the vanguard. During the blackout of 1965, when much of the Northeast lost electricity, the armories provided shelter for people unable to leave Manhattan. When the transit workers went on strike two months later, the armories were opened to commuters stranded in the city. In 1966 the state offered the use of the armories to the city, which had no space in its schools for thirteen thousand kindergarten and prekindergarten schoolchildren. During a cold wave two years later the state allowed more than one hundred New Yorkers whose apartments had no heat to live in the Fifteenth Regiment Armory, which they refused to leave until assured of decent housing. Many armories were used in similar ways in other cities. Newark's First Regiment Armory served as a temporary jail for the large number of people arrested during the riots of 1967. The Concord and Manchester, New Hampshire, armories were turned into temporary prisons in 1977 after thirteen thousand people were arrested in a demonstration against the Seabrook nuclear power plant. And the Chelsea, Massachusetts, Armory was taken over in 1986 by state and local police to process dozens of suspected heroin and cocaine dealers arrested in a dawn roundup.[16]

Several New York City armories have even been turned into shelters for the homeless. Although the Twelfth Regiment Armory provided temporary housing for one hundred evicted tenants in 1919, the city first used armories as shelters on a large scale during the Great Depression, a time when many of its citizens were homeless. Although some lived in "Hoovervilles" and on the streets, others were put up in municipal lodging houses. Most of the homeless had no place to go in the daytime, however, a serious problem in the winter. Thus in 1934 Mayor Fiorello H. LaGuardia decided to turn a few city armories into daytime shelters. If they could be used for dog shows, wrestling matches, and midget auto races, surely they could be used by the victims of the Depression. During the next year or so the city opened half a dozen armories to the homeless. At the Sixty-ninth Regiment Armory, the site of the Armory Show, they played cards, checkers, and shuffleboard and even organized a baseball game. At the Seventy-first, which housed four thousand one frigid winter day, they drank coffee, ate doughnuts, and watched a vaudeville show. When the armories were closed at five in the afternoon, many of the "guests" went to one of the lodging houses for a meal and a night's sleep.[17]

New York began using its armories as shelters again in the 1980s, when homelessness in the city reached what several religious leaders called "crisis proportions." As the U.S. House Committee on Government Operations reported in 1985, homelessness was a problem that plagued most of the country's big cities, including Washington, D.C. An estimated three hundred thousand to three million Americans, many of them women and children, were homeless—more than at any time since the Great Depression, noted New York Governor Mario Cuomo in 1984. With fewer than a hundred thousand beds available in existing shelters, many of these people had no place to live but the streets. And as newspaper stories, magazine articles, and congressional hearings revealed, life on the streets was dreadful, especially in wintertime. But nowhere was homelessness as serious a problem as in New York City, where as many as sixty thousand people lived in the streets and thousands more slept in flophouses and temporary shelters. Homelessness in New York was a product of two things other than the high rate of long-term unemployment in the central city. One was the lack of low-income housing, much of which had been abandoned by landlords, demolished by developers, and replaced by no one. The other was the move toward deinstitutionalization, in the name of which the state had closed many of its mental hospitals. Many former patients, for whom no provision was made, ended up living in the streets.[18]

The growing numbers of homeless soon overwhelmed New York's

existing shelters. And in 1981, two years after the courts had ruled that the homeless had a right to shelter, the city agreed to provide them with clean and safe accommodations. Later in the year, under pressure from Justice Richard W. Wallach, it turned the Flushing Armory in Queens and the Twenty-second Regiment Armory in Manhattan into shelters. By the mid-1980s the city was also housing men in the Seventh and Fifteenth regiment armories in Manhattan, the Kingsbridge and Second Battery armories in the Bronx, and the Thirteenth, Fourteenth, and Twenty-third regiment armories in Brooklyn. A few women were housed in the Sixty-ninth Regiment Armory. At one point the city officials were so desperate for space that they considered converting old ferries and mothballed battleships into shelters. Daytime shelters during the Great Depression, the armories are largely nighttime shelters half a century later. The homeless are bussed to the armories at night and from them in the morning. They sleep in the armories, but eat elsewhere. Their cots, each with sheets, pillow, and blanket, are arranged in long rows in the huge drill sheds—the same drill sheds in which the guardsmen, their uniforms perfectly cut and their weapons at their sides, once marched.[19]

Nowhere were the homeless as incongruous as in the Seventh Regiment Armory, which was opened as a shelter early in 1983— a few years after the regiment had thwarted a proposal by Tishman-Speyer Properties, a New York real estate firm, to buy the building, raze the drill shed, and in its place erect a large hotel and apartment house. The armory housed 150 men, who slept in classrooms on the third floor and a gymnasium on the fifth. Odd as it may seem, they lived in one of the most elegant buildings in the city, rubbing shoulders with prominent New Yorkers on their way to private parties and affluent antique dealers getting ready for the winter show. Things went smoothly until 1984, when the city decided to add another 250 beds, all of which were to be put in the drill shed, thus displacing a tennis club and the Knickerbocker Greys, a drill team for well-to-do youngsters. The regiment and its neighbors objected. "It is like establishing a shelter for the homeless in the Metropolitan Museum of Art," declared a leader of the opposition, which filed suit to block the scheme. Under intense pressure, the city backed down.[20] Still, for the time being New York houses some of its many homeless in the most famous armory in the nation, a building that has been designated a city and state landmark and listed on the National Register of Historic Places, a structure that was designed to intimidate the "dangerous classes," not to accommodate them. In a sense the armory (or, at any rate, part of it) has been turned over to the very people from whom the regiment was supposed to protect the city—a paradox that reveals how much the fears of class warfare that led to the building of the armories in the nineteenth century have waned in the twentieth.

Notes

Prologue. A New Building Type

1. New York *Times,* November 18, 1879; New York *Herald,* November 18, 1879.
2. *The Knapsack: A Daily Journal of the Seventh Regiment New Armory Fair,* November 19, 1879, p. 1.
3. New York *Times,* January 23, 1876, April 10, 1880; Emmons Clark, *History of the Seventh Regiment of New York, 1806–1889* (New York, 1890), II, 291–299; "The New York Seventh Regiment Armory," *National Guardsman,* October 1, 1877, p. 43.
4. Boston *Press,* November 1, 1880, Seventh Regiment Archives, New-York Historical Society, New York; Clarence C. Buel, "The New York Seventh," *Scribner's Monthly,* May 1880, pp. 79–80; New York *Times,* April 10, 1880.
5. Louis Cantor, "The Creation of the Modern National Guard: The Dick Militia Act of 1903" (Ph.D. diss., Duke University, 1963), p. 9. See also Arthur A. Ekirch, Jr., *The Civilian and the Military: A History of the American Anti-militarist Tradition* (Colorado Springs, 1972), chaps. 1–2.
6. John Glendower Westover, "The Evolution of the Missouri Militia 1804–1919" (Ph.D, diss., University of Missouri, 1948), p. 82. See also Ekirch, *The Civilian and the Military,* p. 29; Cantor, "The Modern National Guard," pp. 3–5, 16–17; Marcus Cunliffe, *Soldiers and Civilians: Martial Spirit in America, 1775–1865* (Boston, 1968), pp. 186–212; Stewart Lewis Gates, "Disorder and Social Organization: The Militia in Connecticut Public Life, 1660–1860" (Ph.D. diss., University of Connecticut, 1975), pp. 137–157.
7. Cunliffe, *Soldiers and Civilians,* pp. 215–223; Gates, "The Militia in Connecticut Public Life," pp. 157–167; John K. Mahon, *History of the Militia and the National Guard* (New York, 1983), pp. 83–84.
8. Cunliffe, *Soldiers and Civilians,* pp. 218–230; Gates, "The Militia in Con-

necticut Public Life," pp. 167–169; Westover, "The Evolution of the Missouri Militia," pp. 104–105; Matthew Hall Smith, *Sunshine and Shadow in New York* (Hartford, 1869), pp. 557–558.

9. Frederick P. Todd, "Our National Guard: An Introduction to Its History," *Military Affairs*, Summer 1941, p. 84; Jim Dan Hill, *The Minute Man in Peace and War: A History of the National Guard* (Harrisburg, 1964), pp. 14–15, 24–25, 53–65; Mahon, *History of the Militia*, pp. 67, 86–87, 90–91, 98–99.

10. Cunliffe, *Soldiers and Civilians*, pp. 230–235, 250–252; Gates, "The Militia in Connecticut Public Life," pp. 169–180.

11. *Proceedings of the Military Association of the State of New York: 1867*, p. 48. See also Thomas S. Lanard, *One Hundred Years with the State Fencibles* (Philadelphia, 1913), pp. 78–80; Clark, *History of the Seventh Regiment*, I, 293–294, 313, 361, 374, 383, 388; Theodore G. Gronert, "The First National Pastime in the Middle West," *Indiana Magazine of History*, September 1933, p. 178.

12. *Proceedings of the Military Association of the State of New York: 1855*, p. 18. See also Robert Reinders, "Militia and Public Order in Nineteenth-Century America," *Journal of American Studies*, April 1977, pp. 87–91; Clark, *History of the Seventh Regiment*, I, 215, 221, 243, 254, 276, 344, 413, II, 111–112; John Charles Schneider, "Mob Violence and Public Order in the American City, 1830–1865" (Ph.D. diss. University of Minnesota, 1971), pp. 100–101, 111, 114–115, 166, 174–175.

13. Joseph Jackson, *Encyclopedia of Philadelphia* (Harrisburg, 1931), I, 133–139; Clark, *History of the Seventh Regiment*, I, 93, 95–96, 117–118, 212, 262–263, 308–310; William Hyde and Howard L. Conrad, eds., *Encyclopedia of the History of St. Louis* (New York, 1889), I, 38; Charles Winslow Hall, ed., *Regiments and Armories of Massachusetts* (Boston, 1900), II, 180; Jos. Lapsley Wilson, ed., *Book of the First Troop Philadelphia City Cavalry 1774–1914* (Philadelphia, 1915), pp. 249–251.

14. Clark, *History of the Seventh Regiment*, I, 259, 296–297, 299–300. See also "State Armories," *Massachusetts House Documents* (1853), no. 68, pp. 3–4, 6–8.

15. "State Armories," p. 4; Fred L. Israel, "New York's Citizen Soldiers: The Militia and Their Armories," *New York History*, April 1961, pp. 147–148; Clark, *History of the Seventh Regiment*, I, 258–259, 262, 266, 296–297, 310, 364–365, 391–392, 394–395, 403, 457, 460, 465.

16. Brooklyn *Eagle*, July 6, 1858, July 15, 1864; *A Short History and Photographic Record of the Second Regiment Field Artillery Pennsylvania National Guard* (Philadelphia, 1918); Wilson, ed., *Book of the First Troop*, pp. 251–252; George W. Wingate, *History of the Twenty-second Regiment of the National Guard of the State of New York from Its Organization to 1895* (New York, 1896), pp. 140–141.

17. New York *Atlas*, May 1, 1859, Seventh Regiment Archives; Hall, ed., *Regiments and Armories of Massachusetts*, I, 408, II, 180; Hyde and Conrad, eds., *History of St. Louis*, I, 38.

18. New York *Atlas*, May 1, 1859; Brooklyn *Eagle*, July 15, 1864; Henry R. Stiles, *The Civil, Political, Professional and Ecclesiastical History and Com-*

mercial and Industrial Record of the County of Kings and the City of Brooklyn from 1683 to 1884 (New York, 1884), I, 1195, 1201; New York Times, April 12, 1860; Thomas F. De Voe, The Market Book (New York 1862), I, 556–557.

19. Undated New York World article, Seventh Regiment Archives; Philadelphia Evening Bulletin, July 6, 1874.

1. Fears of Class Warfare

1. Annual Report of the Inspector-General of the State of New York: 1865, pp. 19–23.

2. Boston City Council, Reports of Proceedings, October 9, 1873, pp. 410–411, October 20, 1873, pp. 433–434. See also Annual Report of the Inspector-General of the State of New York: 1866, p. 20; Report of the Adjutant-General of the State of Connecticut: 1873, p. 11.

3. New York Times, July 8, 1871; Boston City Council, Reports of Proceedings, October 20, 1873, pp. 433–434; Annual Report of the Inspector-General of the State of New York: 1865, p. 21, 1866, pp. 118–119.

4. Samuel Bernstein, "The Impact of the Paris Commune in the United States," Massachusetts Review, Summer 1971, pp. 435–439; Proceedings of the Military Association of the State of New York: 1867, pp. 46–47; Report of the Maryland Adjutant-General: 1873, pp. 9–10; Cincinnati Enquirer, August 22, 1869.

5. Henry W. B. Howard, The Eagle and Brooklyn . . . Together with the History of the City of Brooklyn from Its Settlement to the Present Time (Brooklyn, 1893), II, 829; Brooklyn Eagle, July 24, 1874; Jos. Lapsley Wilson, ed., Book of the First Troop Philadelphia City Cavalry 1774–1914 (Philadelphia, 1915), pp. 252–253; Geo. A. Meekins, Fifth Regiment Infantry, Md. Nat. Guard, U.S. Volunteers (Baltimore, 1899), pp. 48–49.

6. Brooklyn Eagle, July 24, 1874. See also ibid., October 29, 1872; Baltimore Sun, February 7, 1873.

7. Boston City Council, Reports of Proceedings, October 9, 1873, pp. 410–411, October 20, 1873, pp. 433–434; James A. Latta, History of the First Regiment Infantry National Guard of Pennsylvania (Gray Reserves) 1861–1911 (Philadelphia, 1912), p. 270; A. T. Andreas, History of Milwaukee (Chicago, 1881), pp. 776–777; Emmons Clark, History of the Seventh Regiment of New York, 1806–1889 (New York, 1890), II, 160, 171, 212, 226, 233, 236.

8. Proceedings of the Third Annual Convention of Officers of the Wisconsin National Guard: 1884, p. 12.

9. William H. Riker, Soldiers of the State: The Role of the National Guard in American Democracy (Washington, D.C., 1958), p. 44; Joseph John Holmes, "The National Guard of Pennsylvania: Policeman of Industry, 1865–1905" (Ph.D. diss., University of Connecticut, 1971), pp. 51–54; Robert Reinders, "Militia and Public Order in Nineteenth-Century America," Journal of American Studies, April 1977, p. 91; Martin K. Gordon, "The Milwaukee Infantry Militia 1865–1892," Historical Messenger of the Milwaukee County Historical Society, March 1968, pp. 6–9; John Glendower Westover, "The Evolution of

the Missouri Militia, 1804–1919" (Ph.D. diss., University of Missouri, 1948), p. 180; George W. Wingate, *History of the Twenty-second Regiment of the National Guard of the State of New York from Its Organization to 1895* (New York, 1896), pp. 349–350.

10. New York *Times,* September 16, 1875. See also Clifton K. Yearley, *The Money Machines: The Breakdown and Reform of Governmental and Party Finance in the North, 1860–1920* (Albany, 1972), chaps. 1–2.

11. David Montgomery, *Beyond Equality: Labor and the Radical Republicans* (New York, 1967), pp. 228–229, 339–340; James Ford Rhodes, *History of the United States from Hayes to McKinley, 1877–1896* (New York, 1919), p. 46; Bernstein, "Impact of the Paris Commune," pp. 435–439.

12. Brooklyn *Eagle,* July 6, 1858.

13. Robert V. Bruce, *1877: Year of Violence* (Indianapolis, 1959), chaps. 2–10; Samuel Yellen, *American Labor Struggles, 1877–1934* (New York, 1974), chap. 1; Marianne Debouzy, "Workers' Self-Organization and Resistance in the 1877 Strikes," in Dirk Hoerder, ed., *American Labor and Immigration History, 1877–1920: Recent European Research* (Urbana, 1983), pp. 71–72.

14. Harry James Brown and Frederick D. Williams, eds., *The Diary of James A. Garfield: Volume III 1875–1877* (East Lansing, 1973), p. 498. See also Bruce, *1877,* chaps. 5–10; Yellen, *American Labor Struggles,* chap. 1.

15. Rhodes, *History of the United States,* p. 46; *Nation,* August 2, 1877, p. 68; New York *Times,* July 26, 1877; Thomas A. Scott, "The Recent Strikes," *North American Review,* September 1877, p. 357.

16. Bruce, *1877,* pp. 311, 314, 315; Frederick Cople Jaher, *Doubters and Dissenters: Cataclysmic Thought in America, 1885–1919* (Glencoe, Ill., 1964), p. 36; Henry David, *History of the Haymarket Affair* (New York, 1963), pp. 185, 436; *Public Opinion,* May 15, 1886, p. 83.

17. Yellen, *American Labor Struggles,* chap. 3. See also Leon Wolff, *Lockout: The Story of the Homestead Strike of 1892* (New York, 1965).

18. Jaher, *Doubters and Dissenters,* p. 42; Yellen, *American Labor Struggles,* chap. 4; Henry F. May, *Protestant Churches and Industrial America* (New York, 1949), pp. 107–109.

19. *Harper's Weekly,* May 22, 1886, p. 322; Fitz John Porter, "How to Quell Mobs," *North American Review,* October 1885, p. 351; Josiah Strong, *Our Country* (New York, 1885), p. 183; Francis Parkman, "The Failure of Universal Suffrage," *North American Review,* July-August 1878, p. 4; Jaher, *Doubters and Dissenters,* p. 43.

20. Bernstein, "Impact of the Paris Commune," pp. 438–439; Charles Loring Brace, *The Dangerous Classes of New York, and Twenty Years Work among Them* (New York, 1880), p. 29; Bruce, *1877,* p. 26; Neil Harris, ed., *The Land of Contrasts* (New York, 1970), p. 17.

21. Bruce, *1877,* p. 310; *Report of the Committee [of the Pennsylvania Senate and House of Representatives] Appointed to Investigate the Railroad Riots of July, 1877* (Harrisburg, 1878), p. 798; Paul Boyer, *Urban Masses and Moral Order in America, 1820–1920* (Cambridge, 1978), pp. 130–131; Norman Pollack, *The Populist Response to Industrial America* (Cambridge, 1962), p. 77; *Public Opinion,* November 14, 1891, p. 130; Jaher, *Doubters and Dissenters,* p. 42.

22. Jaher, *Doubters and Dissenters*, pp. 21–22, 108–122; Bruce, *1877*, p. 319; Boyer, *Urban Masses and Moral Order*, p. 131.

23. James Morris, "No Haymarket for Cincinnati," *Ohio History*, Winter 1974, p. 26. See also Selig Perlman, "Upheaval and Reorganization," pt. 6 of John R. Commons et al., *History of Labour in the United States* (New York, 1946), II, 294–295; Henry B. Leonard, "Ethnic Cleavage and Industrial Conflict in Late Nineteenth Century America: The Cleveland Rolling Mill Company Strikes of 1882 and 1885," *Labor History*, Fall 1979, p. 538; Richard T. Ely, *The Labor Movement in the United States* (New York, 1886), pp. 254–257.

24. Samuel C. Logan, *A City's Danger and Defense* (Scranton, 1887), p. 79; Jaher, *Doubters and Dissenters*, p. 58; *Proceedings of the Third Annual Convention of Officers of the Wisconsin National Guard: 1884*, p. 11; Albert Ordway, ed., *The National Guard in Service* (Washington, D.C., 1891), p. 311.

25. Chicago *Tribune*, May 18, 1878; David, *Haymarket Affair*, pp. 135–136; Ely, *Labor Movement*, p. 289.

26. T. J. Jackson Lears, *No Place of Grace: Antimodernism and the Transformation of American Culture, 1880–1920* (New York, 1981), p. 31; Thomas Lee Philpott, *The Slum and the Ghetto: Neighborhood Deterioration and Middle-Class Reform, Chicago, 1880–1930* (New York, 1978), pp. 44–45; David, *Haymarket Affair*, p. 137; House Select Committee on Existing Labor Troubles in Pennsylvania, *Labor Troubles in the Anthracite Region of Pennsylvania, 1887–1888*, 50th Cong., 2d sess., H. Rept. 4147, viii–ix.

27. John G. Sproat, *"The Best Men": Liberal Reformers in the Gilded Age* (New York, 1968), pp. 225–226; Lears, *No Place of Grace*, pp. 30–31.

28. *Harper's Weekly*, August 11, 1877, p. 618; George B. McClellan, "The Militia and the Army," *Harper's New Monthly Magazine*, January 1886, p. 299. See also Boyer, *Urban Masses and Moral Order*, chaps. 8–12.

29. *Public Opinion*, August 27, 1892, p. 491. See also May, *Protestant Churches and Industrial America*, pp. 92–93; David, *Haymarket Affair*, pp. 183, 185, 187.

30. New York *Herald*, January 21, 1895.

31. *Public Opinion*, May 15, 1886, p. 85; Lears, *No Place of Grace*, p. 29; Ordway, ed., *National Guard in Service*, p. 307; Boyer, *Urban Masses and Moral Order*, p. 128; *National Guardsman*, June 1, 1878; Portland *Oregonian*, August 7, 1887.

32. Bruce, *1877*, pp. 226, 232; Leonard, "Ethnic Cleavage and Industrial Conflict," p. 539; David, *Haymarket Affair*, p. 185; Wallace A. Davies, *Patriotism on Parade: The Story of Veterans' and Hereditary Organizations in America, 1783–1900* (Cambridge, 1955), p. 291.

33. May, *Protestant Churches and Industrial America*, p. 92; *Harper's Weekly*, August 11, 1877, p. 618. See also *Annual Report of the Adjutant-General of the State of New York: 1877*, p. 418.

34. Pauline Maier, "Popular Uprisings and Civil Authority in Eighteenth-Century America," *William and Mary Quarterly*, January 1970, pp. 5–7, 15, 24–26; John Charles Schneider, "Mob Violence and Public Order in the American City, 1830–1865" (Ph.D. diss., University of Minnesota, 1971), pp. 10, 105, 166, 174–175.

35. Maier, "Popular Uprisings and Civil Authority," pp. 33–35; Schneider, "Mob

Violence and Public Order," pp. 104, 176–178; New York *Times*, November 18, 1879; *Biennial Report of the Adjutant General of Illinois: 1891–1892*, p. 11.

36. Cincinnati *Enquirer*, April 5, 1884. See also Charles Theodore Greve, *Centennial History of Cincinnati and Representative Citizens* (Chicago, 1904), I, 998–1004; New York *Times*, March 30, 1884.

37. Frederick Howard Wines, *Report on the Defective, Dependent, and Delinquent Classes of the Population of the United States, as Returned at the Tenth Census (June 1, 1980)* (Washington, D.C., 1888), p. 556.

38. *Report of the Committee Appointed to Investigate the Railroad Riots*, p. 16; U.S. Strike Commission, *Report on the Chicago Strike of June–July, 1894*, 53d Cong., 2d sess., S. Exec. Doc. 7, xliv; New York *Times*, February 24, 1895; *The Knapsack: A Daily Journal of the Seventh Regiment New Armory Fair*, December 4, 1879, p. 1.

39. Reinders, "Militia and Public Order," p. 93; Scott, "The Recent Strikes," pp. 360–361; Riker, *Soldiers of the State*, p. 48–49; *Congressional Record*, May 21, 1878, pp. 3635–37, 3645–46; Henry Ward Beecher, *Patriotic Addresses* (New York, 1891), p. 821; *Nation*, August 9, 1877, p. 86.

40. Bruce, *1877*, p. 88; Providence *Journal*, August 13, 1877; *Congressional Record*, May 18, 1878, pp. 3538–39, May 20, 1878, pp. 3579–86; Reinders, "Militia and Public Order," p. 93.

41. Providence *Journal*, August 13, 1877; *Knapsack*, December 4, 1879, p. 1; *Annual Report of the Adjutant-General of the State of New York: 1874*, pp. 8–9; New York *Herald*, October 14, 1877; *Congressional Record*, May 20, 1878, p. 3584.

42. Thomas F. Edmands to A. H. Berry, July 22, 1882, First Corps of Cadets Archives, Special Collections, Mugar Library, Boston University; Portland *Oregonian*, August 7, 1887; *Souvenir Album and Sketch Book [of Chicago's First Regiment]* (Chicago, ca. 1890), p. 138; *The One Hundred and Fiftieth Anniversary of the Foundation of the First Corps of Cadets, Massachusetts Volunteer Militia, October 19, 1891* (Boston, 1892), p. 31; Latta, *History of the First Regiment Infantry*, p. 773.

43. New York *Times*, July 26, 1877; Reinders, "Militia and Public Order," p. 93; *Congressional Record*, May 21, 1878, p. 3645; *Nation*, August 9, 1877, p. 85.

44. Fred L. Israel, "New York's Citizen Soldiers: The Militia and Their Armories," *New York History*, April 1961, p. 151; Reinders, "Militia and Public Order," p. 93; *Annual Report of the Adjutant-General of the State of New York: 1877*, pp. 44, 630–633; *Nation*, August 9, 1877, p. 85; Bruce, *1877*, chap. 6.

45. New York *Times*, July 26, 1877; *Report of the Committee Appointed to Investigate the Railroad Riots*, pp. 8–10, 18, 27, 28, 34, 35, 117, 266, 385; *Report of the Adjutant General of Pennsylvania: 1877*, p. 89.

46. *Congressional Record*, May 18, 1878, pp. 3538–39. See also New York *Mail*, November 2, 1878, Seventh Regiment Archives, New-York Historical Society, New York; Providence *Journal*, August 13, 1877; New York *Times*, July 26, 1877.

47. Hyman Kuritz, "The Pennsylvania State Government and Labor Controls from 1865 to 1922" (Ph.D. diss., Columbia University, 1954), chap. 7. See also Frederick P. Todd, "Our National Guard: An Introduction to Its History,"

Military Affairs, Fall 1941, p. 158; *Annual Report of the Adjutant General of the Commonwealth of Massachusetts: 1879,* p. 10; Westover, "The Evolution of the Missouri Militia," pp. 191–193; W. C. Colbron, *The Wisconsin National Guard* (Milwaukee, 1894), pp. 31–32.

48. E. L. Molineux, *Riots and Their Suppression* (Boston, 1884), pp. 17, 26; Ordway, ed., *National Guard in Service,* p. 316; *National Guardsman,* July 1, 1878, pp. 202–203; *Proceedings of the Third Annual Convention of Officers of the Wisconsin National Guard: 1884,* pp. 1–13; *Army and Navy Journal,* May 2, 1889, Seventh Regiment Archives; Boston *Herald,* October 14, 1890, Boston *Globe,* October 16, 1890, State Armory Commission Archives, National Guard Supply Depot, Natick, Massachusetts; *Weekly People,* August 17, 1901.

49. Alexander Marshall, "The Necessity for Armories" (No. III), *Bostonian,* May 1895, p. 141. See also *Public Opinion,* July 12, 1894, p. 333; *Annual Report of the Adjutant General of Pennsylvania: 1885,* pp. 141–142; *Proceedings of the Twelfth Annual Convention of Officers of the Wisconsin National Guard: 1893,* p. 89; Ordway, ed., *National Guard in Service,* p. 300; Latta, *History of the First Regiment Infantry,* p. 372.

50. New York *Times,* April 4, 1884; *Nation,* May 13, 1886, p. 391; *Annual Report of the Adjutant-General of the State of New York: 1884,* p. 11; Marshall, "Necessity for Armories," p. 141.

51. Holmes, "National Guard of Pennsylvania;" Winthrop Alexander, "Ten Years of Riot Duty," *Journal of the Military Service Institution of the United States,* July 1896, pp. 1–26; George G. Suggs, *Colorado's War on Militant Unionism: James H. Peabody and the Western Federation of Miners* (Detroit, 1972); Ordway, ed., *National Guard in Service,* p. 300; Wolff, *Lockout,* pp. 228–229; Reinders, "Militia and Public Order," pp. 97–98.

52. Riker, *Soldiers of the State,* pp. 50–51; *The People,* April 5, July 19, 1891; Brooklyn *Eagle,* July 9, 14, 1891; Boston First Corps of Cadets, *Cadet Armory* (ca. 1881), p. 9; Holmes, "National Guard of Pennsylvania," pp. 226, 227, 246; Reinders, "Militia and Public Order," pp. 96–97.

53. *Report of Proceedings of the Twelfth Annual Convention of the American Federation of Labor: 1892,* pp. 12, 32, *Sixteenth Annual Convention: 1896,* pp. 75–76; Detroit *News,* May 1, 1898; New York *Times,* February 4, 1893; *Proceedings of the General Assembly of the Knights of Labor, Seventeenth Regular Session: 1893,* p. 85; Brooklyn *Eagle,* September 24, 1894; *Proceedings of the Fourteenth Annual Convention of Officers of the Wisconsin National Guard: 1895,* p. 15.

54. Pollack, *Populist Response to Industrial America,* pp. 41–42; *The People,* April 5, July 19, 1891; *Social Democratic Herald,* November 30, December 7, 14, 21, 1901; Select Committee on Existing Labor Troubles in Pennsylvania, *Labor Troubles in the Anthracite Region of Pennsylvania,* pp. ix-x.

55. *Annual Report of the Adjutant-General of the State of New York: 1888,* p. 11 (my italics). See also State ex rel. Long v. Brinkman et al., 7 Ohio Cir. Ct. R. 165.

56. Brooklyn *Eagle,* July 14, 1891; New York *Tribune,* January 24, 1887; Thomas F. Edmands to George R. Rogers, December 8, 1890, First Corps of Cadets Archives.

57. Brooklyn *Eagle,* October 12, 1883; *Twelfth Annual Convention of the National*

Guard Association of the State of New York: 1890, p. 23; Annual Reports of the Adjutant General . . . of the State of Rhode Island: 1891, p. 99.

58. Report of the Joint Special Committee of the [Massachusetts] General Court of 1887 on Armories for the Use of the Militia, H. Doc. 392, 3.

59. Ibid. See also Thomas F. Edmands to G. H. Gordon, April 8, 1884, First Corps of Cadets Archives.

60. Annual Report of the Adjutant-General of the State of New York: 1888, p. 12; Edward K. Spann, The New Metropolis: New York City, 1840–1857 (New York, 1981), p. 232; Twelfth Annual Convention of the National Guard Association of the State of New York: 1890, p. 23.

2. The Building of the Armories

1. Emmons Clark, History of the Seventh Regiment of New York, 1806–1889 (New York, 1890), II, 160, 224–225; Emmons Clark to William Seward, Jr., December 15, 1870, Emmons Clark et al., to New York County Board of Supervisors, September 15, 1873, Seventh Regiment Archives, New-York Historical Society, New York; New York Times, February 11, 1873, August 10, 1905.

2. Clark, History of the Seventh Regiment, II, 226; Emmons Clark to W. W. Braman, February 5, 1875, Seventh Regiment Archives; The New Armory of the Seventh Regiment, N.G.S.N.Y. (New York, 1875), pp. 7–11.

3. Clark, History of the Seventh Regiment, II, 229, 233, 236; New York Times, June 4, 1874, September 16, 1875.

4. New York Herald, September 17, 1875, Seventh Regiment Archives; New York Times, January 23, 1876; Clark, History of the Seventh Regiment, II, 238–239.

5. General Committee on New Armory, Seventh Regiment Armory, "To the Citizens and Taxpayers of the City of New York," a circular dated February 16, 1876, New York Public Library. See also Clark, History of the Seventh Regiment, II, 238–239; Clark to Braman, February 5, 1875.

6. New York Herald, January 25, 1876, New York Tribune, February 7, 1876, New York Times, February 29, 1876, Seventh Regiment Archives; Clark, History of the Seventh Regiment, II, 239–240, 253–254.

7. New York Tribune, August 17, 1877, Journal of Commerce, July 30, 1877, Seventh Regiment Archives. See also Robert V. Bruce, 1877: Year of Violence (Indianapolis, 1959), pp. 276–277, 280–281.

8. Clark, History of the Seventh Regiment, II, 261; New York Commercial, August 15, 1877, New York World, August 15, 1877, New York Evening Mail, August 15, 1877, Seventh Regiment Archives.

9. Emmons Clark to Thomas F. Edmands, December 9, 1880, First Corps of Cadets Archives, Special Collection, Mugar Library, Boston University. See also New York Star, November 12, 1878, New York Evening Mail, August 15, 1877, Seventh Regiment Archives; Clark, History of the Seventh Regiment, II, p. 261.

10. New York Sun, November 12, 1878, Seventh Regiment Archives; Clark, History of the Seventh Regiment, II, 268–269, 271–272.

11. Clark, *History of the Seventh Regiment,* II, pp. 274–284.

12. Ibid., 290–301; *The [New York City] Armory Board, 1884–1911* (New York, ca. 1912), p. 6.

13. New York *Times,* November 3, 1877, March 17, 1883; Joseph A. Latta, *History of the First Regiment Infantry National Guard of Pennsylvania (Gray Reserves) 1861–1911* (Philadelphia, 1912), p. 274; *Biennial Report of the Adjutant General of Illinois: 1877–1878,* p. 114; Walter F. Clowes, *The Detroit Light Guard* (Detroit, 1900), p. 465.

14. *Souvenir Album and Sketch Book [of Chicago's First Regiment]* (Chicago, ca. 1890), p. 21; Joseph John Holmes, "The National Guard of Pennsylvania: Policeman of Industry, 1865–1905" (Ph.D. diss., University of Connecticut, 1971), pp. 202, 206; Thomas S. Lanard, *One Hundred Years with the State Fencibles* (Philadelphia, 1913), pp. 297–298; C. Bow Dougherty, *Historical Souvenir of the Ninth Regiment Infantry, N.G.P.* (Wilkes-Barre, 1896); Jesse F. Stevens, "How the Cadet Armory Was Built" (1944), pp. 3–5, First Corps of Cadets Archives.

15. Boston First Corps of Cadets, *Cadet Armory* (Boston, ca. 1881), pp. 5, 26; Thomas F. Edmands to A. H. Berry, July 22, 1882, First Corps of Cadets Archives. See also Holmes, "National Guard of Pennsylvania," pp. 209, 211; Latta, *History of the First Regiment Infantry,* p. 772.

16. Edwin N. Benson, R. Dale Benson, and Theo. E. Wiedersheim, *History of the First Regiment Infantry, National Guard of Pennsylvania* (Philadelphia, 1880), pp. 58–61. See also First Corps of Cadets, *Cadet Armory,* pp. 8–9, 12–19.

17. Latta, *History of the First Regiment Infantry,* pp. 271, 275–276, 662–663; Holmes, "National Guard of Pennsylvania," pp. 205–208; Benson, Benson, and Wiedersheim, *History of the First Regiment Infantry,* pp. 58–59.

18. Stevens, "Cadet Armory," pp. 1–9. See also "Contributions to the Cadet Armory Fund," First Corps of Cadets Archives; Charles M. Green, *Thomas Franklin Edmands, 1840–1906,* First Corps of Cadets Archives; Boston *Transcript,* April 9, 1884, State Armory Commission Archives, National Guard Supply Depot, Natick, Mass.

19. *Souvenir Album and Sketch Book,* pp. 9, 21, 24; A. T. Andreas, *History of Chicago from the Earliest Period to the Present Time* (Chicago, 1886), III, 586; Chicago *Tribune,* July 13, 1890; Thomas Lee Philpott, *The Slum and the Ghetto: Neighborhood Deterioration and Middle-Class Reform, Chicago, 1880–1930* (New York, 1978), pp. 44–45, 59–60.

20. Clowes, *Detroit Light Guard,* pp. 463–488. See also Detroit *Free Press,* October 19, 1897; Paul Leake, *History of Detroit: Chronicle of Its Progress, Its Industries, Its Institutions, and the People of the Fair City of the Straits* (Chicago, 1912), II, 570–573.

21. Holmes, "National Guard of Pennsylvania," p. 208.

22. Ibid., pp. 211–214. See also Samuel C. Logan, *A City's Danger and Defense* (Scranton, 1887), pp. 197–201, 218–237.

23. Holmes, "National Guard of Pennsylvania," pp. 194–200; Latta, *History of the First Regiment Infantry,* pp. 438–441; Geo. A. Meekins, *Fifth Regiment Infantry, Md. Nat. Guard, U.S. Volunteers* (Baltimore, 1899), pp. 166, 169; William J. Watt and James R. H. Spears, eds., *Indiana's Citizen Soldiers: The*

Militia and National Guard in Indiana History (Indianapolis, 1980), pp. 84–85; John Glendower Westover, "The Evolution of the Missouri Militia, 1804–1919" (Ph.D. diss., University of Missouri, 1948), p. 248.

24. St. Louis *Post-Dispatch,* May 9, 1882; Westover, "The Evolution of the Missouri Militia," p. 248; Andreas, *History of Chicago,* III, 588; Cleveland *Plain Dealer,* May 31, 1893; Holmes, "National Guard of Pennsylvania," pp. 203–204, 210–211, 214–216; Jos. Lapsley Wilson, ed., *Book of the First Troop Philadelphia City Cavalry, 1774–1914* (Philadelphia, 1915), pp. 255–257.

25. George W. Wingate, *History of the Twenty-second Regiment of the National Guard of the State of New York from Its Organization to 1895* (New York, 1896), pp. 485–488.

26. Baltimore *Sun,* December 21, 1897; John F. Jones to Mayor of the City of New York et al., April 14, 1884, New York City Sinking Fund Commission Archives, Municipal Archives and Record Center, New York. See also Buffalo *Commercial,* February 1, 1900; *Proceedings of the Commissioners of the Sinking Fund of the City of New York,* December 18, 1883, pp. 2197–2201, September 4, 1884, pp. 2382–83.

27. Baltimore *Sun,* December 21, 1897; *Fifth Annual Convention of the National Guard Association of the State of New York: 1883,* p. 11.

28. *Annual Reports of the Adjutant General . . . of the State of Rhode Island: 1888,* pp. 62–63; *Annual Report of the Adjutant General of Pennsylvania: 1886,* p. 98; *Report of the Adjutant General of Maryland: 1891,* p. 10; unidentified Baltimore newspaper, May 11, 1901, Stewart Scrapbooks, Maryland Historical Society, Baltimore.

29. *Report of the Joint Special Committee of the [Massachusetts] General Court of 1887 on Armories for the Use of the Militia,* H. Doc. 392, 2; Wingate, *History of the Twenty-second Regiment,* pp. 486–488; Buffalo *News,* January 28, 1900; Buffalo *Commercial,* February 1, 1900.

30. *Report of the Joint Special Committee on Armories,* pp. 3–4; Boston City Council, *Reports of Proceedings,* April 25, 1887, pp. 403–404.

31. James C. Malin, *Confounded Rot about Napoleon* (Lawrence, Kans., 1961), pp. 5–10; Wallace Evans Davies, *Patriotism on Parade: The Story of Veterans' and Hereditary Organizations in America, 1783–1900* (Cambridge, 1955), pp. 216–230, 248, 339–342; T. J. Jackson Lears, *No State of Grace: Antimodernism and the Transformation of American Culture, 1880–1920* (New York, 1981), pp. 105–117.

32. Fred L. Israel, "New York's Citizen Soldiers: The Militia and Their Armories," *New York History,* April 1961, p. 153; *Armory in District of Columbia,* 62d Cong., 2d sess., S. Rep. 886, pp. 8–10; Brooklyn *Eagle,* February 1, 1895.

33. Wingate, *History of the Twenty-second Regiment,* pp. 486–488; *The Armory Board,* pp. 1–7, 41–46; Robert Koch, "The Medieval Castle Revival: New York Armories," *Journal of the Society of Architectural Historians,* October 1955, pp. 22–29; *Harper's Weekly,* May 22, 1909, p. 25; U.S. Senate Committee on Public Buildings and Grounds, *Hearings [on] Armory in District of Columbia* (Washington, D.C., 1912), pp. 28–32.

34. Charles Winslow Hall, ed., *Regiments and Armories of Massachusetts* (Boston, 1900), I, 221–254; *Report of the Providence Armory Commission to the General Assembly at its January Session, 1907* (Providence, 1907), pp. 3–11;

Report of the [Connecticut] Arsenal and Armory Commission to the General Assembly of 1907, pp. 1–23; New York *Times*, December 24, 1893; *Annual Report of the Adjutant-General of the State of New Jersey: 1904*, pp. 7–8; *Annual Report of the Adjutant General of Pennsylvania: 1904*, pp. 7–8; *The Armory Board of the State of Pennsylvania: Its Work and Expenditures to December 31, 1912* (Harrisburg, 1913), pp. 1–8.

35. *Proceedings of the Twelfth Annual Convention of Officers of the Wisconsin National Guard: 1893*, p. 90; Cincinnati *Enquirer*, February 17, 1889; Eric Johannesen, *Cleveland Architecture, 1876–1976* (Cleveland, 1979), p. 65; Minneapolis *Tribune*, August 6, 1905; Portland *Oregonian*, August 25, 1968; Seattle *Post-Intelligencer*, April 12, 1909; San Francisco *Call*, August 20, 1909; San Francisco *Examiner*, June 5, 1979.

36. *Fifth Annual Convention of the National Guard Association of the State of New York: 1883*, p. 11; Senate Committee on Public Buildings and Grounds, *Armory in District of Columbia*, p. 29; list of armories built by the Massachusetts Armory Commission dated February 12, 1908, State Armory Commission Archives; *Annual Reports of the Adjutant General . . . of the State of Rhode Island: 1895*, pp. 151–152; *Armory Board of the State of Pennsylvania*, pp. 3, 12–13.

37. New York *Daily Tribune*, January 29, 1890.

38. New York *Times*, March 12, 20, 23, 1892.

39. Brooklyn *Eagle*, January 22, March 9, 16, 1892, March 12, 1893.

40. Ibid., January 26, 1890, February 10, 1893.

41. Ibid., July 14, 1891, February 12, 1893.

42. Ibid., March 12, 1898.

43. *Proceedings of the General Assembly of the Knights of Labor, Seventeenth Regular Session: 1893*, p. 86; Norman Pollack, *The Populist Response to Industrial America* (Cambridge, 1962), pp. 41–42; *The People*, April 5, 1891.

44. B. O. Flower, "Plutocracy's Bastiles: Or Why the Republic is Becoming an Armed Camp," *Arena*, October 1894, pp. 601–621.

45. Joseph Antenucci, Christopher Hugh Ripman, and Kurt Zumwalt, *Armory First Corps of Cadets, 1887–1973* (Boston, 1973), p. 17. Armories were also celebrated in verse. For the dedication of New York's Twelfth Regiment Armory in 1887, Colonel John Ward wrote the following poem:

> Hail fortress [it began],
>   reared in frowning might,
> To guard a noble city's right
>   With soldiers of the State!
> Beneath the Stars and Stripes we stand
> Rejoicing in our honored land,
>   Her heroes render great.

After paying tribute to the Twelfth's heroism in the Civil War, Ward stressed its commitment to public order:

> If riot yet should raise her head,
> And dare New York with banner red;
>   Responsive to their State
> The Guard would meet the bloody scene

Defiantly, and charge between
Communes, like men of Fate.

See *Dedication of the New Armory, Twelfth Reg't. Infantry, N.G.S.N.Y., Tuesday, April 21, 1887*, pp. 18–20.

46. *The People*, April 5, June 21, 1891.

47. Ibid., July 9, 1899.

48. Ibid., December 19, 1897, August 7, 1898; *Weekly People*, April 6, 13, 1901, November 7, 1903. See also Henry F. Bedford, *Socialism and Workers in Massachusetts, 1886–1912* (Amherst, 1966), pp. 75–76.

49. Charles Sidney Clark, "The National Guard of the United States," *United Service Magazine*, June 1908, p. 305; U.S. War Department, Adjutant-General's Office, *The Organized Militia of the United States* (Washington, D.C., 1898), p. 197; *Report of the Chief, Division of Militia Affairs . . . Relative to the Organized Militia of the United States* (Washington, D.C., 1912), p. 18.

50. Watt and Spears, eds., *Indiana's Citizen Soldiers*, p. 101; *Proceedings of the Tenth and Eleventh Annual Conventions of the Interstate National Guard Association of the United States, 1908–1909*, p. 54; W. R. Schwartz and J. T. Milligan, *History of the Fourth Regiment of Infantry Maryland National Guard from Its Organization in 1885 to the Present Day* (Baltimore, 1916), pp. 17, 55, 57; *History of the Eighteenth Regiment Infantry, National Guard of Pennsylvania* (Pittsburgh, 1901), p. 21; Pittsburgh *Dispatch*, June 11, 1911.

51. Senate Committee on Public Buildings and Grounds, *Armory in District of Columbia*, pp. 6–8, 11–13, 20–21.

52. Francis V. Greene, "The New National Guard," *Century Magazine*, February 1892, p. 494; Clark, "National Guard of the United States," p. 307; A. W. A. Pollock, "The 'National Guard': A Hint from the United States," *Nineteenth Century*, November 1909, p. 912.

53. Clark, "National Guard of the United States," pp. 304–307. See also *Annual Report of the Adjutant-General of the State of New York: 1888*, p. 11.

54. Thomas F. Edmands to J. W. Hamilton, March 9, 1883, First Corps of Cadets Archives; Paterson *Morning Call*, May 31, 1894; Portland *Oregonian*, August 7, 1887.

55. "The Seventh Regiment Armory," *Decorator and Furnisher*, May 1885, p. 42; Henry Balch Ingram, "Brooklyn's New Armories," *Harper's Weekly*, July 16, 1892, p. 679; Clark, *History of the Seventh Regiment*, II, 313; Pollock, "The 'National Guard'," pp. 916–917.

56. Julian Ralph, "The First Regiment Armory in Chicago," *Harper's Weekly*, December 3, 1892, p. 1163; Cleveland *Plain Dealer*, May 31, 1893; *Souvenir [of the] Opening of the Armory, Ninth Regiment, N.G.N.Y.* (New York, 1897); Thomas F. Edmands to G. H. Gordon, April 4, 1884, First Corps of Cadets Archives; Clark, *History of the Seventh Regiment*, II, 224; Wingate, *History of the Twenty-second Regiment*, pp. 507–508, 575–576.

57. New York *Herald*, October 14, 1877, Seventh Regiment Archives; Paterson *Morning Call*, May 31, 1894; Latta, *History of the First Regiment Infantry*, p. 773.

58. Chicago *Tribune*, July 13, 1890; Brooklyn *Eagle*, September 21, 1901; Portland *Oregonian*, August 7, 1887.

59. *[Real Estate] Record and Guide*, August 7, 1886, p. 999; Paterson *Morning*

Call, May 31, 1894; *Annual Report of the Adjutant-General of the State of New York: 1874,* pp. 8–9; Clarence C. Buel, "The New York Seventh," *Scribner's Monthly,* May 1880, p. 79.
60. Brooklyn *Eagle,* October 3, 1891.

3. The Location of the Armories

1. New York *Times,* December 29, 1888.
2. *The [New York City] Armory Board, 1884–1911* (New York, ca. 1912), pp. 5–7.
3. Louis Fitzgerald to Hugh J. Grant, February 28, 1889, Mayor Hugh J. Grant Papers, Municipal Archives and Records Center, New York. See also *Report of the Adjutant General of the Commonwealth of Massachusetts: 1880,* p. 17.
4. Buffalo *Express,* April 8, 1900; Baltimore *Sun,* May 13, 1901.
5. New York *Times,* December 29, 1888; Albert Ordway, ed., *The National Guard in Service* (Washington, D.C., 1891), p. 324.
6. New York *Times,* July 8, 1871.
7. Ibid.
8. Ibid.
9. *National Guardsman,* July 1, 1878, p. 202; E. L. Molineux, *Riots in Cities and Their Supression* (Boston, 1884), p. 9.
10. *Proceedings of the Commissioners of the Sinking Fund of the City of New York,* September 4, 1884, p. 2382; New York *Times,* April 4, 1874, September 3, 1886; *Report of the Joint Special Committee of the [Massachusetts] General Court of 1887 on Armories for the Use of the Militia,* H. Doc. 392, 3; Winthrop Alexander, "Ten Years of Riot Duty," *Journal of the Military Service Institution of the United States,* July 1896, p. 43.
11. New York *Times,* April 4, 1874. See also New York *Daily Tribune,* January 24, 1887; Thomas F. Edmands to John Jeffries, May 20, 1888, First Corps of Cadets Archives, Special Collections, Mugar Library, Boston University; Molineux, *Riots in Cities,* p. 18; *Proceedings of the Commissioners of the Sinking Fund,* September 4, 1884, p. 2282.
12. New York *Times,* July 8, 1871.
13. New York *Daily Tribune,* January 24, 1887; Thomas F. Edmands to George R. Rogers, December 8, 1890, First Corps of Cadets Archives.
14. Buffalo *Commercial,* April 2, 1900.
15. *The Armory Board,* pp. 12, 29, 37. See also Boston *Globe,* May 19, 1889; New York City Department of Finance, Bureau of Municipal Investigation and Statistics, *Real Estate Owned by the City of New York under the Jurisdiction of the Armory Board, January 1, 1908* (New York, 1908); "The Finest Armory for Militia in the World," *Harper's Weekly,* May 22, 1909, p. 25.
16. *Investigation of the Departments of the City of New York by a Special Committee of the Senate of the State of New York* (Albany, 1885), I, 269 (hereafter referred to as *Gibbs Committee Investigation).* See also New York *Times,* January 8, 1888; *Report of the [New York State] Tenement House Committee [of 1894]* (Albany, 1895), pp. 272–273.
17. George W. Wingate, *History of the Twenty-second Regiment of the National*

Guard of the State of New York from Its Organization to 1895 (New York, 1896), p. 486. See also *Report of the Tenement House Committee,* pp. 423, 446; Robert H. Bremner, "The Big Flat: History of a New York Tenement House," *American Historical Review,* September 1958, pp. 54, 58; *Gibbs Committee Investigation,* I, 520–535; *[Real Estate] Record and Guide,* February 17, 1883, p. 67, May 3, 1884, p. 466, May 29, 1886, p. 711.

18. New York *Times,* February 22, March 6, 1878.
19. Ibid., February 5, 12, 1878.
20. Ibid., February 19, 24, 1878.
21. Ibid., February 19, 1878.
22. Ibid., February 21, March 5, 1878.
23. Ibid., February 18, 1878.
24. Ibid., February 26, 27, March 5, 1878.
25. Ibid., February 22, March 5, 6, 11, 1878; New York *Daily Tribune,* March 5, 1878.
26. New York *Daily Tribune,* March 5, 1878.
27. New York *Times,* March 6, 13, 1878; New York *Daily Tribune,* March 6, 1878.
28. New York *Times,* March 12, 15, 23, 1878; *Laws of the State of New York Passed at the One Hundred and First Session of the Legislature* (Albany, 1878), p. 459.
29. *The Armory Board,* p. 10; New York *Daily Tribune,* February 20, 1887; New York *Times,* April 23–25, 27–29, May 2, 3, 5, 8, 1909.
30. *The Armory Board,* p. 6; *Gibbs Committee Investigation,* I, 148, 534, 536; New York *Times,* December 1, 5, 1885, January 26–29, April 17, 20, 22, 25, May 12, 1886.
31. *Gibbs Committee Investigation,* I, 527–536.
32. New York *Times,* December 29, 1888.
33. Emmons Clark et al., to New York County Board of Supervisors, September 15, 1873, Seventh Regiment Archives, New-York Historical Society, New York. See also Emmons Clark, *History of the Seventh Regiment of New York, 1806–1889* (New York, 1890), II, 160.
34. *The Knapsack: A Daily Journal of the Seventh Regiment New Armory Fair,* November 27, 1879, p. 2; Clark, *History of the Seventh Regiment,* II, 171, 203; New York *Times,* February 11, 1873.
35. New York *Times,* February 11, 1873, January 23, 1876; Clark, *History of the Seventh Regiment,* II, 212; *National Guardsman,* October 1, 1877, p. 42.
36. New York *Times,* February 11, 1873, September 16, 1875; Clark, *History of the Seventh Regiment,* II, 212.
37. New York *Times,* January 23, 1876; Clark, *History of the Seventh Regiment,* II, 212; *The New Armory of the Seventh Regiment, N.G.S.N.Y.* (New York, 1875), p. 6.
38. New York *Times,* January 23, 1876; Clark, *History of the Seventh Regiment,* II, 224–226.
39. New York *Times,* March 17, 1883; *Proceedings of the Commissioners of the Sinking Fund,* June 8, 1881, pp. 1946–47, December 18, 1883, pp. 2199–2202.
40. *Proceedings of the Commissioners of the Sinking Fund,* September 18, 1884, pp. 2389–90, September 30, 1884, pp. 2400–2401.

41. *The Armory Board*, pp. 5–7, 13–42; *Official Souvenir, Celebration of the Opening of the New Armory, Seventy-first Regiment, N.G.S.N.Y.* (1894), p. 102. See also Robert Koch, "The Medieval Castle Revival: New York Armories," *Journal of the Society of Architectural Historians*, October 1953, pp. 25–28.

42. New York *Times*, March 15, 17, 1889; *Proceedings of the Commissioners of the Sinking Fund*, November 2, 1892, pp. 514–520; *The Armory Board*, p. 15.

43. *Proceedings of the Commissioners of the Sinking Fund*, September 4, 1884, pp. 2382–83. See also the letter from "A member of the 9th regiment" to Mayor Hugh J. Grant, December 1, 1891, Grant Papers.

44. "A member of the 9th regiment" to Hugh J. Grant, December 1, 1891. See also New York *Daily Tribune*, January 24, 1887.

45. New York *Times*, September 6, 1881; New York *Daily Tribune*, January 24, 1887; George A. Hussey and William Todd, *History of the Ninth Regiment . . . 1845–1888* (New York, 1888), pp. 643–644; *Proceedings of the Commissioners of the Sinking Fund*, September 4, 1884, p. 2381, September 18, 1884, pp. 2390–91, October 7, 1885, p. 2697.

46. William Seward, Jr., to Alexander Shaler, November 11, 1884, Mayor Franklin Edson Papers, Municipal Archives and Records Center, New York. See also New York *Daily Tribune*, January 24, 1887; William Seward, Jr., to Alexander Shaler, November 13, 1884, Edson Papers; *Proceedings of the Commissioners of the Sinking Fund*, December 17, 1884, p. 2483.

47. *The Armory Board*, p. 7; New York *Daily Tribune*, January 24, 1887; William Seward, Jr., to Abram S. Hewitt, June 13, 1888, Mayor Abram S. Hewitt Papers, Municipal Archives and Records Center, New York.

48. Minutes of Armory Board Meeting of March 14, 1889, Grant Papers. See also Fitzgerald to Grant, February 28, 1889.

49. New York *Times*, March 15, 1889. See also Richard O'Connor, *Hell's Kitchen* (Philadelphia, 1958), pp. 83–86.

50. Gilbert Osofsky, *Harlem: The Making of a Ghetto* (New York, 1966), chap. 5. See also New York *Times*, May 19, 1985.

51. *The Armory Board*, pp. 11–12; *Proceedings of the Commissioners of the Sinking Fund*, April 23, 1890, pp. 453–454.

52. New York *Daily Tribune*, April 3, 9, 1896; New York *Times*, April 9, 1896.

53. New York *Times*, January 29, 1897; New York *Daily Tribune*, April 9, 1896; *Proceedings of the Commissioners of the Sinking Fund*, May 13, 1897, p. 971.

54. *Proceedings of the Commissioners of the Sinking Fund*, July 2, 1897, pp. 1064–65; *The Armory Board*, p. 15; New York *Daily Tribune*, September 19, 1899.

55. *The Armory Board*, pp. 3, 8.

56. New York *Times*, October 1, 1885, January 27, 28, 1886.

57. Francis V. Greene, "The New National Guard," *Century Magazine*, February 1892, pp. 497–498; *Annual Report of the Adjutant-General of the State of New York: 1884*, p. 436; New York *Times*, December 29, 1888.

58. New York *Times*, July 8, 1871, April 4, 1874, November 2, 1879; *Protest of the Eighth Reg't, N.G.S.N.Y., against the Action of the Board of Aldermen in Assigning Them to the Condemned Building, Corner Ninth Avenue and*

Twenty-seventh Street, a pamphlet that is dated 1877 but was almost certainly published in 1879.

59. Buffalo *Commercial,* February 1, 1900; Meekins, *Fifth Regiment Infantry,* pp. 215–216; Boston First Corps of Cadets, *Cadet Armory* (1887); Buffalo *Express,* March 30, April 8, 1900; *Annual Report of the Adjutant-General of the Commonwealth of Massachusetts: 1880,* p. 17; Seattle *Post-Intelligencer,* December 10, 1903; San Francisco *Call,* September 29, 1909; Hartford *Times,* April 14, 1905, November 12, 1909.

4. The Design of the Armories

1. New York *Times,* April 12, 1860, January 10, 1861; Emmons Clark, *History of the Seventh Regiment of New York, 1806–1889* (New York, 1890), I, 459; undated New York *World* article, Seventh Regiment Archives, New-York Historical Society, New York.

2. George W. Wingate, *History of the Twenty-second Regiment of the National Guard of the State of New York from Its Organization to 1895* (New York, 1896), pp. 140–141; Brooklyn *Eagle,* July 6, 1858; Philadelphia *Public Ledger,* November 16, 17, 1857; Philadelphia *Evening Bulletin,* February 24, 1864; Jos. Lapsley Wilson, ed., *Book of the First Troop Philadelphia City Cavalry, 1774–1914* (Philadelphia, 1915), pp. 251–252.

3. See Willard B. Robinson, *American Forts: Architectural Form and Function* (Urbana, 1977); Quentin Hughes, *Military Architecture* (New York, 1974).

4. Brooklyn *Eagle,* October 29, 1872, September 30, 1873, July 24, 1874; New York *Times,* July 24, 1874; Baltimore *Sun,* February 7, 1873; Geo. A. Meekins, *Fifth Regiment Infantry, Md. Nat. Guard, U.S. Volunteers* (Baltimore, 1899), pp. 48–49.

5. Philadelphia *Evening Bulletin,* July 6, 1874; Wilson, ed., *Book of the First Troop,* pp. 253–254; James C. Massey, "Frank Furness in the 1870s: Some Lesser Known Buildings," *Charette,* January 1963, pp. 13–16; James F. O'Gorman, *The Architecture of Frank Furness* (Philadelphia, 1973), pp. 18, 41, 94, 95.

6. John Maass, *The Gingerbread Age: A View of Victorian America* (New York, 1957), pp. 41–44; *Gleason's Pictorial Drawing-Room Companion,* June 24, 1854, p. 389, September 2, 1854, p. 133; *Harper's Weekly,* June 1, 1861, p. 348; Buffalo *Express,* May 2, 1909; Massey, "Frank Furness in the 1870s," p. 15; Montgomery Schuyler, "A Critique (with Illustrations) of Adler & Sullivan, D. H. Burnham & Co. [and] Henry Ives Cobb," *Architectural Record,* February 1896, p. 64.

7. Undated drawings of the proposed new Seventh Regiment Armory, Seventh Regiment Archives; Clark, *History of the Seventh Regiment,* II, 209; *The New Armory of the Seventh Regiment, N.G.S.N.Y.* (New York, 1875), pp. 14–15 and illustrations following p. 15.

8. Clark, *History of the Seventh Regiment,* II, 291–293; New York *Evening Express,* August 8, 1877, Seventh Regiment Archives; New York *Times,* January 23, 1876, April 10, 1880; *New Armory of the Seventh Regiment,* p. 14.

9. Boston *Press,* November 1, 1880, Seventh Regiment Archives; New York

Times, April 10, 1880; *The [New York City] Armory Board, 1884–1911* (New York, ca. 1912), p. 6.

10. Robert Koch, "The Medieval Castle Revival: New York Armories," *Journal of the Society of Architectural Historians,* October 1955, pp. 25–26; Moses King, *King's Handbook of New York* (New York, 1892), pp. 494–495; *[Real Estate] Record and Guide,* August 7, 1886, p. 999, March 26, 1887, p. 396.

11. New York *Times,* December 2, 1889. See also *American Architect and Building News,* April 11, 1891, pp. 29–30.

12. King, *King's Handbook,* p. 497; Wingate, *History of the Twenty-second Regiment,* pp. 490–492; *Official Souvenir, Celebration of the Opening of the New Armory, Seventy-first Regiment, N.G.S.N.Y.* (1894), pp. 103–105; New York *Times,* December 18, 1892.

13. New York *Daily Tribune,* February 28, 1894, April 18, 1896; New York *Sun,* October 7, 1894; New York *World,* February 28, 1894; New York *Herald,* February 28, 1894, files of Marjorie Johnson of Staten Island, N.Y., the widow of E. A. Sargent's grandson.

14. New York *Times,* November 19, 1893; Brooklyn *Eagle,* November 14, 1891, December 2, 1894; Henry Balch Ingram, "Brooklyn's New Armories," *Harper's Weekly,* July 16, 1892, p. 679.

15. New York *Times,* March 30, 1890, January 25, February 27, 1891, November 19, 1893, April 23, 1894; "Brooklyn's Great Armory," *Harper's Weekly,* April 28, 1894, p. 404; James de Mandeville, comp., *History of the Thirteenth Regiment, N.G.S.N.Y.,* p. 180.

16. Wesley Haynes, "Isaac G. Perry: Architect, Builder and Craftsman" (Master's thesis, Columbia University, 1983), pp. 84–87, 130–135; *Report of the Adjutant-General of the State of New Jersey: 1906,* pp. 115–119; New York *Times,* July 4, 1897.

17. Philadelphia *Public Ledger,* April 19, 1882; Edwin N. Benson, R. Dale Benson, and Theo. E. Wiedersheim, *History of the First Regiment Infantry, National Guard of Pennsylvania* (Philadelphia, 1880), p. 60.

18. Charles Winslow Hall, ed., *Regiments and Armories of Massachusetts* (Boston, 1900), I, 226–251; Boston *Globe,* November 18, 1888, May 19, 1889; *Annual Reports of the Adjutant General . . . of the State of Rhode Island: 1895,* pp. 172–174; William H. Jordy and Christopher P. Monkhouse, *Buildings on Paper: Rhode Island Architectural Drawings, 1825–1945* (Providence, 1982), pp. 237–238.

19. Joseph Antenucci, Christopher Hugh Ripman, and Kurt Zumwalt, *Armory First Corps of Cadets, 1887–1973* (Boston, 1973), pp. 6–11, 18–36; Thomas F. Edmands to J. W. Hamilton, March 9, 1889, First Corps of Cadets Archives, Special Collections, Mugar Library, Boston University.

20. Eric Johannesen, *Cleveland Architecture, 1876–1976* (Cleveland, 1979), pp. 64–65; Cleveland *Plain Dealer,* May 31, 1893; Walter F. Clowes, *The Detroit Light Guard* (Detroit, 1900), p. 471.

21. Julian Ralph, "The First Regiment Armory in Chicago," *Harper's Weekly,* December 3, 1892, p. 1163; *Souvenir Album and Sketch Book [of Chicago's First Regiment]* (Chicago, ca. 1890), p. 17. See also Thomas S. Hines, *Burnham of Chicago: Architect and Planner* (New York, 1974) and Donald Hoffmann, *The Architecture of John Wellborn Root* (Baltimore, 1973).

22. Providence *Journal,* November 5, 1905. See also *American Architect and Building News,* January 14, 1893.

23. "Architectural Aberrations," *Architectural Record,* August 1911, p. 181.

24. *Architecture and Building,* April 7, 14, 21, 28, 1894; *American Architect and Building News,* May 19, 1894, December 11, 1897; Providence Armory Commission, *Conditions of Competition of Designs for the Proposed Armory* (Providence, 1897), p. 7.

25. William A. Coles, ed., *Architecture and Society: Selected Essays of Henry Van Brunt* (Cambridge, 1969), p. 165.

26. Chicago *Times,* July 13, 1890.

27. General Committee on New Armory, Seventh Regiment Armory, "To the Citizens and Taxpayers of the City of New York," a circular dated February 16, 1876, New York Public Library.

28. Henry-Russell Hitchcock and William Seale, *Temples of Democracy: The State Capitols of the U.S.A.* (New York, 1976), p. 161; Edward A. Freeman, "Choice in Architectural Styles," *Architectural Record,* April-June 1892, p. 391.

29. *American Architect and Building News,* October 26, 1878, p. 139; Leopold Eidlitz, *The Nature and Function of Art* (New York, 1881), pp. 39, 54; Talbot Hamlin, *Greek Revival Architecture in America* (New York, 1964), p. 249.

30. Robert de Zurko, *Origins of Functionalist Theory* (New York, 1957), pp. 127, 199–230; William H. Jordy and Ralph Coe, eds., *American Architecture and Other Writings by Montgomery Schuyler* (Cambridge, 1961), I, 160; Harold A. Small, ed., *Form and Function: Remarks on Art by Horatio Greenough* (Berkeley, 1947), pp. 51–68; Roger B. Stein, *John Ruskin and Aesthetic Thought in America, 1840–1900* (Cambridge, 1967), pp. 13–14.

31. A. F. Oakley, "Architect and Client," *American Architect and Building News,* August 26, 1876, p. 277; Emlen T. Littell, "The Church Architecture that We Need," ibid., January 12, 1878, p. 10; J. A. F., "Modern Church Building," ibid., February 15, 1879, p. 51; Barr Ferree, "Utility in Architecture," *Popular Science Monthly,* June 1890, p. 205; Barr Ferree, "What is Architecture?" *Architectural Record,* October-December 1891, p. 206.

32. *Public Opinion,* August 1, 1891, p. 415; Donald Hoffmann, comp., *The Meaning of Architecture: Buildings and Writings by John Wellborn Root* (New York, 1967), p. 28; John R. Thomas, "History of Prison Architecture," *American Architect and Building News,* November 7, 1891, p. 90.

33. Stein, *John Ruskin,* pp. 59–61; James Early, *Romanticism and American Architecture* (New York, 1965), pp. 84–85, 96; William H. Pierson, Jr., *American Buildings and Their Architects,* vol. 2, *Technology and the Picturesque: The Corporate and Early Gothic Styles* (New York, 1978), pp. 310–315.

34. Carroll L. V. Meeks, *The Railroad Station: An Architectural History* (New Haven, 1958), pp. 104–105. See also Henry-Russell Hitchcock, *The Architecture of H. H. Richardson and His Times* (Cambridge, 1966), pts. 3, 4.

35. *Public Opinion,* May 1, 1886, p. 58. See also Heather Tomlinson, "Design and Reform: the 'Separate System' in the Nineteenth-century English Prison," in Anthony D. King, ed., *Buildings and Society* (London, 1980), pp. 111–112.

36. *Nation,* January 27, 1887, p. 7; *American Architect and Building News,* February 2, 1878, pp. 38–40, May 4, 1878, p. 154, May 22, 1886, p. 241, September 3, 1892, pp. 141–142, October 22, 1892, p. 49; T. J. Jackson

Lears, *No Place of Grace: Antimodernism and the Transformation of American Culture, 1880–1920* (New York, 1981), pp. 103–112.

37. Montgomery Schuyler, "Two New Armories," *Architectural Record*, April 1906, pp. 259–261.

38. Thomas F. Edmands to G. H. Gordon, April 4, 1884; Thomas F. Edmands to John Jeffries, May 20, 1888, First Corps of Cadets Archives.

39. *Souvenir Album and Sketch Book*, pp. 18–19. See also *American Architect and Building News*, February 10, 1894, p. 62.

40. *Harper's Weekly*, February 27, 1892, p. 199, April 28, 1894, p. 404; Portland *Oregonian*, May 11, 1887.

41. *Harper's Weekly*, April 28, 1894, p. 404; William G. Preston Architectural Drawings Collection, Fine Arts Department, Boston Public Library; *Dedication of the New Armory, Twelfth Reg't Infantry, N.G.S.N.Y., Tuesday, April 21st, 1887*, p. 16.

42. *New York Supreme Court, Appellate Division-First Department. Horgan & Slattery, Plaintiffs-Respondents, Against The City of New York, Defendant-Appellant. Case on Appeal* (New York, 1905), pp. 35–36, New York County Bar Association Library, New York. See also Benson, Benson, and Wiedersheim, *History of the First Regiment Infantry*, p. 60.

43. *Inland Architect and News Record*, June 1889, p. 90; *Dedication of the New Armory, Twelfth Reg't Infantry*, p. 16; William G. Preston to Thomas F. Edmands, April 13, 1900, First Corps of Cadets Archives.

44. New York *Evening Express*, August 8, 1877, Seventh Regiment Archives; *Dedication of the New Armory, Twelfth Reg't Infantry*, p. 16; Brooklyn *Eagle*, November 14, 1891; *Souvenir Album and Sketch Book*, p. 19; Antenucci, Ripman, and Zumwalt, *Armory First Corps of Cadets*, p. 28.

45. *National Guardsman*, October 1, 1877, p. 43; Newark *Daily Advertiser*, February 22, 1898; *Souvenir Album and Sketch Book*, p. 19; Brooklyn *Eagle*, November 14, 1891.

46. *Souvenir Album and Sketch Book*, p. 19; *Dedication of the New Armory, Twelfth Reg't Infantry*, p. 16; New York *Times*, July 4, 1897; *Harper's Weekly*, April 28, 1894, p. 404; Antenucci, Ripman, and Zumwalt, *Armory First Corps of Cadets*, p. 34.

47. "The Twelfth Regiment Armory," *[Real Estate] Record and Guide*, March 26, 1887, p. 396; *American Architect and Building News*, August 20, 1892, p. 122.

48. Boston First Corps of Cadets, *Cadet Armory* (Boston, 1887). See also J. Hollis Wells, "Armories for the Organized Militia—II," *Brickbuilder*, July 1908, p. 139.

49. *National Guardsman*, June 1, 1878, p. 177; *Biennial Report of the Adjutant General of Illinois: 1891–1892*, p. 11; *The People*, December 25, 1892.

50. *Biennial Report of the Adjutant General of Illinois: 1877–1878*, p. 115; *Fifth Annual Convention of the National Guard Association of the State of New York: 1883*, p. 11; Albert Ordway, ed., *The National Guard in Service* (Washington, D.C., 1891), pp. 307–308.

51. *Proceedings of the Fourteenth Annual Convention of Officers of the Wisconsin National Guard: 1895*, pp. 129–136; Ordway, ed., *National Guard in Service*, pp. 300, 311; *The People*, April 21, 1895.

52. *American Architect and Building News*, February 2, 1878, p. 39, February

23, 1878, p. 63, May 4, 1878, p. 154, May 22, 1886, p. 241, March 29, 1890, p. 193, August 30, 1890, p. 125, September 3, 1892, p. 141; *Architecture and Building,* March 25, 1893, p. 133, January 19, 1895, p. 29.

53. *American Architect and Building News,* February 2, 1878, p. 39, May 4, 1878, p. 154, May 5, 1886, p. 217, March 29, 1890, p. 193, October 22, 1892, p. 49, December 30, 1893, p. 154, November 24, 1894, p. 77; *Architecture and Building,* March 7, 1891, p. 113, July 16, 1892, p. 25.

54. *American Architect and Building News,* April 9, 1887, p. 179.

55. A possible exception is the Cincinnati Courthouse Riots of 1884, during which a mob attacked the armory of the Grand Army of the Republic, stole some weapons, and may have tried to burn it down. The GAR was a veterans' organization, and its armory a small hall in an ordinary building. (Charles Theodore Greve, *Centennial History of Cincinnati and Representative Citizens* (Chicago, 1904), I, 1001–1002; New York *Times,* March 30, 1884.)

56. Adrian Cook, *The Armies of the Streets: The New York City Draft Riots of 1863* (Louisville, 1974), pp. 37, 68–70, 84–85, 101–102, 115–117; New York *Evening Express,* July 14, 16, 1863.

57. New York *Evening Express,* July 14, 16, 1863; Boston *Evening Transcript,* July 15, 1863; Boston *Herald,* March 18, 1877; *American Architect and Building News,* February 10, 1894, p. 62.

58. *Report of the Committee [of the Pennsylvania Senate and House of Representatives] Appointed to Investigate the Railroad Riots in July, 1877* (Harrisburg, 1878), pp. 21, 24–25, 450–453, 521–522; *Report of the Adjutant General of Pennsylvania: 1877,* pp. 14, 34–35, 65, 67–68.

59. *Annual Report of the Adjutant-General of the State of New York: 1877,* pp. 433–434, 459–460; Meekins, *Fifth Regiment Infantry,* pp. 97–99; Robert V. Bruce, *1877: Year of Violence* (Indianapolis, 1959), chap. 6; U.S. Senate Committee on Public Buildings and Grounds, *Hearings [on] Armory in District of Columbia* (Washington, D.C., 1912), pp. 15–16.

60. *Report of the Committee Appointed to Investigate the Railroad Riots,* pp. 521–523. See also E. L. Molineux, *Riots in Cities and Their Suppression* (Boston, 1884), p. 9.

5. The Demise of the Castellated Style

1. Jos. Lapsley Wilson, ed., *Book of the First Troop Philadelphia City Cavalry, 1774–1914* (Philadelphia, 1915), pp. 255–257.

2. New York *Daily Tribune,* November 4, 1900; *American Architect,* February 2, 1907, March 31, 1909; J. Hollis Wells, "Armories for the Organized Militia—III," *Brickbuilder,* August 1908, p. 159; Ernest W. Langdon, "The New Home of Company 'I,'" in *Company 'I' First Infantry Minnesota National Guard* (Minneapolis, 1909), pp. 7–8; Seattle *Post-Intelligencer,* January 20, August 13, 1905.

3. Clinton & Russell, "The New Seventy-first Regiment Armory," *Architects' and Builders' Magazine,* November 1903, pp. 62–66; Montgomery Schuyler, "Two New Armories," *Architectural Record,* April 1906, pp. 260–262; New York *Times,* January 11, 1903.

4. "The Finest Armory for Militia in the World," *Harper's Weekly*, May 22, 1909, p. 25; Buffalo *Express*, May 2, 1909.

5. New York *Daily Tribune*, April 12, 1903; New York *Times*, October 13, 1903; Schuyler, "Two New Armories," pp. 262–263; Hunt & Hunt, "Sixty-ninth Regiment Armory, N.G.N.Y.," *Architects' and Builders' Magazine*, January 1904, pp. 157, 160.

6. Schuyler, "Two New Armories," p. 264; *The [New York City] Armory Board, 1884–1911,* (New York, ca. 1912), pp. 24, 25, 28; Montgomery Schuyler, "An Oasis in the Bronx," *Architectural Record*, February 1917, p. 182; New York *Times*, October 8, 1907, May 8, August 22, 1909.

7. Robert Koch, "The Medieval Castle Revival: New York Armories," *Journal of the Society of Architectural Historians,* October 1955, pp. 26–27; A. D. F. Hamlin, "The State Architect and His Works: I. The State Armories," *Architectural Record*, January 1923, p. 35; *American Architect*, January 13, 1906, p. 15; Clayton Coleman Hall, ed., *Baltimore: Its History and Its People* (New York, 1912), I, 338–339.

8. *Report of the Adjutant-General of the State of New Jersey: 1906*, p. 116; *Architecture*, October 15, 1909, plate 88; J. Hollis Wells, "Armories for the Organized Militia—II," *Brickbuilder*, July 1908, p. 145; Wells, "Armories for the Organized Militia—III," plate 114; St. Paul *Dispatch*, January 7, 1905; San Francisco *Call*, August 22, 31, 1912.

9. Hartford *Times*, November 12, 1909; *The Proposed Arsenal and Armory Building in Hartford, Conn.* (Hartford, 1905), pp. 1–4; *Report of the [Connecticut] Arsenal and Armory Commission to the General Assembly of 1907,* pp. 1–7.

10. *Report of the Connecticut Arsenal and Armory Commission*, pp. 7, 14–20.

11. Hartford *Times*, February 15, 17, 1906. See also Wm. J. Dilthey, "Competitive Design for Arsenal and Armory at Hartford, Conn.," *Architects' and Builders' Magazine*, November 1906, pp. 71–76.

12. Hartford *Times*, March 22, 23, 1906; *Architectural Review*, April 1906, plates 16–21, September 1906, plate 62; Benjamin Wistar Morris, "Connecticut State Armory and Arsenal, Hartford, Conn.," *Architects' and Builders' Magazine*, January 1910, pp. 135–139.

13. *National Guard Armory*, 61st Cong., 2d sess., H. Doc. 860, 3; U.S. House of Representatives Committee on Public Buildings and Grounds, *Hearings [on] Public Buildings and Grounds* (Washington, D.C., 1916), p. 30.

14. San Francisco *Call*, August 22, 31, 1912.

15. *Bulletin of the Beaux-Arts Institute of Design*, September 1925, pp. 3–8.

16. *Program of Competition for the Selection of an Armory Building for the Commonwealth of Massachusetts, to be Built at Allston* (Boston, 1913), p. 9; H. Langford Warren's report to the competitors, enclosed in S. L. Moorhouse to George Howland Cox, August 7, 1913, State Armory Commission Archives, National Guard Supply Depot, Natick, Mass.; James E. McLaughlin, "Commonwealth Armory, Boston, Mass.," *American Architect*, August 9, 1916, pp. 76–82.

17. Frank R. Schwengel, "The New Armory of the 122nd Field Artillery in Chicago," *Field Artillery Journal*, January- February 1926, pp. 1–7.

18. Hamlin, "The State Architect and His Works," pp. 27–43. See also Koch,

"The Medieval Castle Revival," pp. 27–28; New York *Times*, October 8, 1907.

19. *History of the Eighteenth Regiment Infantry, National Guard of Pennsylvania* (Pittsburgh, 1901), p. 17; *Our State Army and Navy Journal*, May 1910, pp. 5–7; Pittsburgh *Press*, June 11, 1911; Pittsburgh *Dispatch*, April 9, June 11, 1911.

20. *National Guard Armory*, pp. 1–4; U.S. Senate Committee on Public Buildings and Grounds, *Hearings [on] Armory in District of Columbia* (Washington, D.C., 1912), pp. 22–23. See also U.S. House of Representatives, Special Subcommittee of the Committee on Public Buildings and Grounds, *Hearings [on] Public Buildings and Grounds* (Washington, D.C., 1919), pp. 19–21.

21. East Liberty *Tribune*, November 23, 1928; Harmon Yerkes Gordon, *History of the First Regiment Infantry of Pennsylvania* (Philadelphia, 1961), pp. 262–263; "New Armory of Mounted Commands," *Providence Magazine*, November 1925, pp. 504, 512.

22. Roy D. Keehn, *The Illinois National Guard and the Armory Building Program: A Report Submitted to the Governor of Illinois and the Sixty-first General Assembly* (1939), p. 6; *Army and Navy Register*, October 22, 1938, p. 3; October 29, 1938, p. 22; Oklahoma City *Daily Oklahoman*, April 12, 1936, Works Progress Administration Archives, National Archives, Washington, D.C.

23. Perry A. Fellows, "To All State Works Progress Administrators," an undated memo accompanying O. K. Yeager, "Preliminary Report on the Armory Construction Program for the National Guard of the United States," September 17, 1935, WPA Archives. See also Keehn, "The Illinois National Guard," p. 27; "National Guard Armories," *Architectural Concrete*, May 1942, pp. 26–31; *North Carolina Municipal News*, December 1937, p. 16.

24. "Illinois State Architecture," *Architectural Record*, June 1931, pp. 73–79; C. W. Short and R. Stanley-Brown, *Public Buildings: A Survey of Architecture of Projects Constructed by the Federal and Other Governmental Bodies between the Years 1933 and 1939 with the Assistance of the Public Works Administration* (Washington, D.C., 1939), pp. 87, 98.

25. Henry W. Desmond and Herbert Croly, "Messrs. McKim, Mead & White," *Architectural Record*, September 1906, p. 218; William A. Coles, ed., *Architecture and Society: Selected Essays of Henry Van Brunt* (Cambridge, 1969), pp. 233–234; John Stewardson, "Architecture in America: A Forecast," *Lippincott's Monthly Magazine*, January 1896, p. 136; A. D. F. Hamlin, "Architecture," *The Forum*, January-March 1904, p. 422.

26. Thomas Hastings, "The Relations of Life to Style in Architecture," *Harper's New Monthly Magazine*, May 1894, p. 961, and "The Evolution of Style in Modern Architecture," *North American Review*, February 1910, p. 198; Coles, ed., *Architecture and Society*, pp. 371–372.

27. Desmond and Croly, "Messrs. McKim, Mead & White," pp. 225–227, 237; William H. Jordy and Ralph Coe, eds., *American Architecture and Other Writings by Montgomery Schuyler* (Cambridge, 1961), II, 557; Coles, ed., *Architecture and Society*, pp. 233–234; Hastings, "The Relations of Life to Style," p. 962.

28. Thomas S. Hines, *Burnham of Chicago: Architect and Planner* (New York, 1974), chaps. 4–5. See also Coles, ed., *Architecture and Society*, p. 233.

29. James Marston Fitch, *American Building* (Cambridge, 1948), p. 123; Hines, *Burnham*, pp. 117–120; Jordy and Coe, eds., *American Architecture*, II, 557–558; Charles Moore, *The Life and Times of Charles Follen McKim* (Boston, 1929), p. 245.

30. Hastings, "The Relations of Life to Style," pp. 958, 961. See also Fiske Kimball, *American Architecture* (Indianapolis, 1928), p. 168.

31. F. W. Fitzpatrick, "The Paucity of Ideas in American Architecture," *Architectural Record*, November 1908, p. 395; John Burchard and Albert Bush-Brown, *The Architecture of America: A Social and Cultural History* (Boston, 1961), pp. 256–268, 276–281; New York *Times*, April 25, 1913.

32. Burchard and Bush-Brown, *The Architecture of America*, pp. 282–291. See also Robert Muccigrosso, *American Gothic: The Mind and Art of Ralph Adams Cram* (Washington, D.C., 1981).

33. T. J. Jackson Lears, *No Place of Grace: Antimodernism and the Transformation of American Culture, 1880–1920* (New York, 1981), pp. 206–207; A. D. F. Hamlin, "Architecture," *The Forum*, July-September 1905, pp. 59–61.

34. Fitzpatrick, "The Paucity of Ideas," pp. 395–396; Jordy and Coe, eds., *American Architecture*, II, 583–587.

35. Louis Sullivan, *Kindergarten Chats on Architecture, Education and Democracy* (Lawrence, Kans., 1934), pp. 30, 31, 179; Stewardson, "Architecture in America," p. 137; Moore, *McKim*, p. 245.

36. *American Architect*, May 31, 1911, pp. 196–197.

37. Senate Committee on Public Buildings and Grounds, *Armory in District of Columbia*, pp. 15–16.

38. *Architectural Record*, August 1911, p. 181; *American Architect*, May 31, 1911, p. 197. See also Chapter 4, note 55.

39. William Gamson Rose, *Cleveland: The Making of a City* (Cleveland, 1950), pp. 562, 572–573, 580, 614, 633; New York *Times*, April 20, 1890.

40. Detroit *News*, September 5, 1969; Walter F. Clowes, *The Detroit Light Guard* (Detroit, 1900), p. 486; Seattle *Post-Intelligencer*, January 20, 1905; Pittsburgh *Dispatch*, June 11, 1911; *Armory in District of Columbia*, 62d Cong., 2d sess., S. Rept. 886, 13.

41. Hall, ed., *Baltimore*, p. 339; *Providence Board of Trade Journal*, January 1908, pp. 19–20; *Providence Magazine*, December 1920, p. 584; Paterson *Herald-News*, August 20, 1982; Seattle *Post-Intelligencer*, May 7, 1909; New York City Landmarks Preservation Commission, "Report on the Seventh Regiment Armory," June 9, 1967, p. 2, Landmarks Preservation Commission Files, New York; Detroit *News*, April 17, 1945, September 5, 1969; Newark *Star-Ledger*, November 30, 1969; Milton W. Brown, *The Story of the Armory Show* (1963), chap. 5.

42. Brooklyn *Eagle*, July 19, 1913; New York *Times*, February 9, 1926.

43. Brooklyn *Eagle*, July 19, 1913; "Using Armories for Recreation," *Playground*, August 1924, p. 302; U.S. Congress, Subcommittees of the Committees on Military Affairs, *Joint Hearings [on] National Guard Armories* (Washington, D.C., 1935), pp. 13, 21; New York *Times*, January 3, 1940.

44. *Statement by the National Guard Association of the United States and the Adjutants General Association of the United States on the Construction Program for the National Guard of the United States* (1936), pp. 5–6; Yeager,

"Armory Construction Program"; Oklahoma City *Daily Oklahoman*, April 12, 1936. All of these items are located in the WPA Archives.

45. Baltimore *Sun*, January 13, April 26, 1933, November 29, 1934, January 31, 1940; unidentified and undated newspapers, Baltimore Public Library newspaper clippings file.

46. Robert I. Goldstein, "The Anarchist Scare of 1908: A Sign of Tensions in the Progressive Era," *American Studies*, Fall 1974, pp. 55–78; Robert K. Murray, *Red Scare: A Study of National Hysteria* (New York, 1964); Maxwell H. Bloomfield, *Alarms and Diversions: The American Mind through American Magazines, 1900–1914* (The Hague, 1967), chap. 3; *American Architect*, April 10, 1918, pp. 432–433, December 3, 1919, p. 694; Frederic Cople Jaher, *Doubters and Dissenters: Cataclysmic Thought in America, 1885–1918* (Glencoe, Ill., 1964), pp. 60–74.

47. Philip Taft, *The A.F. of L. in the Time of Gompers* (New York, 1957), chap. 2; James O. Morris, *Conflict within the AFL: A Study of Craft Versus Industrial Unionism, 1901–1938* (Ithaca, 1983), chap. 1; Daniel Bell, *Marxian Socialism in the United States* (Princeton, 1967); James Weinstein, *The Decline of Socialism in America, 1912–1925* (New York, 1967); Marguerite Green, *The National Civic Federation and the American Labor Movement, 1900–1925* (Washington, D.C., 1956); Stuart Brandes, *American Welfare Capitalism, 1880–1940* (Chicago, 1976).

48. Detroit *Free Press*, October 18, 1897; Brooklyn *Eagle*, September 20, 1901; Baltimore *Sun*, May 12, 1903; Pittsburgh *Dispatch*, June 11, 1911. See also Lears, *No Place of Grace*, pp. 108–117.

49. Louis Cantor, "The Creation of the Modern National Guard: The Dick Militia Act of 1903" (Ph.D. diss., Duke University, 1963), chaps. 4–7. See also Jim Dan Hill, *The Minute Man in Peace and War: A History of the National Guard* (Harrisburg, 1963), chaps. 6–7; John K. Mahon, *History of the Militia and the National Guard* (New York, 1983), chaps. 9–10.

50. Lloyd S. Bryce, "A Service of Love," *North American Review*, September 1887, p. 285; *Scientific American*, January 8, 1916, p. 59, February 19, 1916, p. 197; Detroit *News*, October 19, 1897; Baltimore *Sun*, May 13, 1901.

51. Alan M. Osur, "The Role of the Colorado National Guard in Civil Disturbances," *Military Affairs*, February 1982, p. 2; Mahon, *History of the Militia*, p. 143; *Official Proceedings of [the] Fifty-third Annual Convention [of the] New York State Federation of Labor: 1916*, p. 13; *Annual Report of the Chief of the Militia Bureau: 1922*, p. 47; *Proceedings of the Fourteenth Annual Convention of Officers of the Wisconsin National Guard: 1895*, p. 15; Albert Ordway, ed., *The National Guard in Service* (Washington, D.C., 1891), p. 300.

52. *Annual Report of the Chief of the Militia Bureau: 1922*, p. 43; *Outlook*, April 5, 1916, p. 771; Bruce Smith, *The State Police* (New York, 1925), pp. 30–31; Wilbur F. Sadler, "Efficiency in the National Guard," *North American Review*, October 1915, p. 549.

53. Smith, *State Police*, pp. 37–46; Joseph John Holmes, "The National Guard of Pennsylvania: Policeman of Industry, 1865–1905" (Ph.D. diss., University of Connecticut, 1970), pp. 282–283; *Outlook*, April 5, 1916, p. 771; *Official Proceedings of the Fifty-third Annual Convention of the New York State Federation of Labor: 1916*, p. 41; *Proceedings [of the] Thirty-eighth Annual*

Convention [of the] Illinois State Federation of Labor: 1920, p. 181; Eugene Stanley, *History of the Illinois State Federation of Labor* (Chicago, 1930), pp. 512–519.

54. Holmes, "National Guard of Pennsylvania," pp. 284, 286; Clarence C. Clendenen, "Super Police: The National Guard as a Law Enforcement Agency in the Twentieth Century," in Robin Higham, ed., *Bayonets in the Streets: The Use of Troops in Civil Disturbances* (Lawrence, Kans., 1969), pp. 85–111; Sadler, "Efficiency in the National Guard," pp. 544–550; Bennett M. Rich and Philip H. Burch, Jr., "The Changing Role of the National Guard," *American Political Science Review*, September 1956, pp. 702–706.

55. Stanley, *History of the Illinois State Federation of Labor*, p. 292; New York *Times*, October 23, 26, November 16, 18, 1902; *Report of Proceedings of the Twenty-first Annual Convention of the American Federation of Labor: 1901*, p. 215; Patrick Henry McLatchy, "The Development of the National Guard as an Instrument of Social Control" (Ph.D. diss., University of Washington, 1973), pp. 346–347.

56. "Trade Unionists as Citizen Soldiers," *American Federationist*, March 1910, pp. 22–24; *Report of Proceedings of the Thirty-sixth Annual Convention of the American Federation of Labor: 1916*, p. 383; "A Soldier-Labor Alliance," *Literary Digest*, November 4, 1922, pp. 12–13; New York *Times*, June 11, 1922.

Epilogue. The Fate of the Old Armories

1. Portland *Oregonian*, August 7, 1887, August 25, September 12, 1968; Oregon *Journal*, July 19, September 4, 1968. See also New York *Times*, January 19, 1957, December 29, 1959.
2. New York *Times*, February 23, 1902; Detroit *News*, April 17, 1945. Unless otherwise indicated, the information about the fate of the New Jersey and Philadelphia armories was compiled by Andrew Altman, a former master's student in MIT's Department of Urban Studies and Planning.
3. Buffalo *Courier-Express*, May 7, 8, 1931, July 13, 1982; Buffalo *News*, August 22, 1982, April 12, December 12, 1984.
4. Seattle *Times*, January 20, 1959, January 10, July 11, 1962, March 12, 17, 22, 25, June 2, 1968; Seattle *Post-Intelligencer*, January 7, 8, August 25, 1962, July 28, 1963, February 26, March 11, 19, 1968, Seattle Municipal Reference Library newspaper clippings file.
5. New York *Times*, June 2, 1926, September 20, 1928, January 4, 1929, May 5, 1956, July 7, 1958, April 27, 1962, January 8, 1966, June 26, 1971.
6. Newark *Star-Ledger*, February 9, 1963, November 30, 1969; Camden *Evening Bulletin*, September 28, 1977; Pittsburgh *Press*, August 26, 1966; Commonwealth v. Massachusetts Turnpike Authority, 352 Mass. 143.
7. Minneapolis *Journal*, September 6, 1934; Cleveland *Press*, March 7, 1957, January 6, 1962; Cleveland *Plain Dealer*, July 12, 1962; Frank A. Wittosch to Cristina R. Nelson, December 1, 1985, a letter made available to me by Ms. Nelson; Cincinnati *Post & Times-Star*, November 8, 1960, April 27, 1961, January 12, 1983, November 28, 1984.

8. Cristina R. Nelson, "A Tale of Two Armories: Preservation Politics in New York City" (Master's Thesis, MIT, 1985), pp. 33–46.

9. New York *Daily News,* February 11, 1972, December 11, 1973; *Amsterdam News,* January 26, February 19, 1972; unidentified newspapers, February 23, March 1, 1972, Brooklyn Public Library newspaper clippings file; New York *World-Telegram,* July 24, 1964, Long Island Historical Society newspaper clippings file, Brooklyn, New York; Ann Beha Associates, "The Armory Study" (1987), Executive Summary, an unpublished report that was made available to me by Ann Beha and Pamela Hawkes.

10. Passaic *Herald-News,* August 20, 1982; Boston *Globe,* March 24, September 17, 1983, March 17, 1984; Boston *Phoenix,* March 6, 1984.

11. Ann Beha Associates, "The Armory Study," Executive Summary and pp. 58–59, 77–78, 90–91; New York *Times,* June 12, 1983; *Southern Living,* April 1985, p. 145; San Francisco *Examiner,* September 30, 1986.

12. Craig W. C. Brown, "Some Remarks on the History of the First Corps of Cadets Armory, Boston" (1979), pp. 10–19. See also Boston *Globe,* August 15, 1985.

13. Providence *Journal,* September 11, 1986, October 6, 1987.

14. New York *Times,* July 30, 1953, March 9, 1962, June 17, 1965, May 14, 1977; Boston *Globe,* May 5, 1987; Boston *Phoenix,* March 20, 1984; telephone conversation with General William St. John of the Connecticut National Guard.

15. Ann Beha Associates, "The Armory Study," Executive Summary; New York *Times,* April 30, 1972, February 28, 1987; St. John telephone conversation; telephone conversation with George Vourlojianis, President of the Cleveland Grays; Chicago *Tribune,* July 13, 1981.

16. Bennett M. Rich and Philip H. Burch, Jr., "The Changing Role of the National Guard," *American Political Science Review,* September 1956, pp. 702–706; New York *Times,* November 10, 1965, January 4, October 11, 1966, February 19, 1968, May 14, 1977; Newark *Star-Ledger,* November 30, 1969; Boston *Globe,* October 31, 1986.

17. New York *Times,* October 22, 1919, December 28, 1934, December 28, 1935; "Salvaging Humanity in New York's Armories," *Literary Digest,* February 24, 1934, p. 21.

18. New York *Times,* December 25, 1982; *Washington Post,* January 26, 1984, April 20, 1985; *Newsweek,* January 2, 1984, pp. 20–29, December 16, 1985, p. 22; *U.S. News & World Report,* January 14, 1985; Mark Malone, "Homelessness in an Urban Setting," *Fordham Urban Law Journal* (1981–82), pp. 761–767.

19. New York *Times,* August 27, October 21, December 1, 1981, January 6, 1982, January 23, 1983, March 7, 1984, January 11, 13, 16, November 16, December 6, 1985, February 15, March 24, 1986, January 16, 1987; Washington *Post,* May 12, 1984; Ann Beha Associates, "The Armory Study," Executive Summary; *New Yorker,* December 27, 1982, pp. 28–32.

20. New York *Times,* January 22, 1983, March 24, April 13, 1984; Joe Klein, "The Homeless of Park Avenue," *New York Magazine,* April 16, 1984, pp. 22–26. See also Nelson, "A Tale of Two Armories," pp. 50–57.

Index